Constructive Competition in the Caspian Sea Region?

The Caspian Sea region has hitherto largely been investigated from a 'New Great Game' perspective that depicts the region as a geopolitical battleground between regional and external great powers, where tensions have been exacerbated by the sea's rich natural resources, strategic location, and legal disagreements over its status. This book, by contrast, portrays a new image of the region, which still acknowledges the difficulties and problematic starting situation of power politics there. It, however, seeks to show that there are ways forward by identifying mechanisms and means to transform the 'New Great Game' into processes of functional co-operation. Drawing on theoretical insights from a functionalist framework, this book examines three intertwined case studies, namely the Baku-Tbilisi-Ceyhan pipeline (BTC), the Southern Gas Corridor (SGC), and the Caspian Environmental Program (CEP). It shows that lessons learned from environmental co-operation have influenced the discussion over the uncertain legal status of the sea, which culminated in the signing in 2018 of the Convention on the legal status of the Caspian Sea. This book analyzes the three phases of the BTC and the SGC projects: the planning of the pipeline, its construction, and its use, none of which have been adequately addressed yet. This book illustrates the increasing role of actors beyond and besides the states in the Caspian Sea region, such as transnational corporations, non-governmental organizations, and intergovernment organizations.

Dr. Agha Bayramov is a lecturer in the Department of International Relations at the University of Groningen and in the Institute of Political Science at Leiden University. His research interests include the Geopolitics of Energy in the Caspian Sea region, Azerbaijan, Climate Change and Energy Transition in the South Caucasus.

Europa Regional Perspectives

Providing in-depth analysis with a global reach, this series from Europa examines a wide range of contemporary political, economic, developmental and social issues in regional perspective. Intended to complement the Europa Regional Surveys of the World series, Europa Regional Perspectives will be a valuable resource for academics, students, researchers, policymakers, business people and anyone with an interest in current world affairs with an emphasis on regional issues.

While the Europa World Year Book and its associated Regional Surveys inform on and analyse contemporary economic, political and social developments, the Editors considered the need for more in-depth volumes written and/or edited by specialists in their field, in order to delve into particular regional situations. Volumes in the series are not constrained by any particular template, but may explore recent political, economic, international relations, social, defence, or other issues in order to increase knowledge. Regions are thus not specifically defined, and volumes may focus on small or large group of countries, regions or blocs.

External Powers in Latin America
Geopolitics Between Neo-extractivism and South-South Cooperation
Edited by Gian Luca Gardini

The Blue Economy in Sub-Saharan Africa
Working for a Sustainable Future
Edited by Donald L. Sparks

Catalonia, Scotland and the EU
Visions of Independence and Integration
Niklas Bremberg and Richard Gillespie

Social Welfare Issues in Southern Europe
Edited by Maria Brown and Michael Briguglio

Constructive Competition in the Caspian Sea Region?
An Alternative Image
Agha Bayramov

For more information about this series, please visit: www.routledge.com/Europa-Regional-Perspectives/book-series/ERP.

Constructive Competition in the Caspian Sea Region?
An Alternative Image

Agha Bayramov

LONDON AND NEW YORK

First published 2022
by Routledge
4 Park Square, Milton Park, Abingdon, Oxon OX14 4RN

and by Routledge
605 Third Avenue, New York, NY 10158

Routledge is an imprint of the Taylor & Francis Group, an informa business

© 2022 Agha Bayramov

The right of Agha Bayramov to be identified as author of this work has been asserted in accordance with sections 77 and 78 of the Copyright, Designs and Patents Act 1988.

All rights reserved. No part of this book may be reprinted or reproduced or utilised in any form or by any electronic, mechanical, or other means, now known or hereafter invented, including photocopying and recording, or in any information storage or retrieval system, without permission in writing from the publishers.

Trademark notice: Product or corporate names may be trademarks or registered trademarks, and are used only for identification and explanation without intent to infringe.

British Library Cataloguing in Publication Data
A catalogue record for this book is available from the British Library

Library of Congress Cataloging-in-Publication Data
A catalog record has been requested for this book

ISBN: 978-1-032-03903-9 (hbk)
ISBN: 978-1-032-27554-3 (pbk)
ISBN: 978-1-003-18962-6 (ebk)

DOI: 10.4324/9781003189626

Typeset in Times New Roman
by Taylor & Francis Books

Contents

List of figures	viii
List of Abbreviations	ix
Acknowledgements	xi

Introduction	1

The aim of this book 5
Methodology/case studies 6
Outline of this book 8

1	New Great Game in the Caspian Sea	12

Introduction 12
The original concept of the Great Game 13
From Old to New Great Game 16
    Actors 16
Objective: Survival of the fittest 19
Environmental conflicts 20
Naval advancement 21
What is presented as new and who is presented as
* the winner? 22*
Critiques: Where does the New Great Game literature
* lead us? 24*
Conclusion 27

2	Revisiting functionalism	37

Introduction 37
Underlying assumptions 39
State fixation 40
Sharing interests through functionalist agencies and elites 41

vi *Contents*

The ramification or spill-over approach 45
Critiques of classical functionalism 47
Functionalism revised via social constructivism 52
Social constructivist insights 54
Mediating interfaces: Cross-border and
 transnational infrastructure 56
Functionalist networks 60
Economic leverage 62
Transnational corporations 64
Avoiding Utopic thinking: The ill-fitting
 European benchmark 66
Conclusion 68

3 Environmental issues: Conflict and cooperation potential for the
 Caspian Sea   78

Introduction 78
The Caspian Environmental Program and the Legal
 Status Convention 80
    Environmental cooperation 80
    The long journey to the Legal Status Convention 84
The New Great Game explanation for the Caspian environmental
 cooperation and the Legal Status Convention 88
Economic leverage, networking and technical expertise 90
    Economic leverage 91
    Networking and socialization under the CEP 94
    Technical expertise and construction of
     environmental protocols 96
    From environmental cooperation to the Legal
     Status Convention 100
Conclusion 102

4 Cooperation around post-Soviet transnational infrastructure
 projects in the Caspian Sea   110

Introduction 110
Background of the BTC pipeline 111
The New Great Game views on the BTC pipeline 113
The planning, construction and post-construction phases in the
 functionalist framework 114
    Planning the BTC pipeline: geopolitical uncertainty 114

Contents vii

Construction of the BTC pipeline: challenges
besides geopolitics 116
Network of actors 120
Energy companies 120
Private and public lenders 123
Operating the BTC pipeline 126
Pragmatic cooperation 126
Conclusion 130

5   A new round in the Caspian pipeline game: The Southern
Gas Corridor   139

Introduction 139
Background of the SCG project 140
The New Great Game: the second round 141
*Discussion: the planning, construction and
post-construction phases 145*
Planning the SGC project 145
Constructing the SGC project 151
Network of actors 157
Operating the SGC: expectations versus reality 162
Conclusion 166

Conclusion   176

An alternative image of the Caspian Sea region 177

Index   184

Figures

3.1 Timeline of the Caspian Environmental Program and the Tehran Convention from 1994 until 2018. It shows important meetings, agreements and the date of decisions   82
3.2 List of actors involved in the Caspian Environmental Program and the Tehran Convention   83
3.3 Timeline of the Convention on the Legal Status from 1992 until 2018. It shows important meetings, agreements and the date of decisions   86
4.1 Timeline of the Baku-Tbilisi-Ceyhan oil pipeline from 1994 until 2008   112
4.2 The BTC oil pipeline private shareholders in 2021   121
4.3 List of actors involved in the BTC oil pipeline   124
5.1 Three rounds of internal competition between different natural gas projects   149
5.2 List of actors involved in the Southern Gas Project   158
5.3 International loans from different public banks   161

List of Abbreviations

AIIB	Asian Infrastructure Investment Bank
ANT	Actor Network Theory
BCM	Billion cubic meters
BP	British Petroleum
BSTDB	Black Sea Trade and Development Bank
BTC	Baku-Tbilisi-Ceyhan-Pipeline
BTE	Baku-Tbilisi-Erzurum Pipeline
CEIC	Caspian Environmental Information Centre
CEP	Caspian Environment Program
EBRD	European Bank for Reconstruction and Development
EC	European Commission
ECGD	Export Credit Guarantee Department
ECSC	European Coal and Steel Company
EP	European Parliament
EU	European Union
GEF	Global Environment Facility
IGO	Inter-Governmental Organization
IMF	International Monetary Fund
IR	International Relations
ITGI	Interconnection Turkey Greece Italy
ITU	International Telecommunication Union
LNG	Liquefied Natural Gas
NGO	Non-Governmental Organization
NICO	Naftiran Intertrade Company
NIOC	National Iranian Oil Company
SGC	Southern Gas Corridor
SOCAR	State Oil Company of the Azerbaijan Republic
TACIS	Technical Aid to the Commonwealth of Independent States
TANAP	Trans-Anatolian Gas Pipeline
TAP	Trans-Adriatic Pipeline
TEP	Third Energy Package
TCP	Trans Caspian Pipeline
TNC	Transnational Corporation

x *List of Abbreviations*

TP	Turkish Petroleum
TPA	Third Party Access
TVA	Tennessee Valley Authority
UK	United Kingdom
UNDP	United Nations Development Program
UNEP	United Nations Environment Program
UPU	Universal Postal Union
USA	United States of America
WB	World Bank

Acknowledgements

This book would not have been completed without Professor Jaap de Wilde, who trusted and accompanied me throughout this journey. I am grateful for his insightful guidance, helpful comments, critiques, and patience throughout the researching and writing process of my book. He was always there and always supported me, not just when I faced academic difficulties but also when I faced personal challenges. Thank you Jaap, for your kindness and support, which I will never forget.

I am very grateful to my co-supervisor Christoph Humrich for his valuable and critical 'so what' questions, which encouraged me to push my academic boundaries. His constant encouragement, insightful comments, and suggestions have enriched my research.

I would like to thank many colleagues at the University of Groningen, who have contributed to my research and social life. Particularly thanks to Eric Cezne, Cagri Sagiroglu, Philipp Olbrich, Yara Marusyk, Mustafa Ali Sezal, Sandra Becker, Frank Birkenholzand, Saliha Metinsoy, and Erdogan Aykac for their academic advice, lunch, and coffee breaks. I also wish to thank Xavier Guillaume, Benjamin Herborth, Francesco Giumelli, and Julia Costa López for their reflections on parts of my discussion about classical functionalism. I am grateful to Marijke Wubbolts and Gorus van Oordt for their technical and administrative support.

I would like to thank each one of my interview participants for making time to answer my questions, and for their willingness to share personal experiences with me. I want to thank Dermot Nolan for reading parts of my book at earlier stages of the research. Some parts of chapter 4 were published in *the Caucasus Analytical Digest* and parts of chapter 5 were published in *the East European Politics Journal* in 2019. I would like to thank all anonymous reviewers for their helpful comments.

Without significant help and support from my lovely family and friends, I would not have been able to maintain my motivation and enthusiasm for this project. I am grateful to Gerda, Jan, Anna, and Thomas for making me feel at home. Although I was living far away from my family in Azerbaijan, I never have felt alone in the Netherlands thanks to them. Thanks as well to

xii *Acknowledgements*

Orkhan, Eric, Saliha, and Mustafa for their friendship. I want to thank Mubariz Xalilov and Fazil Fataliyev for their support.

Lastly, I am grateful to my parents, Gadir and Minure, my brother Gurban and my partner Marleen for joining me on this academic adventure and supporting me throughout this journey.

Introduction

The Caspian Sea is an inland body of water between Europe and Asia, the Caucasus, and Central Asia. It is known for its geo-strategic position, hydrocarbon resources, caviar, ecological issues, and bio diversity. During the Cold War, the Caspian Sea was only shared between two littoral states: the Soviet Union and Iran, who had divided the region amongst themselves in the treaties of 1921 and 1940.[1] However, after the collapse of the Soviet Union, the Caspian Sea was divided amongst five littoral states, four of which were newly formed states, namely Azerbaijan, Kazakhstan, Russia, and Turkmenistan.[2]

The dissolution of the Soviet Union created an opportunity for the newly independent states to determine their borders, foreign policies, and language as well as their internal political and economic systems. They also aimed to establish external recognition and relationships with global and regional powers such as the European Union, the United States, China, Turkey, and Iran. In this sense, the unexplored natural resources of the Caspian Sea appeared to be the main economic and political commodity for Azerbaijan, Kazakhstan, and Turkmenistan as these resources allowed them to get the attention of international actors and stabilize their economies. The dissolution of the Soviet Union was also an opportunity for global as well as regional powers like the European Union, the United States, Turkey, and China and their energy companies to diversify their energy resources. In the early 1990s, the three new littoral states started negotiating with a number of international energy companies and Western states the construction of new oil and natural gas pipeline networks.

However, the collapse of the Soviet Union also created new, intertwined issues and challenges, namely the uncertain legal status of the Caspian Sea, the ownership of natural resources, ecological issues, inadequate infrastructure, and determining the proper and safe routes for transporting the natural resources of the region. More specifically, due to the sea's uncertain legal status, it was difficult to determine the ownership of several hydrocarbon fields. The Araz-Sharg-Alov field, for example, sparked disagreement between Azerbaijan and Iran. Kapaz/Sardar is another hydrocarbon field that caused disagreement between Azerbaijan and Turkmenistan.

DOI: 10.4324/9781003189626-1

2   *Introduction*

Additionally, Russia and Kazakhstan struggled to determine which of them owned three fields in the northern part of the Caspian Sea – the Kurmangazy, Khvalynsk, and Tsentralnoye fields. Although the littoral states recognized the need to find universally agreeable solutions for these issues, it was not an easy process in the early 1990s as the littoral states all sought to claim the resources that they felt they had a right to and thus came to conflicting views on the division of the Caspian Sea and its richness.

Aside from that, their colonial past with Russia pushed Azerbaijan, Kazakhstan, and Turkmenistan to diversify their political and economic relations by establishing collaborations with other great powers. In September 1994, for example, Azerbaijan signed its first and biggest energy agreement, called the *Contract of the Century*, with Western energy companies. This deal for the exploitation of large offshore oil fields in the Caspian Sea was also supported by the governments of the United States, the United Kingdom, and Turkey. Following this, Azerbaijan started to explore a number of new pipeline routes to transport its oil to international energy markets since the existing pipeline system of the Soviet Union, the Baku-Novorossiysk pipeline, was constructed in such a manner that natural resources from the Caspian Sea had to be transported through Russia in order to reach world markets. On the other hand, Russia and Iran sought to preserve their regional influence by denying external powers military presence in the Caspian Sea and preventing the establishment of new energy projects in the region. It was for this reason that Iran and Russia criticized the unilateral action Azerbaijan took when it negotiated its energy contract as the issue surrounding the sea's legal status had not been resolved yet and they were initially excluded from the project. In general, these conflicting claims, unilateral actions and the uncertainties surrounding them led to disagreement which slowed the negotiation process among the littoral states down in the early 1990s.

The disagreements, energy projects, and the uncertain legal status of the Caspian Sea naturally captured the attention of academics and the media. Although the region had been virtually unknown to the majority of Westerners, articles on the Caspian Sea region started appearing in *The Guardian, New York Times*, and *Financial Times* in the 1990s (e.g., Bittner 2018; Norton-Taylor 2001; Pannier 2009). For instance, if one were to do a Google Search for 'Caspian Sea' with a timeline between 1980 and 1990, one would only find information about the Caspian sturgeon fish, caviar trade, the environment, and the local people of the region. However, if one changes the time frame and searches between 1990 and 2018, one would find academic articles, newspapers, policy briefs, and other literature about Caspian resource conflicts, geopolitics, a Caspian 'Great Game', the legal dispute about the sea and oil wars (e.g., Ahrari 1994; Alam 2002; Amirova-Mammadova 2017; Bashir 2017; Bittner 2018; Dunlap 2004; Gurbanov 2017a; Kiernan 2012; Kleveman 2003; Norton-Taylor 2001; Saivetz 2003; Smith 1996; Trenin 2003).

Introduction 3

This in turn captured the imagination of the public, as is evidenced by the Caspian Sea featuring as the setting of the James Bond movie *The World is Not Enough*, which was partly filmed in Baku, Azerbaijan in 1999 (Dodds 2003). In this film, Bond is assigned to the Caspian Sea region to help Electra, the daughter of billionaire Sir Robert King, to achieve their family dream of constructing an 800-mile pipeline from Azerbaijan to the Mediterranean. In the Azerbaijani capital Baku, Electra shows Bond a map revealing how this proposed pipeline would provide the West an opportunity to import the oil from the Caspian Sea region while circumventing the existing Russian pipelines. Both Electra and Bond's superior at MI6 note that the Russians will do anything to stop the construction of the pipeline. It can be seen that the bad guys are Russians and Arabic speaking characters, while Western, English-speaking good guys try to save either the world, or at least certain parts of it, from these people. In this regard, the film briefly touches on the geopolitical significance of infrastructure construction, the Russian dominance of the region, and its rivalry with the Western actors, such as Britain, in the Caspian Sea. The idea for the film came from one of the producers, Barbara Broccoli. In 1997, Broccoli saw a TV programme, which showed how the division of unexploited hydrocarbon resources in the Caspian Sea might serve to identify economic progress in the next century. Inspired by this programme, Broccoli asked what would happen if the next Bond movie revolved around a plot to remove all non-Western competition by building an oil pipeline from the Caspian Sea to the Western world owned and operated by the West (as cited in Dodds 2003, 143).

Ironically, the implications of the film can be observed within the relevant academic and media discussion. For example, in 2001, an article published in *The Guardian* argued that:

> ...a new and potentially explosive Great Game is being set up...and the object this time is not so much control of territory. It is the large reserves of oil and gas in the Caucasus, notably the Caspian basin. Pipelines are the counters in this new Great Game.

Similarly, in his journalistic investigation, Kleveman repeats:

> ...more than a hundred years later great empires once again position themselves to control the heart of the Eurasian landmass. The United States has taken over the leading role from the British. Along with the ever present Russians, new regional powers such as China, Iran and Turkey have entered the arena. The New Great Game focuses Caspian energy reserves, principally oil and gas.
>
> (Kleveman 2003, 3)

In the same vein, it is argued that 'access to the Caspian oil and gas resources can decrease the West's energy dependency on the Middle East and can

4 *Introduction*

enhance the independence of the newly independent regional countries' (Cohen 1996, 10). However, the relevant literature also highlights that it is not easy to reach energy resources and secure independence, in part because 'Russia would engage in war with Azerbaijan and Turkmenistan, if its interests were ignored' (Shlapentokh 2013, 155). The relevant literature will be analyzed in greater depth later, but if one reads through this literature one finds that from the 1990s onwards we mainly see a specific image of the Caspian Sea region in academic literature and the media. It is a state-centric, rivalry and sovereignty based 'New Great Game' image.

Over the last two and half decades, the Caspian Sea region has undergone remarkable changes: several new transnational energy pipelines have been constructed (such as the BTC pipeline, the BTE pipeline and the SGC) and new treaties have been signed (such as the *Convention on the Legal Status of the Caspian Sea*). However, as will be illustrated in chapter 1 in depth, since 1990 almost any development or energy project has been described as part of the competition between great powers. Within this discussion, most regional economic and political projects have been depicted as either opposing or favouring the Russian-Iranian hegemony. In light of this, Russia and Iran have been identified as the main transgressors in every single issue (Iseri 2009).

Drawing mainly from the Great Game insights that revolve around the balance of power, the perception of (in)security, attaining and maintaining sovereignty and the influence of the state, scholars have argued that the growing involvement of the Western actors (the US and the EU) and other powers (Turkey and China) increases tension and rivalry in the region as they offer alternative economic, geographical and political choices for the littoral states (Alam 2002). In the same vein, new energy pipelines like the BTC and the SGC have been depicted as a tool to decrease the Russian and Iranian geopolitical dominance and their monopoly over the energy projects in the region (Akiner 2004). The Western powers, (the EU and the US) as well as their energy companies, are then described as the saviours of the newly independent states (Bayulgen 2009).

In light of this, the relevant literature has searched for answers to questions like: Who is the winner of the New Great Game? Can the West save the newly independent states' sovereignty from Russia, Iran and China, and if so, how? In what way can the Caspian natural resources decrease the West's energy dependency on Russia? and Why and how do Russia and Iran seek to re-establish their dominance over the Caspian Sea region? These questions conjure up the image of a desperate place, full of rivalry and conflict. This body of literature sees little room for cooperation, regional integration or exchange. How the Caspian Sea region is seen has consequences in terms of the expectations and perceived potential of the region and possible political action and suggestions for regional stability. However, it is worth asking whether this is the full and true picture of the region and its recent history. Was the Caspian Sea region harmonious, conflict-free and cooperative under

Introduction 5

the Soviet Union and suddenly plunged into disarray with the dissolution of the Soviet Union? Is this a shift in reality or merely a shift of perception?

The aim of this book

The core aim of this book is to propose an alternative reading of the Caspian Sea region. What I will try to do, therefore, is look at the region with another theoretical perspective in mind. In many respects it is a theoretical perspective from the opposite end of the spectrum of International Relations (IR) theory; a perspective which acknowledges the difficulties and problematic starting situation of power politics in the region, but which seeks to show that there are ways forward by identifying mechanisms and means to transform the New Great Game into something else, namely functionalism. The hope is then that a new image of the region emerges which emphasizes the constructive potential and ways to realize it.

Two studies have so far applied the classical functionalist theory to the Caspian Sea region, namely Blum (2002) and Petersen (2016). From an empirical perspective, Petersen (2016) studies the BTC pipeline and only covers Azerbaijan, Georgia, and Turkey, explaining integration among these states, which does not look at the Caspian Sea per se and does not include the relationships between the majority of the littoral states. Blum's study (2002) is one of the few studies which address the Caspian Environmental Program (CEP) and the relationship between the littoral states per se. However, his work needs to be expanded because it was written in 2002 and thus only covered the early stages of the CEP. Both the program and the relationship between the littoral states have changed since then. Due to the infancy of the program at the time of its writing, Blum's work also does not establish any correlation between the CEP and issues in other technical areas, such as the uncertain legal status of the Caspian Sea. From a theoretical perspective, both Petersen (2016, 151) and Blum (2002, 171–172) fall into the common trap of judging the functional developments in the Caspian Sea against an explicitly European benchmark, as do other scholars. Petersen (2016, 151) concluded that 'the integration currently underway in the energy and transport sectors has not placed pressure on other sectors to follow suit, the way that coal and steel integration in Western Europe did in the 1950s.' In the same vein, Blum (2002, 171–172) concluded that unlike the post-Westphalian system, the Caspian littoral states do not share their sovereignties and autonomous decision-making right with the CEP, which means it represents traditional high politics. Both scholars expected to find a European-style cooperation and integration without acknowledging the Caspian Sea's historical, political, economic, material, and normative distinctiveness. By applying a Eurocentric approach, these works ignored the Caspian Sea style of cooperation and its distinct set of political, economic, and social goals set by the littoral states. As a result, while neither Blum nor Petersen repeat the New Great Game arguments, they ended up sceptical and less

6   *Introduction*

convinced by the assumptions of classical functionalism because they were oriented too much on the European experience.

This book is inspired by their work, but it does not follow a European benchmark when discussing the Caspian Sea style of cooperation. To do so, it is necessary to distinguish functionalism as such from its unique European success story that occurred in the early 1950s. The strength of functionalism as a strategy for cooperation has paradoxically been blurred by its success in Western Europe. The specific conditions in Europe are historically unique but the literature has made them absolute requirements for functionalism to work. Hence, I will show that there is (1) not a necessary connection between functionalism and the European case; (2) functionalism has many elements that it claims work independent of the European context on which it builds its identification of 'transformative' means and mechanisms; (3) this does not make it necessary to give up major ideas of functionalism as has been done in the newer liberal theories of IR. I will argue these points while critically revisiting functionalism via social constructivism. This is because similar to classical functionalism, social constructivism addresses issues from a non-traditional angle which makes it easy to cross-fertilize the two debates. In this sense, integrating insights and assumptions from social constructivism broadens the theoretical contours of functionalism and adds a richer understanding of phenomena highlighted by classical functionalism. That way, insights from constructivism can enable classical functionalism to mount a more powerful challenge to the dominant Great Game line of assumptions.

Methodology/case studies

This book examines three intertwined case studies, namely the Baku-Tbilisi-Ceyhan pipeline (BTC), the Southern Gas Corridor (SGC), and the Caspian Environmental Program (CEP). I selected these cases first of all because they explicitly and implicitly include all five of the Caspian littoral states, meaning they are comprehensive enough to uncover what type of relationships and different dynamics formed between the Caspian littoral states in the period from 1990 to 2018. This will also help to explain complex and interconnected mechanisms in the Caspian Sea. Second, two of these cases, the BTC pipeline and the CEP are advanced enough to shed light on the mechanisms of technical cooperation and spill-over.

However, the Caspian littoral states all operate differently and are subject to different dynamics in each case. Therefore, each case serves a specific purpose and offers specific insights into mechanisms of cooperation. I selected the CEP as one of the case studies for three reasons. First, in the early 2000s, achieving cooperation was not easy because of difficult geopolitical problems (e.g., the uncertain legal status of the Caspian Sea, economic issues, internal political struggle). From a New Great Game perspective, we would expect no cooperation to be possible. Despite this, the CEP was established, which brought the littoral governments under its common umbrella. Later, it

Introduction 7

led to the first shared agreement, the *Framework Convention for the Protection of the Marine Environment of the Caspian Sea, the Tehran Convention* (hereinafter referred as the *Tehran Convention*), that has been signed and ratified by all five governments. Thus, it is an example of low politics and technical cooperation among the Caspian littoral states being employed to solve common ecological problems. Second, the CEP is neither unimportant nor inconsequential because it sets the stage for cooperative habits. Third, despite its financial, technical and political difficulties the CEP has made several constructive achievements such as the signing of the *Tehran Convention* and the adaptation of four environmental protocols as well as the construction of new ecological norms, values and principles which are also part of the *Convention on the Legal Status of the Caspian Sea* (hereinafter referred as the Legal Status Convention). This means that, in the broad picture, the CEP is not an isolated case, but is connected to the legal status of the sea and the transportation of oil and natural gas in the Caspian Sea. To understand the complexities of the situation in the Caspian Sea region, this intertwined relationship between the *Tehran Convention* and the *Legal Status Convention* and spill-over between them require a comprehensive explanation. In this regard, it is necessary to highlight CEP's (in)direct relevance (political, economic, and social) to the contemporary Caspian Sea.

I selected the BTC pipeline as a case study because it has been widely depicted as part of the New Great Game and one of the main reasons for conflict and rivalry in the Caspian Sea region. As will be discussed later, the pipeline was expected to trigger rivalry and even war in the region following its construction (Cohen 2002; Kim and Eom 2008). However, the BTC became operational in 2006 and the predictions stemming from the New Great Game scholarship did not come true. Therefore, by analyzing the different results and developments since 2006, I aim to offer a better explanation. Together with the case study of the CEP, this case study serves to validate the claim that the past of the region has not been as bleak as the New Great Game paints the picture.

Finally, I selected the SGC to show that there is improvement in the form of spill-over of established ways of cooperating into new cases which helps to consolidate a brighter future for the region. By using the SGC case study, I aim to show that there are interlinkages between the cases and illustrate how the cooperative habits, established by the CEP and BTC pipeline, have strengthened the conditions for further collaboration in the Caspian Sea. This will help to invalidate the main arguments of the New Great Game.

I conducted 22 semi-structured interviews with local and international institution officials and policymakers holding different positions within 16 regional and international institutions to gain information on decision-making processes by tracing the personal experiences of several experts. These institutions are: the United Nations Environmental Program (UNEP), the Global Environmental Facility (GEF), the CEP Interim Secretariat, British Petroleum, the International Crisis Group, TANAP Corporate, the

8 *Introduction*

Port of Baku, the Ministries of Ecology and Natural Resources of Azerbaijan, Turkmenistan and Iran, the Caspian Barrel, the Regional Studies Centre Armenia, the Georgian Institute of Politics, American University of Armenia, Azerbaijan Diplomacy Academy, the Centre for Strategic Studies of Azerbaijan, and the Azerbaijan Ministry of Foreign Affairs.

The information from the interviews was mainly used to supplement the information from other sources. More concretely, the importance of the interviews was different in each case study. I conducted both online interviews through Skype and email and face-to-face interviews to collect my data. For the latter, I undertook two field research trips to Azerbaijan, Baku. The first from November until December 2017 and the second in May 2018. I choose Baku as the destination of my field trip because of financial, cultural and linguistic reasons. Interviews lasted approximately 30 to 90 minutes each. Due to the limitations of financial resources, safety, and time, I conducted online interviews through Skype and email with differently ranking experts from Armenia, Georgia, Iran, Turkmenistan, Turkey, and the UNEP Office Geneva, Switzerland.

In terms of challenges and limitations, there were certain hurdles during the field trips themselves. First, certain interviews reflected only the official policy line and therefore were not very complementary. I was able to obtain new insights information from some interviews, however. Second, it was difficult to gain access to certain government institutions (e.g., the Ministry of Foreign Affairs and the Ministry of Defence) and certain questions required access to the very top level of decision-making. Therefore, most interviews took place in a private or informal setting. I was not able to meet with any experts from two Caspian Sea states namely, Kazakhstan and Russia. However, my overall fieldwork was useful in terms of getting a broader picture and gaining insight into the personal experience of different experts.

Outline of this book

After the current introduction, the book is divided into five chapters and a conclusion. Chapter 1 critically reviews the main theoretical and empirical works on the New Great Game in view of the Caspian Sea region. In particular, chapter 1 sketches the New Great Game image of the region and the assumptions, concepts, and mechanisms, which revolve around actors, aims, reasons and motivations, this image is based on. It also provides a critique of this view of the region and elaborates on the alternatives to this perspective. Chapter 2 offers such an alternative to the New Great Game view, namely that presented by classical functionalism. It revisits classical functionalism to come to a deeper understanding of the assumptions it is based on.

Chapters 3 through 5 apply the (revised) functionalist perspective to the cases and show that the New Great Game view is wrong and functionalism's expectations are empirically right. More specifically, chapter 3[3] introduces the first case study, namely the study of the CEP. This chapter shows that the

Introduction 9

Caspian Sea region has interconnected and complex dynamics rather than just pure high politics. The similarity of problems faced by the different states produces shared interests and incentives for seeking common solutions; and the CEP has encouraged the littoral states to establish cooperation on other shared issues. In other words, this chapter shows that this cooperation, framed as it was in technical or issue-specific terms, has enhanced interaction patterns, trust, and socialization processes among the littoral states, which eventually fostered further cooperation, common interests, and interaction, culminating in the signing of the *Legal Status Convention*.

Chapter 4 revisits the BTC pipeline.[4] This case study illustrates that the stage for cooperative habits, which was set by the CEP, continued and strengthened through the BTC pipeline. In doing so, the chapter explains the three phases of the pipeline project, namely its planning, construction and use. Chapter 4 shows that, contrary to the predications of the New Great Game scholarship, transnational infrastructure projects like the BTC are mediating interfaces as they connect several actors, state, non-state and semi-state, encouraging them to cooperate and enhance regional and international interaction capacities in the Caspian Sea region. The chapter argues that it is not only geopolitical but economic, technical, environmental, and social challenges that led to the delays and investigations which almost stopped the pipeline project. The findings of chapter 3 serve to illustrate that the past of the Caspian Sea region has not been as miserable as the New Great Game paints the picture.

By using a similar analysis, chapter 5 moves the discussion to the trans-national gas pipeline and analyses the SGC. This chapter shows that coop-eration on the CEP and the BTC pipeline has spilled over to the SGC project. With the help of the logic of revised functionalism, this chapter unpacks the effects of the SGC to the strategies of regional cooperation, conflicts, and exchange in the Caspian Sea region which have largely gone unnoticed. This chapter shows that transnational infrastructures do not infringe on sovereignty, but they help to create trans-governmental influences within the ministries and state-owned companies of the participating states.

Finally, the concluding chapter reviews the case studies and presents the new and comprehensive image of the Caspian Sea region on the basis of their findings.

Notes

1 Treaty of Friendship between the Russian Soviet Federal Socialist Republic and Iran (Persia) was signed on February 26, 1921, and the Soviet-Iranian Trade and Navigation Agreement was signed on March 25, 1940.
2 The official names of the five Caspian littoral states are the Republic of Azerbai-jan, the Republic of Kazakhstan, the Republic of Turkmenistan, the Russian Federation, and the Islamic Republic of Iran.
3 Some parts of chapter 3 were published in *the Caucasus Analytical Digest* in 2019.

10 *Introduction*

4 This chapter was published in the *East European Politics Journal* in 2019 except for the Introduction, section 3 and subsection 4.2.2. It also includes subsection 3.2 from the Introduction chapter. The link for the article is: https://doi.org/10.1080/21599165.2019.1612372.

Bibliography

Ahrari, Ehsan M. 1994. 'The dynamics of the new great game in Muslim Central Asia.' *Central Asian Survey* 13 (4): 525–539.

Akiner, Shirin. 2004. *The Caspian: Politics, Energy and Security.* London: Routledge.

Alam, Shah. 2002. 'Pipeline politics in the Caspian Sea Basin.' *Strategic Analysis* 26 (1): 5–26.

Amirova-Mammadova, Sevinj. 2017. *Pipeline Politics and Natural Gas Supply from Azerbaijan to Europe.* Wiesbaden: Springer.

Bashir, Omar S. 2017. 'The Great Games Never Played: Explaining Variation in International Competition Over Energy.' *Journal of Global Security Studies* 2 (4): 288–306.

Bayulgen, Oksan. 2009. 'Caspian energy wealth: social impacts and implications for regional stability.' In *The Politics of Transition in Central Asia and the Caucasus*, by Amanda E Wooden and Christoph H Stefes, 163–189. New York: Routledge.

Bittner, Jochen. 2018. 'Who Will Win the New Great Game?' April 26. Accessed July 10, 2018. https://www.nytimes.com/2018/04/26/opinion/russia-china-west-power.html.

Blum, Douglas. 2002. 'Beyond Reciprocity: Governance and Cooperation around the Caspian Sea.' In *Environmental Peacemaking*, by Ken Conca and Geoffrey Dabelko, 161–190. Baltimore: The John Hopkins University Press.

Cohen, Ariel. 2002. *Iran's Calims over Caspian Sea Resources Threaten Energy Security.* Washington: The Heritage Foundation.

Cohen, Ariel. 1996. *The New 'Great Game': Oil Politics in the Caucasus and Central Asia.* Washington: The Heritage Foundation.

Dodds, Klaus. 2005. 'Screening Geopolitics: James Bond and the Early Cold War films (1962–1967).' *Geopolitics* 10 (2): 266–289.

Dodds, Klaus. 2003. 'Licensed to Stereotype: Geopolitics, James Bond and the Spectre of Balkanism.' *Geopolitics* 8 (2): 125–156.

Dunlap, Ben. 2004. 'Divide and conquer? The Russian plan for ownership for the Caspian Sea.' *Boston College International Comparative Law Review* 27 (1): 115–130.

Gurbanov, Ilgar. 2018. 'Caspian Convention and Perspective of Turkmenistan's Gas Export to Europe' *Caucasus International*, 8 (2): 159–179.

Gurbanov, Ilgar. 2017a. 'Propaganda Against Trans-Adriatic Pipeline Continues Under 'Environmental Concerns'.' April 26. Accessed May 20, 2017. https://jamestown.org/program/propaganda-trans-adriatic-pipeline-continues-environmental-concerns/.

Iseri, Emre. 2009. 'The US Grand Strategy and the Eurasian Heartland in the Twenty-First Century.' *Geopolitics* 14 (1): 26–46.

Kiernan, Peter. 2012. 'The Great Game for gas in the Caspian.' *The Economist.* http://www.energianews.com/newsletter/files/ddf2b1fcc6f999dd6d96ff5605b022c1.pdf.

Kim, Younkyoo, and Guho Eom. 2008. 'The Geopolitics of Caspian Oil: Rivalries of the US, Russia, and Turkey in the South Caucasus.' *Global Economic Review* 37 (1): 85–106.

Kleveman, Lutz. 2003. *The New Great Game: Blood and Oil in the Central Asia.* New York: Grove Press.

Norton-Taylor, Richard. 2001. 'The New Great Game.' March 5. Accessed July 10, 2018. https://www.theguardian.com/comment/story/0,3604,446490,00.html.

Pannier, Bruce. 2009. 'China, EU Wait In The Wings For Access To Central Asia.' August 2. Accessed July 10, 2018. https://www.rferl.org/a/China_EU_Wait_In_The_Wings_For_Access_To_Central_Asia/1790745.html.

Petersen, Alexandros. 2016. *Integration in Energy and Transport*. London: Lexington Books.

Saivetz, Carol. 2003. 'Perspectives on the Caspian Sea Dilemma: Russian Policies Since the Soviet Demise.' *Eurasian Geography and Economics* 44 (8): 588–606.

Shlapentokh, Dmitry. 2013. 'Turkmenistan and military buildup in the Caspian region: A small state in the post-unipolar era.' *Journal of Eurasian Studies* 4: 154–159.

Smith, Dianne L. 1996. 'Central Asia: A New Great Game?' *Asian Affairs* 23 (3): 147–175.

Trenin, Dmitri. 2003. 'A Farewell to the Great Game? Prospects for Russian-American Security Cooperation in Central Asia.' *European Security* 12 (3–4): 21–35.

1 New Great Game in the Caspian Sea

Introduction

Since the early 1990s, the notion of the New Great Game has been used as a shorthand tool for explaining the competition between great powers over religious influence, military power, geopolitical hegemony, and economic profit (e.g., the oil and gas industries, and transport) in regions such as, the Caspian Sea, the Arctic Sea, the Black Sea, and the South China Sea (Borgerson 2009; Clover and Hornby 2015; Hunter 2017; Kim and Eom 2008; Rinna 2013). Besides being written into academic journals, the concept is also regularly used by popular media, such as Radio Free Europe, *Financial Times, New York Times, The Guardian*, due to its journalistic attractiveness (e.g., Bittner 2018; Pannier 2009; Norton-Taylor 2001). It is argued that great powers compete with each other to establish their political, cultural and economic influence over them. This competition has also been called 'the grand chessboard' (Brzezinski 1997, 64) and is understood as a zero-sum game or the re-establishment of China's and/or Russia's traditional vassal relations over these regional seas (Swanstrom 2005, 581). Although these regional seas exhibit complex patterns of cooperation and conflict at all levels from the local to the global, they are often depicted as prime arenas of the great powers' competition due to their geographical location, natural resources, and contested borders. In depicting them as such, the relevant literature has paid systematic attention to the significance of the New Great Game as an explanatory paradigm to facilitate understanding of the political and economic developments in these regional seas.

This chapter critically reviews the main theoretical and empirical works on the New Great Game. The latter mainly focused on the Caspian Sea region. This review is based on prominent academic journals, newspapers, reports, and policy briefs. In doing so, the chapter will answer the following questions: What do authors mean by the (New) Great Game? Why do they use this phrase and what do they consider to be at stake? Is there a difference between Old and New Great Games? With the answers to these questions, I will turn to the Caspian Sea region and ascertain: How the academic literature interprets the impact of competition between great powers on social,

DOI: 10.4324/9781003189626-2

New Great Game in the Caspian Sea   13

political and economic developments in the Caspian Sea region? And: Who are presented as the dominant actors? Answering these questions offers a crucial insight into the relevant academic discussion, its logic and preferred vocabulary and it shows the main gaps and limits of the mainstream academic literature. More specifically, identifying the gaps and limits of extant scholarship will provide this research with new avenues for alternative theoretical and empirical interpretations.

The chapter is divided into five sections. Following the introduction, the second section traces the evolution of the scholarly conception of the Old Great Game. The third section critically engages with the main theoretical and empirical arguments of the New Great Game. The fourth section introduces the existing criticism of the New Great Game concept and alternative concepts that have been put forward so far. In the concluding section, I will present the main findings.

The original concept of the Great Game

According to Fromkin (1980, 936) and Hopkirk (1990, prologue), it was a British officer, Arthur Conolly, who first coined the phrase. Conolly was sent to Bukhara by the East Indian Company to convince the Uzbek Amir to side with them against the Russians. However, the Uzbek emir imprisoned him for two months and beheaded him. Later, a historian of the First Afghan War found the term 'Great Game' in his diary and quoted it (Fromkin 1980, 937). However, the term only became widespread and popularized during the first years of the 20th century after being used in the novel *Kim* by Rudyard Kipling, first published in McClure's and Cassell's magazines in 1900.[1] Considering this, it can be argued that the concept is originally based on a fictitious novel or imaginative fiction, on which some authors based their academic discussions.

The relevant literature follows the classical realist line of reasoning which claims that territorial control, power, prestige, economic profit, and imperial domination were the main aims of the Old Great Game (Campbell 2014; Deutschmann 2014; Fromkin 1980, Hopkirk 1990; Ingram 1980; Morrison 2017; Sergeev 2013; van der Oye 2014; Williams 1980). More precisely, it holds that the Old Great Game is a narrative of sovereign states' political struggle for power. Great powers, namely Britain and Russia, are presented as the dominant actors from an empirical perspective but the local rulers, the khanates, and their people being marginalized and side-lined in the academic discussion.

Much of the existing empirical work on this Great Game relies on historical studies, biographies, monographs, and archival documents (e.g., diplomatic correspondence) from Russia, Britain, India and Uzbekistan (Campbell 2014; Morrison 2017; Sergeev 2013; van der Oye 2014; Williams 1980). Each relevant empirical work uses these diverse sources to cover a particular timeframe, a war or an event that transpired between Britain and

14 *New Great Game in the Caspian Sea*

Russia (from 1800 until 1907). In light of this, the relevant scholarship claims various reasons to explain the rivalry between Britain and Russia. However, focusing only on the British-Russian rivalry, the relevant literature neglects and over-simplifies the complex web of alliances and conflicts that existed between Russia, the Kazakhs, and the Central Asian khanates.

The empirical literature should be divided into two bodies of scholarly works in accordance with the opposing and diverse conclusions they arrive at about who the aggressor was in the Old Great Game. The first body of scholarly works argues that the Russian authorities aimed to extend Russia's territorial, economic and political control, while challenging the British imperial dominance. According to this body of work Great Britain was possessed by the fear that Russia would march across Asia to attack the British position in India throughout the 19th century. Fromkin (1980, 939–940) argues that Britain had no less than five reasons for opposing the continuing Russian expansion: (1) the expansion would change the balance of power in the world by making Russia much stronger than the other European powers; (2) it would facilitate a Russian invasion of British India; (3) it would motivate India to revolt against Britain; (4) it would cause the Islamic regimes of Asia to collapse which in turn would lead to the outbreak of a general war between the European Powers; and (5) it would threaten British trade with Asia and the naval communication line upon which Britain's commercial and political positions in the world depended. Queen Victoria tellingly claimed that 'it is a question of Russian or British supremacy in the world' (Fromkin 1980, 940).

Similarly, Cooley (2012, Ch.1) adds that in response to the Russian expansion, Great Britain formulated a strategy to resist the Russian influence, which included contesting frontier areas, persuading local rulers to side with Great Britain, and deploying a vast network of secret agents to gather intelligence. To prevent the Russian expansion, Britain first attacked Afghanistan in 1838, which is called the First Anglo-Afghan War of 1838–42. Later, Russia encouraged Persia to move against Afghanistan in response to this war, which led to the Anglo-Persian War of 1856–57. More concretely, Britain attached Persia to prevent the Persian expansion. In 1878 Britain attacked Afghanistan for a second time in response to the Russian imperial army's annexation of the Central Asian khanates of Kokand and Bukhara (Cooley 2012, Ch.1; Hopkirk 1990, Ch.19). When Russian border patrols reached the Afghan frontier, during the Penjdeh crisis of 1885, Britain and Russia nearly went to war with each other (Fromkin 1980). The Old Great Game ended in 1907 with the signing of the *Anglo-Russian Convention* (Hopkirk 1990; Sergeev 2013, Ch. 6). In August of that year, this historic convention was signed in Petersburg by Count Izovolsky and Sir Arthur Nicolson, the British ambassador (Hopkirk 1990, 427). However, considering these historical facts and arguments, it can be argued that this first body of scholarly works on the Old Great Game implicitly presents Russia as the aggressor and Britain as a responding actor in it. The reason for this is that the relations between both countries have mostly been examined through British and other western sources. This body of scholarly works mainly focused on the one-sided, British perception of the conflict and rivalry. In doing so, this group ignores the Russian intentions, the importance of Central Asia to Russian history, and local interpretations of the Great Game conquest.

By contrast, the second body of scholarly works has tried to address this problem of one-sidedness by using the Russian, Uzbek and the Soviet Union archives (e.g., Malikov 2014; Mamadaliev 2014; Morrison 2017; Sergeev 2013). In 2014 *the Journal of Central Asian Survey* dedicated one of its special issues to the Russian conquest of Central Asia.[2] By studying different episodes of the conquest through archival documents, the issue outlines Russia's motives and ideologies and, above all, the meaning and experience of the conquest from a Central Asian perspective. This body of scholarly works collectively argues that the main aim of the Russian expansion was to strengthen its borders, break cultural resistance against Russian assimilation, and prevent the growing British influence from reaching the khanates in the region (Gorshenina 2014; Mamadaliev 2014). According to the relevant works, the Russians were worried about British economic imperialism, which threatened to push Russian goods and merchants out of Central Asia. This second body of scholarly works thus shows that there was outside pressure on Russia to define its political and economic spheres of interest in Central Asia to its own advantage (Williams 1980). Despite this contribution, one may argue that similar to the western perspective espoused by the first body of scholarly works, the second body one-sidedly describes Russia as a responding actor and Britain as an expansionist empire. In this regard, it can be argued that the relevant literature as a whole offers both British and Russian perspectives of the Old Great Game. However, one needs to read works espousing both perspectives in order to understand the full picture. Moreover, while the relevant works mainly focus on these two empires, scant attention has been paid to the local actors' motivations, roles, and responses to the British-Russian rivalry in Central Asia.

Overall, considering the discussion above, it can be argued that the term Great Game has been used to describe the competition and rivalry between two empires, Russia and Great Britain. According to the relevant scholarship, the goal of the original Great Game was to extend and preserve Russian and British imperial dominance in politics as well as economics in Central and Southeast Asia. In doing so, these empires mainly pursued military alliances and strategies to achieve their goals. To achieve their long-term goals, both empires used local actors and neighbouring empires such as Persia as Great Game strategies. However, the relevant authors do not explain why they prefer to use the term 'Great Game' or what the theoretical or analytical advantage of using the term in their discussion is. This gives the impression that the term is only used by the relevant literature because of its journalistic appeal or literariness rather than its analytical or theoretical value. This is an issue because the lack of analytical value makes it difficult to

16 *New Great Game in the Caspian Sea*

determine its conceptual utility, methodological choice, patterns, empirical categories, and the scope of its analysis (Marks 2011). Therefore, it can be argued that the relevant literature prefers to use the Great Game metaphor because of its linguistic attractiveness. Despite its journalistic appeal, it can be argued that the Old Great Game actually took place because in the 19th century Russia and Great Britain confronted each other both directly, in military altercations, and indirectly. With this in mind the main question becomes whether and how the New Great Game is connected to the Old Great Game.

From Old to New Great Game

Actors

The contrast between the actors that are said to be involved in Old Great Game and the New Great Game is one of the most striking differences between the two. Like the literature on the Old Great Game, the scholarship on the New Great Game views great external powers as the main competitors in it. In the New Great Game these permanent players are the US, Russia and China (Alam 2002; Karasac 2002). Unlike the literature on the Old Great Game, however, the literature on the New Great Game (in the Caspian Sea Region) considers regional powers, such as India, China, Saudi Arabia, Turkey, Iran, Pakistan, the European Union, Kazakhstan, Turkmenistan, Azerbaijan, Georgia, and Armenia each with their own aims, objectives, and methods of attaining them (Sheng 2017). These regional powers are seen to join the permanent players' political and economic blocks in situational coalitions to achieve their own goals. Examples of these coalitions from existing scholarship are Iran, Russia and Armenia contra Turkey, the US, and the EU; Russia and China contra Turkey and the US; Iran and Russia contra the US and the EU (Khanna 2008; Rywkin 2004; Scott 2008; Swanstrom 2005). This means that the relevant literature recognizes local actors as part of the New Great Game, which in turn means that the discussion is more comprehensive. However, similar to the Old Great Game, the literature on the New Great Game is also state-centric because non-governmental actors are neglected.

In discussing its main players, the literature on the New Great Game should be divided into two bodies of works based on the diverse and opposing assumptions. The first body of works explains the competition and rivalry as mainly existing between the great powers, e.g. the US, China and Russia (Alam 2002; Flikke and Wilhelmsen 2008; Iseri 2009; Khanna 2008; Kim and Eom 2008; Kubicek 2013; Swanstrom 2005). In doing so, this literature recognizes the local actors as 'primitive states' (Khanna 2008, 93). Similar to the literature on the Old Great Game, local states and their peoples are marginalized or ignored completely in this body of works. For example, Swanstrom argues that:

New Great Game in the Caspian Sea   17

...the principal actors today are China and the US, especially following the US intervention in Afghanistan. Neither China nor the US is concerned over Russian pressure in the long term, since they know Russia has severe economic and social problems of its own to deal with.

(Swanstrom 2005, 581)

It is apparent that China has begun to use financial means to make the Central Asian states more dependent on it, a dependence in terms of gas and oil as well as political and military cooperation (Swanstrom 2005). Similarly, Rywkin (2004) argues that the New Great Game is between the US and Russia. All eight republics of Central Asia and the Southern Caucasus need good relations with both Russia and the US in order to ensure their independence and peaceful development in the 21st century (Kim and Indeo 2013). Nevertheless, despite their contribution, this body of works presents oversimplified conclusions, as they do not offer a new way of understanding the regional dynamics. More concretely, this group neglects that times have changed since the Old Great Game. States that were not around in the 19th century emerged in the early 1990s, and they can follow different foreign policy directions, such as joining different alliances or intergovernmental organizations than they were expected to. Meanwhile, the political and economic costs of interstate wars have grown unaffordable. The inability to incorporate these developments shows that this body of works is written with a 19th century mindset and uses a 'one size-fits-all' toolbox to view current developments and events which are far more intertwined and co-influential than those in the Old Great Game.

In contrast to the first group, the second body of works advances the debate by recognizing the role of regional actors such as, Azerbaijan, Armenia, Kazakhstan, Iran, Turkey, and Turkmenistan (Collins and Bekenova 2016; Edwards 2003; Kavaliski 2010; Kubicek 2013; Orazgaliyev 2017; Smith 1996). This body of works advances the New Great Game argument while also recognizing the influence of newly independent states and regional powers. According to Kanet (2010, 81) 'the local states are not mere pawns in the hands of the great powers. In fact, local leaders have been able to use their command of energy resources, their location and other factors to play off the outside states to their own advantage.' They are their own actors who can play the game for their own advantage and out of their own motivation and self-interest (Collings and Bekenova 2017). Denison argues that:

...newly independent regional states rapidly moved from being consumers of externally constructed geopolitical plays to a position of agency, thus the West's protectionist work is done in the region. The sovereignty of the region's states is established and unlikely to be reversed.

(Denison 2012, 148)

18 *New Great Game in the Caspian Sea*

According to the relevant works, the dynamics of the New Great Game allowed Central Asian and Caspian elites to play off the external actors against each other. The local actors have developed closer ties with Washington when needed and they have moved away towards Moscow or Beijing when their threat perceptions changed (Collins and Bekenova 2017). For example, according to the second body of works, the composition of interests of the Azerbaijani oil consortia are not only a direct result of economic forces, but also the result of a very deliberate weighing-up of Azerbaijani foreign policy interests (Orazgaliyev 2017). In the same vein, Kennedy (2010, 132) finds that 'power has shifted from outside actors to Kazakhstan itself as the government handles effectively external alternatives (China, Russia and the West) and uses interest in its petroleum resources to bolster its international role.' In other words, the countries in the region try to preserve the balance between external powers to satisfy their own economic and political interests.

Overall, the current scholarly debate on the New Great Game recognizes local states as well as external powers as actors. However, the advancement of the New Great Game argument stopped after the development that instigated its second body of works. In other words, following the recognition of the local states as actors, the literature has failed to move one-step further to include actors besides and beyond states in its examination of this New Great Game. As a result, the rest of the players again are side-lined. States are still presented as the main players and the rest, companies, banks, financial institutions, and NGOs, are only ever considered tools of the states. Scant scholarship has been devoted to the motivations and preferences of actors besides or in spite of states, such as, companies, financial institutions, lobby groups, banks, NGOs and intergovernmental organizations. For example, Ismailzade argues that:

> ...Putin has actively used energy companies as a tool to promote a 'liberal empire'. For this purpose, energy giants such as RAO-UES, Gazprom, Rosneft and Transneft – controlled by the Kremlin – became the harbingers of a new Russian policy in the Caucasus. This policy has consisted of obtaining as many local energy assets as possible across the Former Soviet Union, thus placing the Caucasus republics into a position of economic, and thus political, dependence on Russia.
>
> (Ismailzade 2006, 2)

In this sense, some of the New Great Game scholars do discuss the influence of non-governmental actors, albeit only superficially and only because for them these non-governmental actors represent states' national interests. Additionally, little academic literature has been devoted to the technical, social, diplomatic, security, and networking power of other actors. The literature fails to see, for example, how the network of different financial institutions and NGOs with differing interests autonomously coordinated

New Great Game in the Caspian Sea 19

regional developments. With this in mind, I will take the advancement of the New Great Game argument one-step further and include actors besides states without emphasizing Great Game politics.

Objective: Survival of the fittest

According to the relevant literature, the first aim of the states engaged in the New Great Game is controlling the transnational infrastructure of the region (Alam 2002; Allison and Jonson 2001; Amineh 1999; Blank 2004; 2012; Karasac 2002; Kubicek 2013; Labban 2009; Monshipouri 2016; Uddin 1997). Because the Caspian Sea is landlocked, it is difficult to export the resources extracted from it to global markets. One of the important ways of exporting goods is through transnational infrastructure, that is, through pipelines, railways, highways, and ports. Therefore, the questions of how infrastructure access is managed – what routes should be provided, who should be responsible for their construction and safety, who charges tolls and profits from them as well as the question of who composes the consortia and firms responsible for this – are portrayed as a whole subsection of the New Great Game hypobook (Dodds 2005; Karasac 2002; Iseri 2009; Collins and Bekenova 2016; Smith 1996; Stegen and Kusznir 2015). Thus, events like building of gas or oil pipelines between Azerbaijan and the EU, Kazakhstan and Russia, or Turkmenistan and China have been framed as a rebalancing of forces between these great powers.

The proponents of classical geopolitics have portrayed the process of planning and constructing transnational infrastructure projects, namely the BTC, the SGC, the Baku-Tbilisi-Kars railway and the Baku International Sea Trade Port, as the new round of the Great Game in the Caspian Sea (see e.g., Alam 2002; Bayulgen 2009; Cohen 2002; Economist Intelligence Unit 2013; Karasac 2002; Kim and Eom 2008; Kober 2000). In this conception of the New Great Game, Russia and Iran are depicted as the main opponents to the development of the pipelines because these infrastructures are viewed as a way to avoid Russian and Iranian infrastructural imperialism and its monopoly on infrastructure. The US, Turkey, and the EU are described as saviours of local actors on the other hand, because they are taken to be the alternative to Russian and Iranian imperial plans. In the New Great Game scholarship, Russia, Iran and Armenia are claimed to be among the main causes of almost every technical, economic and political issue (see e.g., Assenova and Shiriyev 2015; Frappi and Valigi 2015; Kober 2000; Lussac 2008; Rukhadze 2016; Rzayev and Huseynov 2018). Absurdly, those projects are all different, but the proposed arguments are the same.

For example, Kusznir (2013, 5) argues that 'Russia will not renounce its own position in the region and will use different methods of pressure (cultural, political and energy leverage) on gas producing countries and the transit country Turkey.' Along the same lines, Dodds (2005) described the Caspian Sea basin as part of a gigantic strategic triangle (along with the South China

20 *New Great Game in the Caspian Sea*

Sea and West Asia) that would come to shape the patterns of potential (resource) wars in the 21st century. According to existing literature, a notable development in this new round is that besides Russia and Iran, China now plays a main role in these transnational infrastructure projects. The reason for this is China's 'One Belt One Road' project. The Caspian Sea countries invested billions of dollars in transnational projects to connect Asia to Europe. While supporting the idea of great power competition in the Caspian Sea, Yenikeyeff (2011) argues that 'in this new game Russia prefers the active involvement of China, rather than that of the EU and the US, because Russia views China as a partner against EU-US bloc.' Therefore, according to scholars advancing the New Great Game reading, the new round is a competition between two blocks: Russia, China and Iran contra the EU, Turkey, the US and Azerbaijan (Kusznir 2013).

What these scholarly works have in common is that they constantly ask how power politics influence transnational infrastructure and how regional conflicts threaten infrastructure. Scant scholarship has been devoted to the effects of transnational infrastructure projects on the strategies of regional cooperation and exchange. The New Great Game literature constantly predicts war and conflict in the long term and is unable to explain the peaceful developments and exchanges in the Caspian Sea. This is also the dominant way in which infrastructure is presented in the media and in official speeches by politicians.

Environmental conflicts

The literature divides environmental resources into two main groups: renewable (e.g., land, forest, water, fish, caviar) and non-renewable resources (e.g., oil, natural gas, diamond and gold). According to the literature, the second goal of the states engaged in the New Great Game relates to politics of non-renewable resources and who controls how much of them (Alabi 2013; Labban 2009; Monshipouri 2016; Uddin 1997). By using the scarcity framework, the relevant literature argues that environmental competition has intensified in recent times due to the rapid growth of the influence of great powers, which has increased the demand for the non-renewable natural resources, primarily oil, natural gas, gold, and diamonds (Diehl and Gleditsch 2001; Moyo 2012). More concretely, the relevant literature argues that the Caspian Sea environmental resources (oil and natural gas) are one of the main reasons for competition and rivalry between external great powers, such as the US and China, and regional ones such as Russia, Turkey, and Iran (Borgerson 2009; Klare 2001; Moyo 2012). Because of the landlocked nature of the Caspian Sea, it is extremely difficult to export natural gas and oil to external markets. In light of this, the regional powers compete to control the infrastructure facilitating the export of these resources. Therefore, works on the New Great Game argue that the essence of the entire geopolitical competition is creating an uninterrupted flow of oil from the region to the Western energy markets. For the

Western great powers this means restricting Russian and Iranian monopoly on the search for oil and gas fields and their exploitation (Karasac 2002; Kubicek 2013).

To support these arguments, the relevant literature constantly exaggerates the natural resource reserves of the Caspian Sea. When comparing the Caspian Sea with the Middle East, the literature depicts Caspian natural gas and oil reserves as an alternative source of fuel large enough to save the world (Alam 2002). The relevant literature tends to cite reserve figures that range from optimistic to unrealistic. The most commonly used estimate for the region's oil reserves is 200 billion barrels, with no distinction made between 'proven' and 'possible' reserves (see e.g., Alam 2002; Bahgat 2003; Kim and Blank 2016; Jaffe and Manning 1998; Ruseckas 1998). This exaggeration might seem unimportant but it has created a false image of the sea and increased international attention to it.

Lastly, the New Great Game literature sees the way environmental issues were handled mainly to support its geopolitical arguments and power politics. For example, Ismailzade (2006, 22) argues that the BTC project was hindered or postponed because environmental issues were raised. Many consider Russia to be behind these environmental protests or obstacles, as it seeks to stop the regional projects.[3]

Naval advancement

Military security is portrayed as another goal of the states engaged in the New Great Game. The topic has gained prominence since the early 2000s due to several reasons, such as the uncertain legal status of the Caspian Sea, the 9/11 attacks, and subsequent US intervention in Afghanistan, the NATO Partnership for Peace (PfP) program, and regional ethnic conflicts. According to the relevant literature, one of the main reasons the states involved had for building up their naval forces was the uncertain legal status of the Caspian Sea.

Alam (2002, 22) argues that 'there are two burning issues in the Caspian Sea Basin—the legal status of the Caspian Sea and the ethnic conflicts. These two sensitive issues can at anytime jeopardize the security of the region. Thus, these issues should be properly and carefully resolved.' Similarly, Haghayeghi (2003, 36) claims that 'Azerbaijan, Turkmenistan and Kazakhstan have small naval forces but are increasing them as the legal status of the Caspian Sea continues to be contested.' According to these authors, the increase in military movement corresponds with the rising tension about the uncertain legal status of the Caspian Sea. The relevant scholars argue that Russia and Iran are by far the most dominant naval powers in the region and have already shown a willingness to use their military might to intimidate their neighbours (Karasac 2002; Saivetz 2003; Shlapentokh 2013). It has been argued that 'Russia would engage in war with Azerbaijan and Turkmenistan, if its interests were ignored' (Shlapentokh 2013, 155). In light of this,

22 *New Great Game in the Caspian Sea*

the relevant literature takes the build-up of naval forces to be one of the ways in which littoral states to protect their legal status in the Caspian Sea (Laruelle and Peyrouse 2009; Shlapentokh 2013).

Furthermore, in the aftermath of the 9/11 terror attacks and the subsequent American-led military action in Afghanistan, the whole question of a New Great Game was revisited because following the 9/11 terror attacks, the Caspian Sea came to be considered a strategically important sector for NATO (Alam 2002). With the signing of the PfP, NATO has sought to set up close military relations with Azerbaijan, Turkmenistan, and Kazakhstan.[4]Laruelle and Peyrouse (2009) propose a number of reasons for these Western military activities in the region. First, they argue that the integrity of the newly independent states might be under the threat of Moscow and Tehran because of the presence of Russia and Iran, which would make the area susceptible to instability in the long-term which would in turn be detrimental to Western interests. Second, they state the security of American companies participating in international consortiums exploiting Azerbaijani and Kazakhstani oil has to be ensured. Lastly, the security of eastern Turkey and the export routes from the Caspian to the Caucasus and the Black Sea requires Western supervision.

In short, almost every argument of the New Great Game literature is based on the myth of absolute state sovereignty and state-centric geopolitics based on constant fear and preparation for war. However, this (mainly pessimistic) scholarship neglects how times have changed between the 19th and 21st centuries and that the attitude towards warfare has changed. Up to the First World War, waging a successful war was seen as the highest goal for rulers. If they wanted to claim a heroic legacy, they had to conquer new territories or regain those lost in previous wars. However, in the 21th century warfare is seen as a failure of diplomacy while avoiding warfare became the highest loftiest aim of diplomacy.

What is presented as new and who is presented as the winner?

Often the adjective 'new' is added to distinguish contemporary changes, frameworks from older developments as seen in the usage of 'new regionalism', 'new political science' and 'new security studies'. 'New' in 'Great Game' is employed in the same way by scholars who try to explain the post-Cold War developments and changes in different regions. Considering both theoretical and empirical perspectives, it can be asked what is 'new' in this Great Game. From a theoretical perspective, it can be argued that the existing works use a logic to explain the current developments that is similar to the logic used in the Old Great Game literature, e.g., the logic of foregrounding states, establishing monopolies over natural resources, pursuing power maximization, prioritizing their own survival, establishing cultural and religious influence over others, and aspiring to military dominance and geopolitical hegemony. In other words, it is still coloured by a logic of quasi-Darwinian survival of the fittest among sovereign giants. The literature does not recognize the present-day complexities, recent geopolitical trends, the effects of globalization or the distinction between the 19th and the 21th centuries. In this regard, it can be argued that it is misleading to call it 'new' because there is nothing new in this conception of a so-called Great Game. The aim that scholars argue to be underlying this game is influence at political, economic, and cultural levels. Therefore, the New Great Game literature is not 'new' because it fails to move away from orthodox and outdated state-centric assumptions and considers states and regions as given.

From an empirical perspective, the relevant literature describes almost every event, case or regional project, such as the construction of transnational infrastructure, legal disputes, environmental disagreements and transportation of natural resources, as part of this so-called New Great Game. Therefore, there is a clear logic in the New Great Game scholarship (as there was in the Old Great Game scholarship) but whether this logic accurately predicts conflict or cooperation is not clear. Additionally, unlike the Old Great Game scholarship, the New Great Game recognizes the role of regional states. Unlike the Old Great Game scholarship however, what is described in New Great Game literature is purely the imagination of authors based on newspaper articles. The reason for this is that in the 19th century Britain and Russia had wars and clashes in Central Asia. However, since the 1990s the great powers have not openly clashed in the Caspian Sea. This means that the causes for events and occurrences that the Old Great Game literature described are more substantial than those the New Great Game literature describes. It also makes the arguments of the New Great Game literature less strong because they give no real reason for this lack of conflict. By indulging in this, the New Great Game literature tends to interpret the present and future developments in terms of outdated 19th century insights rather than the 21st-century condition of world politics.

The next question is who the winner of the New Great Game is. Unfortunately, there is no agreement between the different New Great Game scholars. The studies examining the outcomes of the New Great Game have generated a wide range of contradicting empirical findings, which do not allow for a clear-cut conclusion. Kavalski (2010) argues that no country has yet come out as the dominant force – a position that seems increasingly untenable given the number of international actors who are involved in the New Great Game. The reason that no one force has yet become dominant despite the involvement of so many actors with diverse aims and interests, is that all of them prefer stability and peace in the region to war and conflict (Kavalski 2010; Smith 1996). According to Smith (1996) the players of the New Great Game, in particular Iran, Pakistan, India, Russia, and China, seek to promote stability in the region while expanding and protecting their own regional influence, unlike the players of the Old Great Game.

In contrast to these assumptions, Kazantsev (2008, 1084) claims that 'up to the middle of 2006, Russia had achieved its aim to preserve its dominance

24 *New Great Game in the Caspian Sea*

of the region and restrict access of other powers.' He therefore considered Russia the winner of the New Great Game. Similarly, Stegen and Kusznir (2015, 102) declared 'China and the Caspian Sea states themselves the winners of the New Great Game.' The reason for this outcome is the irritating behaviour of other great powers, Russia in particular. These irritating behaviours included Russia's aggressive intervention in Georgia and Ukraine, which decreased the trust that the Caspian Sea states had in Russian intentions. Similarly, the democratizing pressures of the US and the EU, which were taken to be a threat to the existing system of the Caspian Sea states, were considered irritating and were counterproductive to the US' and EU's aims of building influence in the region (Stegen and Kusznir 2015).

These examples illustrate that the relevant scholars present different and contradictory findings, which makes it difficult to follow the debate or to see one systematic New Great Game discussion. These contradicting findings also illustrate that pessimistic vocabularies and assumptions dominate the scholarly debate about the future of the Caspian Sea region. Despite all the positive developments in the region, the New Great Game literature does not expect a peaceful resolution to the existing issues because rivalry, not cooperation, is presented as the essence of the region's diplomacy.

Critiques: Where does the New Great Game literature lead us?

The arguments put forward in relation to the New Great Game reading of developments in the Caspian Sea region have been challenged by a number of scholars (e.g., Amirova-Mammadova 2017; Bashir 2017; Casier 2016; Cooley 2012; Edwards 2003; Fettweis 2011; Grigas 2017; Jaffe and Manning 1998; Orazgaliyev 2017; Stulberg 2012; Trenin 2003). These critics question the theoretical, conceptual and empirical assumptions and relevance of the New Great Game literature mainly by using geo-economic and liberal theories and lines of reasoning.

From a theoretical perspective, these critics argue that using the toolbox of (neo)realism (e.g., state, power, geostrategic interests, rivalries, wars, and threat perception) is not sufficient to critically examine and explain the intertwined contemporary dynamics in the region (Edwards 2003; Orazgaliyev 2017). More concretely, the relevant literature claims that the (neo)realist approach misses a number of fundamental tools and theoretical instruments to shed light on the more complex developments in the global arena. To counter this, critics offer insights from the liberalist theory as an alternative way to analyse the conflict, competition and cooperation between different actors, both regional and global. The liberalist insights include the influence of private actors, mutual interdependence, cooperation and economic power rather than just insisting on military causes for all developments.

Critics question the validity of the concept of the New Great Game in relation to the interactions in the Caspian Sea region from a conceptual perspective as well. According to some critics, today, the number of external players is large and their aims are far more complex than the rather black-and-white imperatives of the Old Great Game, and there is no longer a convenient regional power vacuum for the external players to fight over (Bashir 2017; Casier 2016; Cooley 2012; Edwards 2003). Casier (2016) argues that considering the complexity of contemporary energy markets, the Western-Russian energy-related geopolitics should be viewed from a broader and more pluralist perspective that accounts for the preferences and interactions of private, governmental, and individual actors. In doing so, a distinction should be made between collective and bilateral interactions in order to accommodate the fact that the process is not only about energy politics, but also about economics and environmental concerns and has to contend with social and cultural preferences as well (Casier 2016). It will also help scholars to see that energy politics is only one part of the complex geopolitical and geo-economic picture rather than its only part.

From an empirical point of view, critics argue that most New Great Game authors have a wrong picture of the Caspian Sea region because they use inadequate conceptual tools. That is to say, the New Great Game literature ignores cooperation in specific sectors when assessing the relationship between great powers and regional states (Bashir 2017; Casier 2016; Cooley 2012; Trenin 2003). One of these cooperation examples is the war on terror after the 9/11 terror attacks. Trenin (2003) explains that Russia and the US, contrary to what advocates of the New Great Game reading think, have been cooperating in their policies toward Afghanistan since the tragedy of 9/11, which made them allies in the war on terror. Russian President Putin initially agreed to allow US forces to establish temporary military bases in Uzbekistan and Kyrgyzstan in support of its campaign in Afghanistan. Putin not only offered President Bush support in Afghanistan, which included providing valuable intelligence information, but raised no objection to a US military presence in Central Asia. According to Trenin (2003), the reason for this is that it became clear that Russia and America were facing similar challenges, and that their enemies were closely allied. In addition, Russia did not prevent Azerbaijan's involvement in PfP.

Another example of this cooperation is the way energy companies have been allowed to do business in the region. More specifically, American energy companies collaborated with Russian companies in order to build the Caspian-Pipeline-Consortium (CPC) pipeline (Orazgaliyev 2017). Rather than competing over the routing of pipelines from the Caspian region, Western and Russian oil companies have cooperated on the commercially appealing and strategically important projects, such as the South Caucasus Pipeline (SCP)[5] consortium in which Iranian, Russian, and Western companies are shareholders (Edwards 2003; Orazgaliyev 2017; Trenin 2003).

According to Cooley (2012), many of Russia's policies regarding the Caspian Sea region have been tactical reactions to American and Chinese initiatives or reflections of the broader state of its relations with these great

26   *New Great Game in the Caspian Sea*

powers. The interaction between the US, Russia, and China in the region has intensified over the decade, but zero-sum competition or the pursuit of relative gains have not been the exclusive or even the dominant form of great power interaction. At times their agendas have generated some flashpoints, tensions, and direct retaliations, but for the most part they have coexisted in the region without nearly the level of conflict that New Great Game scholars perceive. According to Kaczmarski (2018) Russia and China deliberately try to avoid a clash between their economic initiatives (Silk Road and Eurasian Union) or an open rivalry. The reasons for this are that China is more interested in the practical benefits of regional cooperation and that cooperation is beneficial to Russia as it is struggling to maintain the image of a strategic leader in Eurasia.

Additionally, the relevant critics argue that the natural resource reserves of the Caspian Sea are exaggerated. According to Jaffe and Manning (1998), the idea from the 1990s that the oil reserves in the Caspian Sea region can offer long-term energy security to the West was a misconception. In this regard, the suggestions that these newly independent states could solve Western energy problems and give the West geopolitical advantages against Russia, Iran, and China were exaggerated myths (Jaffe and Manning 1998). This misinformed estimation of the region's richness in resources also inflated the region's commercial and strategic significance and distorted the US foreign policy calculations, which led the US to risk ultimately unnecessary tensions with other actors, particularly Russia and Iran (Bashir 2017). In short, the energy reserves in the Caspian region are much less important than many political analyses have implied (Bashir 2017; Jaffe and Manning 1998).

Considering the latest findings, Grigas (2017), argues that since the 2010s, changes in the global gas markets, such as competition from Liquified Natural Gas (LNG) and the shale gas-boom, have reduced the significance of Caspian or Central Asian gas for Russia, Europe, and China. Both Europe and China now have a number of alternatives because of their gas diversification and supply strategy, especially in the form of LNG. Similarly, Rzayeva (2013, 2015) argues that the gas volume that the Shah Deniz (SD) consortium will be offering on the markets (10 bcm/a on the European market and 6bcm/a on the Turkish market) is near-negligible when compared to Gazprom's gas volume (130 bcm/a). Not even the SD as a whole can compete with Russian gas.

Finally, by using the geo-economic perspectives Stulberg (2012) argues that the main competition over Caspian oil reserves essentially boils down to commercial competition among energy companies and financial interests, as opposed to geopolitical rivalry among states. Scant attention has been paid to understanding the conditions under which a weakened Russian government can manipulate markets and domestic regulatory mechanisms in interdependent energy networks for the purposes of statecraft. The tone of Russian diplomacy has become decidedly pragmatic, with primary emphasis placed on securing Russia's competitive economic interests (Stulberg 2012).

New Great Game in the Caspian Sea   27

In the oil sector, neither Russia nor Iran wields sufficient geo-economic clout, not even combined, to shape the course of the search for oil in the Caspian region or the direction of its main exports. Russia's geo-economic short-comings in the oil sector limit Moscow's ability to manipulate support for favoured oil exploration and exporting projects, or to impose restraint on regional energy diversification (Stulberg 2012). These geo-economic factors undermine the credibility of Russian threats to dictate proposals for extract-ing and exporting Caspian crude oil or to obstruct alternative proposals. Similarly, Edwards (2003) claims that the import-export of oil and gas requires economic as well as political cooperation as there is no one state that is able to dominate the market. Even states that are supposed by New Great Game scholars to be directly competing for political influence – Russia and China for instance – work with each other. Russia may still view Central Asia and the Caucasus as lying within her geopolitical space, but it seems to have a willingness to accept that there can be no monopoly of influence on those states, either in the political or economic sense. In the same vein, Fettweis (2011) claims that unlike the (neo)realist expectations, neither of the two burning regional issues, that is the uncertain legal status of the Caspian Sea and the ethnic conflicts, have sparked conflict. Despite the *realpolitik* language of the great powers, they use economic tools to achieve their objectives or strengthen their positions.

In short, taking these critiques into account, it can be argued that the number of scholars who are sceptical about the theoretical, conceptual and empirical arguments of the New Great Game reading is growing. These scholars challenge the theoretical, conceptual and empirical findings of previous works by offering alternative views that take better account of the geo-economic situation.

Conclusion

Kipling wrote his novel *Kim* based on his 19th-century imagination and a series of anecdotes. Today's literature borrowed its central term from Kipling. The concept of the New Great Game has been structured and explained differently by different scholars at different times. Nevertheless, the relevant literature suffers from theoretical, conceptual and empirical over-simplification. The relevant literature does not recognize the fundamental difference between the 19th-century state-centric system and the modern system of the 21st century. Many of the analyses that use this concept do so without any qualification or reservation. In the following, I focus on the persistent shortcomings that are characteristic of the studies discussed. More concretely, I will list five shortcomings in this conclusion.

The first shortcoming is that the existing literature barely studies the Cas-pian Sea per se. The relevant works view the sea merely as a separating entity between the Caucasus and Central Asia rather than as a bridge that unifies the littoral states. As a result, the existing literature mainly explores either

28   *New Great Game in the Caspian Sea*

the relationship between Armenia, Azerbaijan and Georgia as part of the South Caucasus on the one hand or the relationship between the five Central Asian states, Kazakhstan, Kirgizstan, Uzbekistan, Turkmenistan and Tajikistan. The literature includes Russia and Iran in both regional discussions, since they share border with both the South Caucasus and Central Asia. This book, by contrast, is interested particularly in understanding and explaining the role of the Caspian Sea, its natural resources, material infrastructures and the type of relationship between the five Caspian littoral states per se.

The second shortcoming is that the relevant literature includes too much empirical action with too few facts. More concretely, the relevant literature uses a mixture of unreliable information and evidence (e.g., the Caspian Sea's oil reserves measuring 200 billion barrels) to support its geopolitical arguments. In doing so, these academics neglect the intertwined connections between different issues in the broader picture, such as the legal status of the Caspian Sea, cooperation on environmental issues, and transportation of natural resources. They are therefore unable to adequately explain new developments, changes, and disagreements on these issues. This is the reason why the relevant scholarship is mainly pessimistic on the prospects for cooperation among the Caspian Sea states. Additionally, the scholarship uses a fixed mindset revolving around power, sovereignty issues, forging alliances, and insecurity to view all developments in the region. In doing so, a false image of the events in the modern Caspian Sea region has taken shape. Despite the distinctiveness of the issues faced by the states in the Caspian Sea region, their complexity cannot be understood in isolation. This interconnectivity means that the struggle in fixing one these issues may unexpectedly impact the other issues just as cooperation on one issue may create suitable conditions for tackling other issues.

The third shortcoming is that the relevant literature does not explain why, when, and how technical challenges lead to unanticipated economic, political, and social consequences. Instead, the relevant scholarship has investigated every challenge exclusively along the lines of rivalries between great powers and from a (neo)realist perspective without concrete evidence addressing transnational infrastructure developments. In this discussion, states, primarily Iran, China, and Russia, have been identified as the driving force behind every development, political, economic, technical, and social as well as environmental, and setback in the planning and construction phases of transnational infrastructure projects. In the same vein, this scholarship expects transnational infrastructure projects to always trigger rivalries or even wars in the region following their construction or even in their planning phase (as was predicted for the energy pipelines). However, as will be shown in chapters 4, 5, and 6, when one reviews the facts and ascertains the real causes of the above-mentioned issues, one can see that it was not Russia, Armenia, or Iran but one of the BTC pipeline's key stakeholders, Georgia, who blocked the pipeline's construction because of environmental issues. In the same vein, it was one of the core Western supporters of the project, the

UK, who investigated and questioned the involvement of BP and ECGD in the project for their technical and material failures, as will be shown in chapter 5. Finally, the project got delayed due to massive protests by workers. They protested against their poor working conditions, as will be shown in chapter 5. These examples point out that the resolution of technical issues cannot be fully explained by the New Great Game hypobook alone. In light of this, we can say it is crucial to have alternative theoretical and conceptual frameworks to distort this oversimplified debate and offer a more nuanced reading of the issues surrounding transnational infrastructures.

The fourth shortcoming, and one that is in line with the previous shortcoming, is that when addressing the impact of the infrastructural projects on the region, the existing scholarship (e.g., the scholarship with a geopolitical perspective and that with a geo-economic perspective), focuses mainly on conflict between states and/or companies while neglecting the material power of infrastructure. This is because, despite the diversity of the existent literature, scant research has explained how transnational infrastructure influences the interaction between different actors, or what kind of changes infrastructure brings and how the BTC influenced the relationship between the Caspian littoral states after its construction and whether the BTC has led to cooperation or to enhanced regional rivalry since its construction. It is necessary to consider these questions as they address the problems that arise when trying to think about the importance of transnational infrastructures. However, the relevant literature moves on to other issues or projects without answering these questions.

The final shortcoming is that the relevant works neglect the increasing role of other actors, such as companies, NGO, IGO, and banks by putting them into a state-centric analysis. In the 1990s, the New Great Game literature viewed the great powers as the only players in the Caspian Sea. Since 2000 the newly independent regional states have also been recognized as the players of the new great game due to their economic and political positions. Nevertheless, this advancement of the debate has not moved forward. By using a purely state-centric model, it has become increasingly difficult to understand new developments, changes, disagreements and conditions in the Caspian Sea region. To remedy this, I will continue developing the debate without emphasizing the New Great Game. Until relatively recently, scant scholarly attention was paid to the significance of non-governmental actors as an explanatory paradigm to assist in understanding the geopolitics of the Caspian Sea region. For example, both the New Great Game literature and geo-economic scholarship fail to explain what the role of transnational energy cooperation within the littoral states is. Or how non-governmental actors promote or undermine strategies of regional cooperation. It is important to answer these questions because transnational infrastructure projects involve other actors besides governments. To see the complete picture it is important to explain the role of these actors and their preferences.

30 *New Great Game in the Caspian Sea*

If one only considers the New Great Game literature, one would assume that the Caspian Sea is a hopeless place, which is wholly preoccupied with geopolitics, rivalries, and competition between regional and great powers. One would also assume that due to the rivalry between great powers, the newly independent Caspian states have to choose to pledge allegiance to either Russia and Iran, or the West. Thus, one would come to the conclusion that cooperation, regional integration and exchange for joint gains are extremely rare. It would lead one to believe that there is no hope for a bright future because the region is rife with political tension, ready to blow up and be destroyed sooner or later. The reason for this is that the New Great Game literature perceives attitudes as constant or fixed irrespective of the potential positive outcomes of cooperation processes. Another reason for this is that the literature wears the same black glasses and assumes that everything is dark, which makes them to miss any light and or different colour. However, is this the full picture? This is not, however, the complete picture of the situation in the Caspian Sea region, as will be shown in chapters 4, 5, and 6, because viewing the Caspian Sea first and foremost as a geopolitical battleground obscures important layers of a more complex reality. Because they describe every development from a black and white perspective, the New Great Game scholars ignore the cooperation that takes place in areas such as environmental policy, energy politics, and the legal status of the Caspian Sea. In the early 1990s, it was understandable to work with uncertain assumptions or misleading perceptions because of uncertainty in the region. It was difficult for (Western) scholars to gain access to the region in the 1990s. However, continuing to work with the same exaggerated and oversimplified assumptions now without detailed research or critical attitudes would produce inaccurate results unnecessarily, as the region is now open to the outside world and it is possible to work with more accurate information.

Overall, relying solely on the New Great Game paradigm to analyze the Caspian Sea region leaves several important questions unanswered. Therefore, this literature misses several complex dynamics and processes that are taking place in the Caspian Sea region.

Notes

1 It appeared as a book, namely Kipling, Rudyard. 1901. *Kim.* London: Macmillan and Co Ltd. Website for McClure's Magazine: http://www.kiplingsociety.co.uk/m embers/paper_richardskim.htm.
2 Link for the journal: http://www.tandfonline.com/toc/rjpp20/12/2?nav=tocList.
3 Besides energy politics, competition for cultural and religious dominance is proposed as another facet of the New Great Game. Since the beginning of the 1990s, it has been widely anticipated that there would be a struggle for cultural and religious influence (pan-Turkism, pan-Arabism, and/or pan-Islamism) in Central Asia and South Caucasus between Iran, Saudi Arabia, Pakistan, India and Turkey (Ahrari 1994; Hunter 2017; Kim and Eom 2008; Monshipouri 2016). However, since cultural and religious aspects are outside the scope of this research and not relevant to the discussion, they are not included in the main discussion.

New Great Game in the Caspian Sea 31

4 The Partnership for Peace (PfP) is a programme of practical bilateral cooperation between individual Euro-Atlantic partner countries and NATO. It was established in 1994 and allows partners to build up an individual relationship with NATO, choosing their own priorities for cooperation and pace of progress. Currently, there are 21 countries in the Partnership for Peace programme (as cited in NATO (2017)).

5 The South Caucasus Pipeline (SCP) was built to export Shah Deniz gas from Azerbaijan to Georgia and Turkey. The pipeline starts from the Sangachal terminal near Baku. It follows the route of the BTC crude oil pipeline through Azerbaijan and Georgia to Turkey, where it is linked to the Turkish gas distribution system (BP Azerbaijan 2018).

Bibliography

Ahrari, Ehsan M. 1994. 'The dynamics of the new great game in Muslim Central Asia.' *Central Asian Survey* 13 (4): 525–539.

Alabi, Joshua. 2013. 'Resource conflicts: energy worth fighting for?' In *International Handbook of Energy Security*, by Hugh Dyer and Julia Maria, 41–78. Cheltenham: Edward Elgar.

Alam, Shah. 2002. 'Pipeline Politics in the Caspian Sea Basin.' *Strategic Analysis* 26 (1): 5–26.

Allison, Roy, and Lena Jonson. 2001. *Central Asian Security: the New International Context*. Washington: Brookings Institution Press.

Amineh, Perviz Mehdi. 1999. *Towards the Control of Oil Resources in the Caspian Region*. New York: St. Martin's Press.

Amirova-Mammadova, Sevinj. 2017. *Pipeline Politics and Natural Gas Supply from Azerbaijan to Europe*. Wiesbaden: Springer.

Assenova, Margarita, and Zaur Shiriyev. 2015. *Azerbaijan and the New Energy Geopolitics of Southeastern Europe*. Washington: Jamestown Foundation.

Bahgat, Gawdat. 2003. 'Pipeline Diplomacy: The Geopolitics of the Caspian Sea Region.' *International Studies Perspective* 3 (3): 310–327.

Bashir, Omar S. 2017. 'The Great Games Never Played: Explaining Variation in International Competition Over Energy.' *Journal of Global Security Studies* 2 (4): 288–306.

Bayramov, Agha. 2019. 'Great game visions and the reality of cooperation around post-Soviet transnational infrastructure projects in the Caspian Sea region.' *East European Politics* 35 (2): 159–181.

Bayulgen, Oksan. 2009. 'Caspian energy wealth: social impacts and implications for regional stability.' In *The Politics of Transition in Central Asia and the Caucasus*, by Amanda E Wooden and Christoph H Stefes, 163–189. New York: Routledge.

Bittner, Jochen. 2018. 'Who Will Win the New Great Game?' 26 April. Accessed July 10,2018. https://www.nytimes.com/2018/04/26/opinion/russia-china-west-power.html.

Blank, Stephen. 2012. 'Whither the new great game in Central Asia?' *Journal of Eurasian Studies* 3: 147–160.

Blank, Stephen. 2004. 'Infrastructural policy and national strategies in Central Asia: the Russian example.' *Central Asia Survey* 23 (3): 225–248.

Borgerson, Scott G. 2009. 'The Great Game Moves North.' March 25. Accessed April 6, 2018. https://www.foreignaffairs.com/articles/global-commons/2009-03-25/great-game-moves-north.

32 *New Great Game in the Caspian Sea*

Brzezinski, Zbigniew. 1997. *The Grand Chessboard*. New York: Basic Books.

BP Azerbaijan. 2018. 'First Quarter 2018 Results. May 17.' Accessed May 23, 2016. https://www.bp.com/en_az/caspian/press/businessupdates/first-quarter-2018-results. html.

Campbell, Ian. 2014. 'Our friendly rivals': rethinking the Great Game in Ya'qub Beg's Kashgaria, 1867–77.' *Central Asian Survey* 33 (2): 199–214.

Casier, Tom. 2016. 'Great Game or Great Confusion: The Geopolitical Understanding of EU-Russia Energy Relations.' *Geopolitics* 21 (4): 763–778.

Clover, Charles, and Lucy Hornby. 2015. 'China's Great Game: Road to a new empire.' 12 October. Accessed July 10, 2018. https://www.ft.com/content/6e098274 -587a-11e5-a28b-50226830d644.

Cohen, Ariel. 2002. *Iran's Calims over Caspian Sea Resources Threaten Energy Security.* Washington: The Heritage Foundation.

Collins, Neil, and Kristina Bekenova. 2017. 'Fuelling the New Great Game: Kazakhstan, energy policy and the EU.' *Asia Europe Journal* 15 (1): 20–40.

Cooley, Alexander. 2012. *Great Games, Local Rules*. New York: Oxford University Press.

Denison, Michael. 2012. 'Game Over? Shifting Energy Geopolitics in Central Asia.' Policy Brief. Washington: Elliott School of International Affairs.

De Wilde, Jaap. 2017. 'Anachronistic Research in International Relations and Security Studies.' In *Rethinking Security in the Twenty-First Century*, by Edwin Daniel Jacob, 29–41. New York: Springer.

Diehl, Paul F, and Nils Petter Gleditsch. 2001. *Environmental Conflict*. Colorado: Westview Press.

Deutschmann, Moritz. 2014. 'The Great Game, 1856–1907.' *European Review of History* (21) 3: 435–436.

Dodds, Klaus. 2005. *Global Geopolitics: A Critical Introduction*. Essex: Pearson Education Ltd.

Economist Intelligence Unit. 2013. 'The Great Game for gas in the Caspian.' *The Economist.* http://www.energianews.com/newsletter/files/ddf2b1fcc6f999dd6d96ff56 05b022c1.pdf.

Edwards, Matthew. 2003. 'The New Great Game and the new great gamers: Disciples of Kipling and Mackinder.' *Central Asian Survey* 22 (1): 83–102.

Fettweis, Christopher. 2011. 'Is oil worth fighting for? Evidence from three cases.' In *Beyond Resource Wars*, by Shlomi Dinar, 201–239. London: MIT Press.

Flikke, Geir, and Julie Wilhelmsen. 2008. *Central Asia: A Testing Ground for New Great-Power Relations*. Oslo: Norwegian Institute of International Affairs (NUPI), 1–58.

Freire, Maria Raquel, and Roger E. Kanet. 2010. *Key Players and Regional Dynamics in Eurasia The Return of the 'Great Game'*. Basingstoke: Palgrave Macmillan.

Frappi, Carlo, and Marco Valigi. 2015. 'Patterns of Cooperation in the South Caucasus Area.' Working Paper, ISIPI. https://www.ispionline.it/it/pubblicazione/pa tterns-cooperation-southern-caucasus-area-azerbaijan-georgia-and-turkey-triangul ar-diplomacy-shadow-energy-strategy-13623.

Fromkin, David. 1980. 'The Great Game in Asia.' *Foreign Affairs* 58 (4): 936–952.

Gorshenina, Svetlana. 2014. 'Samarkand and its cultural heritage: perceptions and persistence of the Russian colonial construction of monuments.' *Central Asian Survey* 33 (2): 246–269.

Grigas, Agnia. 2017. *The New Geopolitics of Natural Gas*. London: Harvard University Press.

Gurbanov, Ilgar. 2017. 'Propaganda Against Trans-Adriatic Pipeline Continues Under "Environmental Concerns".' April 26. Accessed May 20, 2017. https://jamestown.org/program/propaganda-trans-adriatic-pipeline-continues-environmental-concerns/.

Haghayeghi, Mehrdad. 2003. 'The Coming of Conflict to the Caspian Sea.' *Problems of Post-Communism* 50 (3): 32–41.

Hopkirk, Peter. 1990. *The Great Game.* London: John Murray.

Hunter, Shireen T. 2017. *The New Geopolitics of South Caucasus.* New York: Lexington Books.

Ingram, Edward. 1980. 'Great Britain's Great Game: An Introduction.' *The International History Review* 2 (2).

Iseri, Emre. 2009. 'The US Grand Strategy and the Eurasian Heartland in the Twenty-First Century.' *Geopolitics* 14 (1): 26–46.

Ismailzade, Fariz. 2006. *Russia's Energy Interests in Azerbaijan.* London: GMB Publishing Ltd.

Jaffe, Amy Myers, and Robert Manning. 1998. 'The Myth of the Caspian Great Game: The Real Geopolitics of Energy.' *Survival* 40 (4): 112–129.

Kaczmarski, Marcin. 2018. 'Russian-Chinese relations in Eurasia: Harmonization or subordination?' *The Finnish Institute of International Affairs.* April 9. Accessed April 9, 2018. https://www.fiia.fi/en/publication/russian-chinese-relations-in-eurasia.

Kamrava, Mehran. 2016. *The Great Game in West Asia.* New York: Oxford University Press.

Kanet, Roger E. 2010. 'Russia and the Greater Caspian Basin: Withstanding the US Challenge.' In *Key Players and Regional Dynamics in Eurasia The Return of the 'Great Game',* by Raquel Maria Freire and Roger E Kanet, 81–103. New York: Palgrave Macmillan.

Karasac, Hasene. 2002. 'Actors of the New Great Game Caspian Oil Politics.' *Journal of Southern Europe and the Balkans Online* 4 (1): 15–27.

Kavalski, Emilian. 2010. *The New Central Asia: The Regional Impact of International Actors.* Singapore: World Scientific Publishing Co. Pte. Ltd.

Kazantsev, Andrei. 2008. 'Russian Policy in Central Asia and the Caspian Sea Region.' *Europe-Asia Studies* 60 (6): 1073–1088.

Kennedy, Ryan. 2010. 'In the new 'Great Game', who is getting played? Chinese investment in Kazakhstan's petroleum sector.' In *Caspian Energy Politics Azerbaijan, Kazakhstan and Turkmenistan,* by Indra Overland, Heidi Kjaernet and Andrea Kendall-Taylor, 116–136. New York: Routledge.

Khanna, Parag. 2008. 'The Silk Road and the Great Game.' In *The Second World,* by Parag Khanna, 93–100. New York: Random House.

Kiernan, Peter. 2012. *The Great Game for gas in the Caspian.* London: The Economist.

Kim, Younkyoo, and Stephen Blank. 2016. 'The New Great Game of Caspian energy in 2013–14: 'Turk Stream', Russia and Turkey.' *Journal of Balkan and Near Eastern Studies* 18 (1): 37–55.

Kim, Younkyoo, and Fabio Indeo. 2013. 'The new great game in Central Asia post 2014: The US 'New Silk Road' strategy and Sino-Russian rivalry.' *Communist and Post-Communist Studies* 46: 275–286.

Kim, Younkyoo, and Guho Eom. 2008. 'The Geopolitics of Caspian Oil: Rivalries of the US, Russia, and Turkey in the South Caucasus.' *Global Economic Review* 37 (1): 85–106.

34 *New Great Game in the Caspian Sea*

Klare, Michael. 2001. *Resource Wars*. New York: Metropolitan Books.

Kleveman, Lutz. 2003. *The New Great Game: Blood and Oil in the Central Asia*. New York: Grove Press.

Kober, Stanley. 2000. 'The Great Game Round 2.' *Foreign Policy Briefing* 63: 1–11.

Kubicek, Paul. 2013. 'Energy politics and geopolitical competition in the Caspian Basin.' *Journal of Eurasian Studies* 4: 171–180.

Kusznir, Julia. 2013. 'TAP, Nabucco West, and South Stream: The Pipeline Dilemma in the Caspian Sea Basin and Its Consequences for the Development of the Southern Gas Corridor.' *Caucasus Analytical Digest* 47: 1–7.

Labban, Mazen. 2009. 'The Struggle for the Heartland: Hybrid Geopolitics in the Transcaspian.' *Geopolitics* 14 (1): 1–25.

Laruelle, Marlène, and Sébastien Peyrouse. 2009. 'The Militarization of the Caspian Sea:'Great Games' and 'Small Games' Over the Caspian Fleets.' *China and Eurasia Forum Quarterly* 7 (2): 17–35.

Laruelle, Marlène, Jean-François Huchet, SébastienPeyrouse, and Bayram Balci. 2010. *China and India in Central Asia A New 'Great Game'?*Basingstoke: Palgrave Macmillan.

Lelyveld, Michael. 2001. 'Caspian: Tempers Flare In Iran-Azerbaijan Border Incident.' July 25. Accessed March 21, 2018. https://www.rferl.org/a/1097012.html.

Lussac, Samuel. 2008. 'Tha Baku Tbilisi Kars Railroad and its geopolitical implications for the South Caucasus.' *Caucasus Review of International Affairs* 2 (4): 1–13.

Malikov, Azim M. 2014. 'The Russian conquest of the Bukharan Emirate: military and diplomatic aspects.' *Central Asian Survey* 2 (33): 180–198.

Mamadaliev, Inomjon. 2014. 'The defence of Khujand in 1866 through the eyes of Russian officers.' *Central Asian Survey* 33 (2): 170–179.

Martel, Gordon. 1980. 'Documenting the Great Game: 'World Policy' and the 'Turbulent Frontier' in the 1890s.' *The International History Review* 2 (2): 288–308.

Marks, Michael. 2011. *Metaphors in International Relations Theory*. Berlin: Springer.

Matthew, Edward. 2003. 'The New Great Game and the new great gamers: Disciples of Kipling and Mackinder.' *Central Asian Survey* 22 (1): 83–102.

Monshipouri, Mahmood. 2016. 'Pipeline politics in Iran, Turkey and South Caucasus.' In *The Great Game in West Asia*, by Mehran Kamrava, 57–83. New York: Oxford Press.

Morningstar, Richard. 2003. *From Pipe Dream to Pipeline: The Realization of the Baku-Tbilisi-Ceyhan Pipeline*. Harvard: Council on Library Resources.

Morrison, Alexander. 2017. 'Beyond the 'Great Game': The Russian origins of the second Anglo–Afghan War.' *Modern Asian Studies* 51 (3): 686–735.

Moyo, Dambisa. 2012. *Winner Take All*. Penguin Books: London.

NATO. 2017. 'Partnership for Peace programme.' June 7. Accessed April 10, 2018. https://www.nato.int/cps/su/natohq/topics_50349.htm.

Norton-Taylor, Richard. 2001. 'The New Great Game.' 5 March. Accessed July 10, 2018. https://www.theguardian.com/comment/story/0,3604,446490,00.html.

Orazgaliyev, Serik. 2017. 'Competition for pipeline export routes in the Caspian region: The new Great Game of the new Silk Road?' *Cambridge Journal of Eurasian Studies* 1: 1–24.

Pannier, Bruce. 2009. 'China, EU Wait In The Wings For Access To Central Asia.' 2 August. Accessed July 10, 2018. https://www.rferl.org/a/China_EU_Wait_In_The_Wings_For_Access_To_Central_Asia/1790745.html.

Pilati, Paola. 2014. 'Non restate nelle mani di Mosca.' 20 November. Accessed May 23, 2018. http://espresso.repubblica.it/plus/articoli/2014/10/16/news/non-restate-nelle-mani-di-mosca-1.184470?refresh_ce.

Raphael, Sam, and Doug Stokes. 2014. 'US oil strategy in the Caspian Basin: Hegemony through interdependence.' *International Relations* 28 (2): 183–206.

Rasizade, Alec. 2003. 'Entering the Old Great Game in Central Asia.' *Orbis* 47 (1): 41–58.

Rinna, Anthony. 2013. 'Journal of Energy Security.' November 20. Accessed April 2, 2018. http://ensec.org/index.php?option=com_content&view=article&id=471:stepping-out-of-the-shadows-turkmenistan-and-its-feisty-neighbors&catid=139:issue-content&itemid=425.

Rukhadze, Vasili. 2016. 'Completion of Baku–Tbilisi–Kars Railway Project Postponed Again.' March 2. Accessed November 1, 2018. https://jamestown.org/program/completion-of-baku-tbilisi-kars-railway-project-postponed-again/.

Ruseckas, Laurent. 1998. *Energy and Politics in Central Asia and the Caucasus.* Seattle: The National Bureau of Asian Research.

Rywkin, Michael. 2004. 'The Great Game Revisited.' *American Foreign Policy Interests* 26: 467–475.

Rzayev, Ayaz, and Vasif Huseynov. 2018. 'South Caucasus Eyes Becoming a Hub Along EU–China Transportation Route.' November 9. Accessed November 10, 2018. https://jamestown.org/program/south-caucasus-eyes-becoming-a-hub-along-eu-china-transportation route/?fbclid=IwAR2bjaeSXo4tigkMtRwYgd6sCDaTMbciM04KHC4XIY3adu7t0LIUAeM-AKg.

Rzayeva, Gulmira. 2015. *The Outlook for Azerbaijani Gas Supplies to Europe Challenges and Perspectives.* Oxford: The Oxford Institute for Energy Studies.

Rzayeva, Gulmira. 2013. 'Azerbaijan and Energy Security of Europe.' Hazar Strateji Enstitusu, Caspian Report. https://www.academia.edu/4752309/Why_The_Caspian_matters_.

Saivetz, Carol. 2003. 'Perspectives on the Caspian Sea Dilemma: Russian Policies Since the Soviet Demise.' *Eurasian Geography and Economics* 44 (8): 588–606.

Scott, David. 2008. 'The Great Power 'Great Game' between India and China: 'The Logic of Geography.' *Geopolitics* 13 (1): 1–26.

Sergeev, Evgeny. 2013. *The Great Game, 1856–1907.* Baltimore: Johns Hopkins University.

Sheng, Andrew. 2017. 'OBOR and EuroAsia's New Great Game.' *China Report* 53 (2): 232–252.

Shlapentokh, Dmitry. 2013. 'Turkmenistan and military buildup in the Caspian region: A small state in the post-unipolar era.' *Journal of Eurasian Studies* 4: 154–159.

Smith, Dianne L. 1996. 'Central Asia: A New Great Game?' *Asian Affairs* 23 (3): 147–175.

Stegen, Karen Smith, and Julia Kusznir. 2015. 'Outcomes and strategies in the 'New Great Game': China and the Caspian states emerge as winners.' *Journal of Eurasian Studies* 6: 91–106.

Stevens, Paul. 2009. *Transit Troubles: Pipelines as a Source of Conflict.* London: Chatham House, Royal Institute of International Affairs.

Stulberg, Adam. 2012. 'Strategic bargaining and pipeline politics: Confronting the credible commitment problem in Eurasian energy transit.' *Review of International Political Economy* 19 (5): 808–836.

36 New Great Game in the Caspian Sea

Stulberg, Adam N. 2005. 'Moving Beyond the Great Game: The Geoeconomics of Russia's Influence in the Caspian Energy Bonanza.' *Geopolitics* 10 (1): 1–25.

Suny, Ronald Grigor. 2010. 'The pawn of great powers: The East–West competition for Caucasia.' *Journal of Eurasian Studies* 1: 10–25.

Swanstrom, Niklas. 2005. 'China and Central Asia: a new Great Game or traditional vassal relations?' *Journal of Contemporary China* 14 (45): 569–584.

The Economist. 2007. 'The Great Game revisited.' March 22. Accessed February 19, 2018. https://www.economist.com/node/8896853.

The Economist. 2001. 'Storm in a precious teacup: Little naval clashes over oil rights could be serious.' August 2. Accessed March 12, 2018. https://www.economist.com/node/719184.

Trenin, Dmitri. 2003. 'A Farewell to the Great Game? Prospects for Russian-American Security Cooperation in Central Asia.' *European Security* 12 (3–4):21–35.

Uddin, Shams. 1997. 'The New Great Game in Central Asia.' *International Studies* 34 (3): 1–13.

van der Oye, DavidSchimmelpenninck. 2014. 'Paul's great game: Russia's plan to invade British India.' *Central Asia Survey* 33 (2): 143–152.

Williams, Beryl. 1980. 'Approach to the Second Afghan War: Central Asia during the Great Eastern Crisis, 1875–1978.' *The International History Review* 2 (2): 216–238.

Yenikeyeff, Shamil Midkhatovich. 2011. 'Energy Interests of the 'Great Powers' in Central Asia: Cooperation or Conflict?' *The International Spectator* 46 (3): 61–78.

Yusin, Lee. 2005. 'Toward a New International Regime for the Caspian Sea.' *Problems of Post-Communism* 52 (3): 37–48.

2 Revisiting functionalism

Introduction

In this regard, my revision integrates contributions from scholars who do not conceive of themselves as working in the functionalist tradition per se (Adler 1997; Checkel 1998; Finnemore and Sikkink 1998, 2001; Price and Reus-Smit 1998; Ruggie 1998; Wendt 1992). Classical functionalism embodied a number of insights that can be argued to be social constructivist in character (e.g., insights concerning the logics of appropriateness, acknowledging the role of organizations and experts, explaining changes within social and material relations), but classical functionalism did so implicitly, since the social constructivist turn in Sociology and the study of International Relations (IR) had not yet taken place. With these insights having since been explicated and integrated, it is easy to relate debates on classical functionalism to those on social constructivism. Each theory has distinctive weak aspects that are complemented by the other's strengths. Social constructivism addresses many issues that are similar to those that classical functionalism has addressed from a different angle. In light of this, the current chapter aims to illustrate how social constructivism echoes a number of arguments expressed earlier by Mitrany (1948, 1965, 1966, 1975). By doing this, it is able to offer a richer understanding of some phenomena which is lacking within classical functionalism.

Functionalism is both a theory and an empirical observation, which seeks to survey different nations through their common societal interests and problems without emphasizing power politics, nationalism or religious, cultural and ideological differences (Mitrany 1966). It can be characterized as an issue-specific and technocratic approach to politics. Because of this it is more explicit about its prescriptive consequence as it suggests instructions on how to soften antagonism among different actors. David Mitrany (1888–1975), who was a Romanian born British scholar, is considered a key theorist of functionalist theory.[1] His pamphlet *A Working Peace System: An Argument for the Functional Development of International Organization* from 1943 is a detailed expression of the aims of functionalism.[2] At the core of functionalism is the prioritization of human needs and public welfare through the practical appreciation of their technical aspects. The reason for this

DOI: 10.4324/9781003189626-3

38   *Revisiting functionalism*

foregrounding of technical aspects is to side line the restrictions created by nationalism and differing ideologies. The functionalist perspective has been widely influential, and it has been applied to the analysis of integration, international organizations, multilevel governance and in interdependence literature. Yet, it has also been marginalized for being 'idealistic.'

Following the creation of the European Coal and Steel Community (ECSC) in 1952, neofunctionalism was developed to explain how the ECSC's regulatory harmonization efforts had 'spilled over' into broader economic integration, through the European Economic Community (EEC) and energy integration, through the European Atomic Energy Community (Euratom). The term neofunctionalism was first introduced by Ernst B. Haas (1924–2003), a German-born American political scientist. It was originally based on Haas' analysis of the ECSC, but was extended to include his conclusions on both the EEC and Euratom (Haas 1958, 1961, 1964, 1975, 1980, 2001). Later, Lindberg and Scheingold (1963) contributed to neofunctionalism by explaining the formation of the EEC. While Haas mainly concentrated on the role of nongovernmental elites, Lindberg largely focused on governmental elites, socialization processes and engrenage (Niemann 2006).[3]

After the 1960s, the popularity of the theory decreased and there was a gap until the late 1980s. The theory regained its status for a short term in the early 1990s, which saw a more historical reading of Mitrany, his personal knowledge of Balkans and origins of his assumptions (see e.g., Anderson 1998; Ashworth 2005; Long 1993). Despite its popularity in the 1950s, 1960s, and the 1990s, the theory does not figure prominently in recent contributions to the rapidly growing body of literature on cooperation, international organizations or regional integration. The last time the theory was discussed systematically was in the *Journal of European Public Policy* in 2005, which dedicated one of its special issues to the nostalgic review of neofunctionalism.[4] Ernst B. Haas passed away, in March of 2003 and this special issue paid tribute to one of the greatest thinkers in European integration studies (Börzel 2005, Preface of the special issue).

The theory is briefly mentioned in a few recent publications and it is mainly applied to explain the bureaucratic and administrative governance of the European Union, such as negotiation and decision making processes among different European Institutions, local and regional policy formation, EU-wide regulations, the admittance of new members and barriers during this process (see for instance Börzel 2006; Farrell and Héritier 2005; Holthaus 2018; Macmillan 2009; Niemann and Ioannou 2015; Weiss and Wilkinson 2014; Zwolski 2018). Overall, the theory has come to be ignored by its erstwhile critics as well as its proponents. This is an unfortunate oversight since several of its insights are as relevant to present-day debates as they were during the decades of their initial development by Mitrany. These insights include emphasizing both non-material and material cooperation, approaching the subject matter non-state-centrically, recognizing intrinsic dynamics, acknowledging the role diverse experts, a logic of appropriateness, and being pragmatic in terms of

Revisiting functionalism 39

preferences. The unique feature of functionalism is that it is more explicit about its prescriptive consequence as it suggests how to avoid antagonism among different actors. The knowledge produced by functionalism is generally more useful in changing the view of the world as mainly made up of antagonistic relationships than in working within it.

This chapter lays out the theory of (neo)functionalism in order to demonstrate where the theory ought to be revised to take into account the valid critiques it has met with. To that end, this chapter is divided into five sections. Following the introduction, the second section critically engages with the core arguments of functionalism and neofunctionalism. This section seeks to delineate the origin of functionalism and its applicability, benefitting from Mitrany's and Haas' original conceptualizations. The third section discusses the existing critiques of functionalism and responds to them. The fourth section offers my interpretation of the discussion, in which I take into account global developments, historical and geographical changes, and social constructivist turn in IR. Fifth and finally, the conclusion presents the chapter's findings.

Underlying assumptions

In order to establish the groundwork for the revised functionalism I intend to develop and use, it is necessary to first selectively and briefly recall the classical functionalist assumptions of David Mitrany, Ernst Haas and Leon Lindberg, and synthesize their main points. This will provide the basis for replying to existing critiques and specifying what the revised functionalist framework will encompass. The reason for this selectiveness is that there are already a number of works in existence that comprehensively address most principles of both functionalism and neofunctionalism (e.g., Alexandrescu 2007; Ashworth and Long 1999; Holthaus 2018; Imber 2002; Oneal et al. 1996; Rosamond 2005; Groom and Taylor 1975; Zwolski 2018). Therefore, it is unnecessary to walk the same pathways.

Following the early works of Mitrany (1948, 1965, 1966), Haas (1958), and Lindberg Scheingold (1963), the essence of the classical functionalist theory can be said to have been derived from five core observations. These observations are that: (1) states are not unified actors and not the only actors in the international arena, meaning that the international system is constructed by a multitude of diverse actors. Classical functionalism offers both specific and broad theoretical implications to cover the preferences, roles, networks, and power of actors besides and beyond states. Although new institutionalism also places the analytical focus on this aspect, it grants only a restricted role to institutions and organizations as neoliberal institutionalists consider them to be the creations of states. (2) Preferences should not be perceived as constant or fixed since they tend to change through cooperation processes since actors undergo learning over time. (3) The similarity of problems, which challenge the different sub-systems of the world – individual states or

40 *Revisiting functionalism*

blocs of states – produces shared interests which in turn act as incentives for seeking common solutions. These problems cannot be solved in any other way than by joint efforts, or can be solved on a national level but at much higher costs. Classical functionalism highlights intrinsic dynamics of issues and cooperation, which means the characteristics of an issue determine its geographical scope, the expertise required to solve it, who the functionally involved actors are and other dimensions. (4) Functional cooperation is pragmatic, technocratic, and flexible rather than political. This means that technical problems should be left to specialists because they focus on the root causes of a problem and the best means to solve it without emphasizing political feelings or the balance of power. Civil servants, technicians, and scientists can link sectors of their national societies and sections of their national institutions together into vast and growing networks of international relations that are peaceful and beneficial to their work. The new ideologies of the time (communism, fascism, and liberal-capitalism) had to be circumvented, leading to the advent of new habits and interests which diluted these ideologies over time. In this regard, modern national and international issues require not only the involvement of state-centric politicians, but also the contribution of social, economic and technical experts. (5) Each and every problem has to be tackled as a practical issue in itself. This means cooperation in one field should be left to generate others gradually. This is called 'ramification'.

However, it is worth mentioning that while some ideas overlap between functionalism and neofunctionalism, they are partly based on different assumptions. For example, while functionalism did not define integration to be limited by any territorial scope, neofunctionalism gave it a specific regional focus. Furthermore, Mitrany argued that the form, scope and purpose of a functional agency would be determined by the issue-specific task that it was designed to fulfil, while neo-functionalists attach considerable importance to the autonomous influence of supranational institutions. Another difference is that spill-over is extended and diversified in neofunctionalism. Finally, Mitrany asserted the importance of changes in popular support, the needs of people and the functional arrangements that help fulfil those needs. However, by using the cost-benefit assumptions, neo-functionalists emphasize the attitudes of the elite and self-interest.

State fixation

Writing at a time of international crisis (i.e., the Second World War), Mitrany advocated that global integration should be based on administrative and technical cooperation, rather than political cooperation among nation-states. In this regard, the idea of the nation-state has been described by Mitrany as one of the 'basic enemies.' In his publications, Mitrany sought to refute the 'state fixation' attitude toward international politics. According to Mitrany, state fixation should not be one of the primary principles of international politics because it is an obstacle to innovative thought and obstructs international affairs (Mitrany 1966). While criticizing state fixation and nationalistic feelings, Mitrany argued that by clinging to them, people would not be able to end rivalries and conflicts. States are not absolute and should not be the predominant actors in the regional or international system of cooperation and negotiation due to modern technologies, new inventions, complex economic developments, and trans-border issues (Mitrany 1966, 9). Mitrany criticized scholars from Machiavelli to Treitschke, who exaggerated the importance of the state for the social development of the community (Mitrany 1975, 86–114). According to him, their political approaches were restricted by 'dogmatic narrow mindedness' which meant they were victim to the 'state fixation of political writers' (Mitrany 1975, 97–114). According to Mitrany:

> …trade and finance, culture and communication, were integrated at different levels and periods, not through political union but through changes and advances in particular fields of activity. Every new invention, every new discovery is now apt to breed problems which for the first time in history are global in their very nature and in their scale. And that, inescapably, also projects the scale of the coming international system. New issues and inventions yet to come are free of any sovereign land or air limits. The new problems are leading states not to create sovereignty but to deny it and not to exclusive political integration but to collective functional integrations.
>
> (Mitrany 1975, 27)

Mitrany highlighted that putting economic and social activities under a particular ideological dogma would not bring cooperation and stability. He argued that states would be more effective and peaceful without traditional political dogmas. Therefore, flexibility and open-mindedness in the international system should be the key ideas (Mitrany 1966, 138). Overall, the argument against state fixation is one of the important insights of classical functionalism because it emphasizes global changes, interconnected issues, the role of non-state actors, non-political issues and fields and the limits of state-centrism to address these things. However, it is worth mentioning that while he was right in saying that when issues are perceived as technical, cooperation is easier, Mitrany was wrong in distinguishing technical aspects from political aspects. Therefore, this distinction should be viewed as a matter of framing, which will be discussed in detail later in this chapter.

Sharing interests through functionalist agencies and elites

According to Mitrany:

> …not all interests are common to all, and common interests do not concern all countries in the same degree. In this regard, unity within

42 *Revisiting functionalism*

diversity can be done by making use of the present social and scientific opportunities to link together particular activities and interests, one at a time, according to need and acceptability, giving each a joint authority and policy limited to that activity alone.

(Mitrany 1966, 200)

The habit of coming together to deal with shared issues might flourish in the countries of a region, and they may discover a new interest and a new pride in solving their shared problems. Mitrany (1966, 115–116) argues that 'it is important to determine those activities that are common, where they are common and the extent to which they are common.' Also, while states are part of these activities with respect to their interests and resources, there should not be an obligation to either participate in all of the activities or stay out of any of them (Mitrany 1966, 116–125). One way of making sure this is the case is to divide issues into specific economic, technical, and social parts that can be dealt with as separate cases (Mitrany 1966, 200–203). This offers the assurance of non-domination and equality of opportunity to even the weakest of countries as the benefits of any functional cooperation it participates in (Mitrany 1966, 205). The task itself can never be defined or limited in advance but must remain continuously variable, reflecting that situations have the propensity to change. In the vocabulary of functionalism, cooperation for the common good is the task, both for the sake of peace and that of a better life, and it is essential for that cooperation that certain interests and activities should be taken out of the realm of competition and worked on together (Mitrany 1975, 123). In other words, the key component of a functional approach is that it can be employed across borders, across allegiances and identities, because it works towards the common needs of individuals, regardless of allegiance or group rivalries (Steele 2011).

In this regard, Mitrany found the approach in the New Deal, particularly that of the Tennessee Valley Authority (TVA), a good example of functionalism because its aim was to deal with practical issues without changing the general system of government or challenging the Constitution. It was the wholly pragmatic response to the 'felt necessities' of a pressing situation. Although the Tennessee River crosses several states, the TVA was able to circumvent most of the local juridical barriers due to its technical, issue-specific aim. To address the common issues and needs of people, the TVA oversaw irrigation works, canalization, industrialization, and reforestation in the Tennessee River basin and combined it with social measures like the extra taxing of high incomes, extending loans to people with mounted mortgages, and building extra houses in suburbs (De Wilde 1991). The TVA side lined ideology, religion, and bureaucratic interests by dealing directly with the technical aspects of the given problem. In this regard, the TVA became a remarkable example of Mitrany's functionalist ideas as it incorporated a particular public dimension without directly contradicting old-fashioned constitutional and territorial areas of state authority.[5]

Revisiting functionalism 43

Mitrany (1966, 115) proposed global service agencies forming a strong network with other agencies and performing the required tasks while side lining ideological, national, and geopolitical differences. Under the general name of technical assistance, these agencies would establish, shape and articulate new and acceptable norms, interests and identities among different countries (developed or underdeveloped) and address their communal needs. According to Mitrany (1966, 159), the common index of needs could be made by joint agencies set up to deal with the common and specific needs. Such functional agencies could be started up by a small coalition of countries, initially to deal with logistics, for instances, and could later be broadened to include new members or reduced to let reluctant members drop out, while functions could equally be added or abandoned without devastating the system as a whole. In other words, no states would have to be forced to come in and no state would be excluded from the cooperation. States can participate in specific tasks based on their specific resources. The aim of these agencies should be made on practical cooperation such as on social, technical or economic issues.

> The issue-specific task can determine scope and purpose of a functional agency. These agencies can be flexible to give service wherever needed, so it would clearly be their duty to deny service where it was not obviously needed, or might be abused
>
> (Mitrany 1975, 183)

The way of working that Mitrany proposed was modelled after the examples of international organizations and unions, such as the Universal Postal Union (UPU), International Telecommunications Unions (ITU), and International Labour Organization (ILO). The UPU is one of the best-known examples. It was established in 1875 by 20 European countries, Egypt, and the USA. Later, its services were extended to other countries as well, which made it one of the first global service networks. The UPU still exists and has 192 member-states.[6] The International Telegraph Union (1865), predecessor of the International Telecommunications Union (ITU), developed similarly. The ILO, which also had a strong influence on Mitrany's ideas, had been created in 1919 by the Treaty of Versailles to improve labour rights and living and working conditions. It was an agency of the League of Nations and was unique because it gave an equal voice to both government representatives and non-state actors such as workers and trade unions regarding technical assistance. It survived the Second World War and became the first specialized agency of the UN in 1946 (International Labour Organization 2019). Considering he wrote in the early 1950s, these can be said to have been the prime examples for Mitrany at the time. The number of specialized organizations has increased, but this has not led to the world peace Mitrany expected.

In their works, Haas and Lindberg decreased the scope of functionalist agency from the global to the regional level by discussing the European

44 *Revisiting functionalism*

Commission. Like functionalism, neofunctionalism emphasizes the mechanisms of technocratic decision-making, incremental design and learning processes. Similar to Mitrany, Haas and Lindberg portrayed the relationship between nation-states and a functionalist agency as a win-win endeavour rather than zero-sum one. In the ECSC example, Haas and Lindberg described functionalist agencies as one of the main kinds of actors strengthening the regional political and economic integration between different nation-states. One way of doing this was to bring the different national elites together under the ECSC's umbrella to nullify the differences and emphasize the shared interests. Therefore, unlike Mitrany, who indirectly suggested diminishing the future role of nation-states, Haas (1958, Ch. 5) and Lindberg and Scheingold (1963) proposed dividing this role between functionalist agencies and nation-states.

In contrast to Mitrany, who prioritized human needs in his approach, Haas (1958, Ch. 5 and Ch. 6) and Lindberg and Scheingold (1963, 6) emphasized the needs of elite groups in their neofunctionalism. In this sense, they emphasized the importance of self-interest and cost-benefit cooperation among different elite groups. For Haas, the integration between Western European states is based on the self-interest of dominant elites and policy-makers (Haas 1958, Ch. 5 and Ch. 6). He claimed that European integration advanced due to the strong support of elites, both in the governmental and private sectors. According to Haas (1958, Ch. 6), 'interest politics' is a determinative factor for the success of international cooperation among different governments rather than a natural harmony of interests. Eliminating their interest in politics would complicate interpreting and understanding relations between experts. According to Haas:

> ...all political action is purposively linked with individual or group perception of interests. Cooperation among groups is thus the result of convergences of separate perceptions of interest and not a spontaneous surrender to the myth of the common good.
>
> (Haas 1964, 34)

Haas (1970, 627) argued that rational and self-interested actors have the capacity to learn and to change their preferences and loyalties. Their preferences and loyalties are likely to change during the integration process, as actors benefit from regional policies and learn from their experiences in cooperative decision-making (Haas 1958, 291). Because of this, interest-driven national and supranational elites, recognizing the limitations of national solutions, provide the key impetus for international integration.

For neo-functionalists, the integration process is always supported in the long run by a change of attitudes and expectations (Lindberg, 1963). Lindberg (1963) drew attention to the proliferation of EEC working groups and sub-committees, which, by bringing thousands of national officials into frequent contact with each other and with committee officials, had given rise to a complex system of bureaucratic interpenetration. These kinds of interaction patterns, Lindberg argued, increase the likelihood of socialization processes occurring amongst national civil servants within the 'Council framework.' It has further been implied that these socialization processes, which foster consensus formation amongst agents of member governments, would eventually lead to more integrative outcomes, which is also called 'engrenage' (Lindberg 1963: Ch. 1 and 4; Lindberg and Scheingold 1970, 119). As opposed to lowest-common-denominator bargaining, which Lindberg saw as inherent in intergovernmental decision-making, supranational systems were characterized by 'splitting the difference' and more significantly a bargaining process of 'upgrading common interests.' Common interests are advanced to the extent that each participant feels that, by conceding something, they have gained something else (Niemann and Schmitter 2009). Engrenage is the process whereby national civil servants are encouraged to take integrative decisions through their increasing involvement with each other (Lindberg and Scheingold 1970; Niemann 1998).

While Haas and Lindberg strengthened functionalism by accounting for the needs and preferences of elites, they shifted the debate to discussing a cost-benefit logic. Mitrany had, however, emphasized that participation is not primarily related to calculating profits or preferences, but instead relies on interpretations of reasonability, human need, natural cause and moral good. In other words, Mitrany's original argument includes both cost-benefit logic and logic of appropriateness. According to March and Olsen:

> ...actor action is driven by rules of appropriate or exemplary behavior, organized into institutions. Actors do what they see as appropriate for themselves in a specific type of situation. Within the logic of appropriateness perspective, preference or self-interest is seen as one of many possible rules that actors may come to believe is exemplary for specific roles in specific settings and situations, which means actors combine several modes of action in their behavior.
>
> (March and Olsen 2011, 479)

Considering this approach, it can be argued that actors broadened the role of the ECSC because they saw the given action as right, appropriate and exemplary. For them, sharing in the ECSC becomes a way of meeting obligations stemming from their roles, identity and membership of their political community.

The ramification or spill-over approach

The idea of ramification is another significant aspect of functionalism. It claims that collaboration in one field could result in new cooperation in another area (Mitrany 1966). According to the ramification approach, if A and B could cooperate in one shared field or to address one shared need, it becomes likely that they will establish cooperation on other issues. In that

46 *Revisiting functionalism*

respect, the ramification approach would contribute to a change of attitude among the states in favour of widening and broadening cooperation (Mitrany 1966). Mitrany explained that:

> every function was left to generate others gradually, like the functional subdivision of organic cells, and in every case the appropriate authority was left to grow and develop out of actual performance.
>
> (Mitrany 1966, 56)

In other words, Mitrany argued that it is important to establish cooperation in technical, social, and economic fields first, increasing trust between parties and decreasing nationalistic feelings, after which political cooperation would likely follow. In accordance with the concept of ramification, Mitrany argued that the broadening and widening of cooperation would diminish the probability of war breaking out and eventually eliminate war through an incremental transformation from adversarial to cooperative patterns of behaviour. The transformation of behavioural patterns is incremental or gradual because the ramification effect takes time. The significant point in that emergency action was that each and every problem was tackled as a practical issue in itself. Its character would be the same for certain purposes; only the range would be new (Mitrany 1966, 56). Mitrany explained this assumption in a limited manner and he left a number of questions unanswered, which have been addressed by Haas, Lindberg and others later. This idea was later named 'spill-over' by neo-functionalists (Haas 1958).

Similar to Mitrany, Haas (1970) argued that integration at the regional level in one sector is only tenable in combination with integration in other sectors, as problems arising from the functional integration in one task can only be solved by integrating yet more tasks. At first, the term was applied in two distinctive manners: (1) it was used as a sort of shorthand for describing the occurrence of (further) integration; and (2) it was used to identify the driving force and inherent logic of integration via increased functional/economic/technical interdependence (Petersen 2016, Ch. 1). Haas identified that the integration of coal and steel production placed pressure on European transportation networks to deliver the products to markets, which encouraged countries to cooperate more closely in secondary sectors. Similar to Mitrany, both Lindberg and Haas were optimistic regarding the 'automatic' spill-over, which has been criticized by a number of scholars (see e.g., Niemann 1998, 2009, Rosamond 2003).

However, Haas and Lindberg put considerable emphasis on the role of economic and political elites in supporting the automatic spill-over process. National elites were assumed to realise that problems of substantial interest cannot be satisfactorily solved at the national level. This would lead to a gradual learning process whereby elites shift their expectations, political activities and – according to Haas – even loyalties to a new centre. As a result, national elites would promote further integration, thus adding a political stimulus to the process. In this regard, it can be argued that unlike Mitrany, Haas, and Lindberg emphasized that integration could be started and extended from high political level. The result of the pressure emanating from that high political level is that political parties, business and professional associations, trade unions, or other interest groups alter their perception of the proposed integration. Presuming that they would perceive integration to have positive benefits, these private organizations should support further integration (Haas 1958).

Critiques of classical functionalism

Functionalism is a strongly criticized theory (e.g., Hoffmann 1995; Holland 1980; Milward 1992; Moravcsik 1993, 2005; Risse-Kappen 1996; Taylor 1983). The theory has been criticized from within the functionalist camp itself by various scholars. While some critiques contributed to the further development of the theory, a number of critiques levelled against functionalism misrepresented its claims, distorted its arguments or interpreted the theory selectively and narrowly. Therefore, only some of the critiques of (neo) functionalist theory are entirely justified.

The first critique concerns the concept of automatic spill-over. In the 1990s, some scholars argued that the definition of spill-over was not specific enough and lacked a comprehensive, refined, and integrated specification of the conditions under which spill-over might occur (Groom 1994; Lelieveldt and Princen 2015; Nieman and Schmitter 2009; Schmitter 2005, 1969; Tranholm-Mikkelsen 1991). In doing so, a series of adjectives have come to be considered applicable to the term, such as: functional, political, economic, induced and dialectical; and new terms such as 'spillback' have been proposed. According to Tranholm-Mikkelsen (1991), 'functional spillover' is a mechanism arising from the inherent technical characteristics of the functional tasks themselves. The idea is that some sectors within industrial economies are so interdependent that it is impossible to treat them in isolation. In other words, 'projects of integration engender new problems which, in turn, can only be solved by further integration' (Tranholm-Mikkelsen 1991, 4–6). 'Political spill-over' encompasses the integrative pressures exerted by national elites, who realize that problems of substantial interest cannot be satisfactorily solved at the domestic level (Groom 1994; Niemann 1998). As a result, national elites promote further integration, having developed the perception that their interests are better served by seeking supranational rather than national solutions. 'Cultivated spill-over' is linked to supranational organizations actively fostering further integration with actors seen as policy entrepreneurs (Lelieveldt and Princen 2015, 28–36). 'Induced spill-over' refers to 'involuntary motives', such as extra-community demands and unforeseen threats to community interests. Sharing preferences with external actors is the unexpected result of this process and may be influenced by international interdependence or utility-maximizing outsiders inspired by the success of a

48 Revisiting functionalism

regional bloc or the ineffectiveness of purely national solutions (Niemann 1998). Finally, due the deadlock that occurred in the early 1960s, the term 'spillback' was created to explain a halt to integration (Niemann and Schmitter 2009). It is argued that the spillback, or a reverse of spill-over, can occur when leaders (such as Charles de Gaulle or Margaret Thatcher) or interest groups, lobbies, or opposition parties, or even public opinion, are wary of further integration and stall the process (Niemann 2006; Petersen 2016).

Nevertheless, while recognizing the niche utility of these terms, it can be argued that their added value is very limited as some of them give off the impression of being moves in a language game among different scholars. Spill-over is not limited to being economic, cultivated or political, it can also be environmental, legal, social and technical. Thinking of concepts such as spill-over in such a limited way puts specific requirements and constraints on concepts and their operationalization. With such strict standards of verification and proof there is very little of significance that can be said about spill-over. Spill-over was not intended to be a measurable concept, but a heuristic one or even just a metaphor to indicate an expectation about the consequence of pragmatic cooperation on one issue. For example, if one looks at spill-over from a constructivist perspective one will encounter certain specific operational demands. From a critical theory perspective, one may interpret spill-over in light of progressive change – a means to side line the power of the sovereignty discourse. Considering this, it can be argued that the classical term spill-over is sufficient to indicate a process triggering further cooperation among different nations. The classical spill-over does not restrict cooperation to any specific form. Therefore, there is no problem with ramification in Mitrany's functionalist approach because unlike his critics he did not make assumptions about the relationship between issues. Rather, Mitrany (1966, 56) argued that any theory of integration should include an account of the transferability of lessons because social, political and economic issues constantly change and transferability is therefore desirable.

The second critique argues that neofunctionalism exaggerated the power supranational institutional have over states. Neo-functionalist scholars argued that supranational entities like the European Commission would challenge the power of nation-states. However, in the early 1960s, neo-functionalism ran into difficulty as European integration stalled for several years due to political difficulties in countries like France, undermining the central tenet of the theory. After its heyday in the mid-1960s, critiques of neo-functionalism emerged from inter-governmentalist scholarship (e.g., Hoffmann 1995, 84) and also increasingly from within the neo-functionalist camp itself, not least from its self-critical founding father (Haas 1975, 175). This critique is partly a myth since the existing literature exaggerates the failure of theory to explain the period of stagnation. Despite the stagnation phase in the 1960s, the integration has continued in Europe and even the role and number of functional agencies has increased during and since 1960s, most notably the development of European Law.

Revisiting functionalism 49

The third critique concerns the applicability of the theory outside Europe. In his early work Haas observed and studied integration not only in Europe but also in other parts of the world, such as Latin America, Africa, the European members of the Soviet bloc, and the Arab world. In one of the most important articles on regionalism published in 1961, Haas concluded that the conditions required for integration in the EEC area, such as an industrial economy and liberal politics, did not apply elsewhere. He concluded that 'whatever assurance may be warranted in our discussion of European integration is not readily transferable to other regional contexts' (Haas 1961, 378). Later, by misinterpreting Haas' assumption, other scholars argued that the theory is not useful or even applicable outside Europe (Jensen 2003; McGowan 2007, Risse-Kappen 2005). The reason for this misperception is that when the theory is applied to other regions, the scholars often expect European style integration (Blum 2002; Mattli 2005; Macmillan 2009; Petersen 2016; Schubert 1978). If the regional developments do not lead to the new organization or regional cooperation similar to the EU-style cooperation, they argue that functionalism failed. One weakness in previous thought is that too often regions are considered desirable and good (Söderbaum 2016). It is indisputable that regionalism can solve a variety of collective action dilemmas, but it is equally clear that it may sometimes be exploitative, reinforce asymmetric power relations or lead to a range of detrimental outcomes. Thus, it should not be assumed beforehand that regionalism is either positive or negative (Söderbaum 2016).

Having said that, Acharya (2012) argues that Haas did not imply that regional integration in other parts of the world, driven by different functional pursuits than Western Europe and responding to a different set of converging interests, would not succeed. On the contrary, Haas warned that other regions have their own functional objectives and approaches to integration or impulses peculiar to them. These differences in purpose and trajectory meant that there could be no universal law of integration deduced from the European example (Haas 1961). While styles of cooperation and integration are different, some regions besides Europe are also integrating, economically at least, but not along the European pathway. East Asia has pursued a market-led rather than organization-driven integration. Regional institutions in Africa, Asia, and Latin America have all contributed to peace and security in a way that is consistent with their own set goals or objectives. In this regard, Haas' prescient warning seemed to have been ignored by those latter-day advocates of the European example, who tend to judge, explicitly or implicitly, the performance of non-European regional institutions on the basis of the European benchmark. In this regard one may say that because the theory has been applied to explain developments and changes in EU, its applicability outside the field of EU studies has come to be restricted.

In other words, the reason the European example does not translate is because the EU is a unique organization. However, classical functionalism does not argue or expect the creation of closed regional organizations like

50 *Revisiting functionalism*

the EU and even Mitrany (1965, 125–130) argued that there should not be utopian expectations. Originally, Mitrany's aim was not to develop a theory of European integration, but to assemble a generic portfolio of propositions about the dynamics of cooperation in any context. The theory possesses certain analytical tools to deal with a certain kind of developments, e.g., those related to explaining integration. By looking at these studies from a post-colonial perspective, one may ask if non-Western regions can do what the West can do, which they cannot. The principles of functionalism as formulated by Mitrany are more subtle and much closer to historical practice. Moreover, why should Latin American or African states integrate into confederal states? Unlike European integration, the purpose of much of the non-EU regionalist interaction was to seek autonomy, secure independence from colonial rule, and limit the influence of outside powers in regional affairs (Acharya 2016, 6). The EEC was basically conceived as a project to tame nationalism and constrain state sovereignty; non-Western regionalisms were inspired by exactly the opposite motivations, to advance nationalism and preserve sovereignty after centuries of colonial rule. It is obvious that scholars in European Studies are normatively strongly influenced by the ideals specific to Europe. In all, it is limiting and ethnocentric to use the EU as a benchmark to explain the regional cooperation and development in the post-colonial world.

The fourth critique centres around the distinction that functionalism makes between political and technical issues. Mitrany (1966, 132–135) argued that due to the strong impact of state fixation, politicians view every issue, even human needs issues, from the perspective of politics, balance of power, and rivalry. According to Mitrany (1966, 27–38) however, one should detach the functional core of a problem from its political shell, as it is difficult and complex to achieve cooperation among political elites because of their differing security needs and political agendas. This has been criticized by several scholars (De Wilde 1991, Ch. 7; Hammerlund 2005, Ch. 2–3; Haas 1958). More specifically, it is argued that it is difficult to find clear distinction between political, economic, and technical issues.

However, Mitrany envisions a new way of conducting politics based on service and needs, rather than on traditional power-struggle. This does not mean that functionalism really side lines politics (as Mitrany argued), but it changes the rules of the game. The power of language is that it structures our conceptualizations of issues to some extent. By separating the political from the technical, language is used to divide issues into multiple levels, which creates a conceptualization in which different actors' needs are prioritized at different levels (Diez 1999). By labelling or framing something political, an actor claims a need and a right to treat it by extraordinary means, which raises political management questions such as distribution of cost-benefit, sovereignty, autonomy and regime formation. Since politicization enables emergency measures outside democratic control, Mitrany argued that the technical should generally be preferred over the politicized mode of problem

Revisiting functionalism 51

solving, addressing human needs and necessities. One of the linguistic functions of the term functionalism is to show the irrationality or counterproductiveness of the political mode of reasoning. In this regard, this distinction is better understood and seen as a speech-act, where the main point is not to stress whether issues are political or not, but the ways in which a certain issue (pipeline construction, building a transnational railway; facilitating caviar trade; environmental cooperation) can be socially constructed as political (meaning the issue is part of public policy, requiring government decision and resource allocation).

Finally, a number of authors (Hoffmann 1995; Nieman and Schmitter 2009; Söderbaum 2016) have argued that (neo)functionalists failed to take the broader international context into account adequately as the theory restricted its scope to regions. This argument is not completely sound because classical functionalism adequately considers the broader international developments. Therefore, it is clear that the critics who levelled this critique had failed to appreciate the assumptions of classical functionalists. Mitrany argued that:

> ...the argument about the need of an intermediate step is obviously only valid if the regional unions are to be open unions; whereas if they are to be closed and exclusive unions, the more fully and effectively they are integrated the deeper must in fact be the division they cause in the emergent unity of the world.
>
> (Mitrany 1965, 123)

Any (regional) cooperation's level of embeddedness in a global context depends on whether it is meant to promote closed and exclusive regional unions or administrative devolution with a universal system. The regional idea would have vastly different consequences if used to set up closed political units (Mitrany 1966, 178–185). These new units would then not support but cut across the jurisdiction and authority of any international system. While explaining cooperation between different actors regional or international, Mitrany highlighted that it is necessary to adequately consider the wider issues of interdependency and the global context. More concretely, Mitrany explained that 'all, the emergence of unforeseen and irreducible global issues, with others yet in the making. None of these can be dealt with by regional or continental unions' (1975, 244). This is also the reason for Mitrany's earlier claim that 'the League system did not fail because it was not regional, but rather because it was regional in effect' (1966, 183). Mitrany was against isolated regional cooperation and institutions that draw a border between a region and the outside world. Even when criticizing Europe Mitrany mentioned that 'as to the limits of the union, the search for a true European solution requires more than a solution of little Europe' (1965, 127). Nevertheless, the relevant literature has neglected Mitrany's original arguments and blamed functionalism for being a regionalist approach.

52 *Revisiting functionalism*

In short, it can be argued that functionalism's success as a source of inspiration for the creation of the European communities, such as the ECSC and the EEC, has killed its success as a theory. European integration has become the benchmark for judging functional cooperation elsewhere, meaning that other regions' performance is not viewed in terms of goals set by those regions themselves. By using positivist logic, the existing scholarship has tried to test the assumptions of functionalism, such as the occurrence of spill-over, socialization, and technical cooperation in different regions. In doing so, scholars expected these regions to follow the (West-)European example – which had its own specific spatial and temporal circumstances, however. The orthodox, fixed assumptions about problem-solving and having a rationalist focus on regional organizations side lined alternative questions and answers about cooperation outside Europe. Considering the historical, political, economic, and normative differences, it can be argued that the EU model has not and will not travel well in the developing world. Moreover, it can be argued that functionalism has not been applied in the context of the specialized agencies of the United Nations (UN). They are clearly based on the logic of issue-specific cooperation. Therefore, it can be said that the relevant literature has been remarkably silent on the specialized agencies of the UN.

Functionalism revised via social constructivism

To determine exactly what functionalism stands for is no straightforward undertaking, as the theory has come to mean different things to different people at different times. Therefore, it has become increasingly difficult to distinguish what exactly qualified as functionalist thought because the theory underwent a series of reformulations in the late 1960s and early 1970s. As discussed, Mitrany's original functionalism was revised and modified by Ernst Haas and Leon Lindberg. Later, neofunctionalism was also revised and modified by a number of writers, such as Philippe Schmitter, Stuart Scheingold, and Arne Niemann. However, they mainly discussed European cases (e.g., Holthaus 2018; Macmillan 2009; Niemann 2009; Schmitter 2005). In light of this, this section offers my own interpretation of the existing discussion, which keeps the most important original functionalist assumptions, while dropping the positivist attitude towards functionalism and adopting one influenced by social constructivism instead.[7] The aim of this revision of functionalism is to slightly broaden its theoretical scope. This revised functionalism is thus the result of the cross-fertilization, on multiple levels, between classical functionalist insights and social constructivist insights.

Any discussion of functionalism should start with establishing an understanding of the trends of the time and the significant recent changes in the international system, which many critics fail to do. This includes the end of the Cold War, the emergence of the complex and interconnected economic, political, environmental, material, and cultural issues, macro-electronic revolution, and the spread of transnational corporations (TNCs) and non-governmental and international governmental organizations (NGOs and IGOs), which are all glossed over in the existing functionalist scholarship. My revised functionalism on the other hand recognizes that the role of states relative to that of TNCs, NGOs, and IGOs is changing remarkably. In this sense, I take the functionalist discussion further by acknowledging TNCs, NGOs and IGOs. My revision also integrates contributions from scholars who do not conceive themselves as working in the (neo-)functionalist tradition (e.g., Barry 2013a, 2013b; Bijker 2001; Chandler 2013; Coole 2013; Edward 2016; Latour 2005; Verbeek 2005).

The five points summarized below are addressed in revised functionalism and will be discussed in detail later in this chapter. The first point is that the revised functionalism extends the idea of technical cooperation to the construction of material infrastructures such as pipelines, railways, ports, fibre-optic cables and roads. This enriches the theoretical tools of functionalism and gives the research empirical insight in the transnational movements of things, people, and ideas that lie at the heart of most projects of the contemporary time. In doing so, revised functionalism does not include Mitrany's misleading admonition about distinguishing between the political and the technical. However, drawing insights from social constructivism, I argue that when political aspects are perceived as technical, cooperation is easier, which means that the distinction is just a matter of framing. The second point is that revised functionalism includes TNCs as functionalist agencies since they offer the required resources and instruments that most states do not have or cannot afford. Related to this point is the third point; that revised functionalism puts more emphasis on the importance of different functionalist agencies, such as companies, IGOs, financial institutions, and NGOs networking. The fourth point is that while considering the importance of spill-over, revised functionalism includes stop and go rhythms of spill-over. The final point is that besides the bureaucratic power of functionalist agencies, revised functionalism mainly emphasizes the economic leverage of agencies.

While dropping some of the assumptions of classical functionalism, such as the expected disappearance of nation states and the automaticity of spill-over, several of its assumptions remain unchanged: (1) States are not unified actors and certainly not the only actors in the international arena. This system is also built up and influenced by multiple and diverse other actors, some of them private, some of them state-owned but non-political (like state-owned companies) or semi-public (like state-owned or capital-dominated media), some of them sub-state (like cities) or trans-governmental (networks of civil servants). (2) Preferences are not constant or fixed, but likely to change during cooperation processes since actors gain new insights all throughout it. Revised functionalism intends to show the irrationality or counter-productiveness of the political mode of reasoning about fixed preferences. (3) The problems faced by the different systems of the

54 *Revisiting functionalism*

world – individual states or blocs of states – are similar to some extent, which produces common interests between these systems, which in turn act as incentive for seeking common solutions. (4) Functional cooperation tends to be pragmatic, technocratic, and flexible. This means that we must try to circumvent the influence of ideologies and national/ethnic identities, since we have not been able to sidestep them entirely, leaving it to the growth of new habits and interests to dilute them over time. (5) Each and every problem should be tackled as a practical issue in itself.

Social constructivist insights

To establish the groundwork for cross-fertilization, it is necessary to selectively and briefly outline three core features of social constructivists that are relevant for this research. The reason for this selectiveness is that there are already several excellent works that broadly discuss the intellectual history of the constructivist school (e.g., Adler 1997; Barnett and Finnemore 1999; Burr 2015; Finnemore and Sikkink 2001; Guzzini 2000; Peltonen 2017). Therefore, it is unnecessary to re-tread the same paths.

In the 1990s, social constructivism was a new turn in the study of IR, which was developed in response to the dominant (neo-)realist and (neo-) liberal paradigms. The essence of social constructivism can be derived from a number of key underlying arguments. A first defining feature of social constructivism is its attention to the ways in which the material world is socially conceptualized. Constructivists argue that 'objects shape and are shaped by human action, and interaction depends on dynamic, normative and epistemic interpretations of the objects' (Adler 1997, 322). This assumption means that material objects (e.g., a pipe, musical instrument or a totem pole) are assigned meaning, significance and value by the social, historical, and cultural contexts, through which they are defined and interpreted (Checkel 1998; Finnemore and Sikkink 2001). For example, railways, roads and infrastructures do not exist in nature but once constructed each of them is attributed a special meaning and use by diverse social groups. In light of this, the meaning and use of an object can never be said to be singular because the different social groups that encounter and use any given object may attribute different uses and meanings to it (Bijker 2001). It also means that language and framing influence how people think about objects and issues. Framing influences how people perceive objects and issues, whether they are technical, (geo)political, economic, or social, which accordingly influences how people behave. Therefore, unlike Mitrany (1966, 134–135), who emphasized the distinction between political and technical dimensions to objects, constructivists argue that the meaning of an object is dependent on how it is framed, increasing or decreasing any object's value and role.

Conversely, social interaction is also shaped by the particulars of an object or artefact. Once a technological artefact (e.g., a railway) is established, it can facilitate or restrict interaction, communication and the transportation

Revisiting functionalism 55

of people, information or artefacts (Bijker 2001). This aspect is emphasized by scholars who work on socially constructed elements of technology and actor-network theory (see e.g., Barry 2013a, 2013b; Bijker 2001; Sismondo 2009). The following sections will offer a more detailed description of this point.

A second defining feature of the constructivist approach is that it, like functionalism, does not view states as the only actors in the international arena. In the constructivist approach, 'actors' may be individuals, inter-governmental organizations, non-governmental organizations, governments within states and international institutions (Keck and Sikkink 1998). Actors depend on their social environment and its shared systems of meaning (Risse-Kappen 2005). More concretely, constructivism emphasizes that actors and international structures are mutually constituted and they influence each other. For example, Finnemore and Sikkink (2001) explain that international organizations frame issues, identify agendas, adjust the existing norms and rules or generate and even 'teach' states new norms and rules. According to Keck and Sikkink (1998), a number of techniques and tools (e. g., economic or political leverage, issue framing, strategic use of information, and naming and shaming) are implemented to construct or promote norms, rules and interests. Besides this, international organizations play a key role in promoting socialization between different actors, as Checkel (2005) highlights.

Related to this, the third defining feature of social constructivism is how it perceives the construction of relationship among different actors. In contrast to realism, constructivism argues that social relations and interests among different actors are not fixed or given. A similar argument is suggested by liberal theories. However, what distinguishes the social constructivist argument about the interests of actors is that it holds that actors' interests and identities are influenced and constructed by their interaction with others and with their social environment (Hurd 2008). In light of this, a relationship of enmity or friendship is seen by social constructivist as the result of ongoing socialization between actors in their social context. This socialization may reinforce the enmity or friendship. It may also reinforce or change the broader social structures in which the actors exist, including norms and other forms of shared meaning regarding sovereignty, threats, and interests (Adler 1997). By looking at the ways actors influence each other and the social context in which they interact, as well as how this context influences them, social constructivists seek to understand and explain changes in the relationship between diverse actors, most importantly the change from conflict to cooperation or from war to peace.

This section briefly introduced the constructivist insights that are relevant to this research. The following sections will provide in-depth discussion of the abovementioned features by incorporating them into classical functionalism. This will help to establish a comprehensive theoretical background and give rise to insights of revised functionalism.

56 *Revisiting functionalism*

Mediating interfaces: Cross-border and transnational infrastructure

The literature on functionalism views cooperation mostly as a set of inter-governmental treaties, institutional agreements, passages of policies, the formation of regional and international institutions and organizational frameworks. As a result, it focuses primarily on the bureaucratic conceptualization of treaties, norms, agreements, and regulations. While the literature acknowledges the importance of technical cooperation, it rarely explains or acknowledges the its proclivity to bring different societies together and increase their capacity to interact (Högselius, Van de Vleuten, and Kaijser 2016). The existing literature also fails to consider necessary transnational perspectives to adequately analyse the technical networks. Mitrany believed that it was on specific technical issues that cooperation would advance primarily and most efficiently (Ashworth 1999, 6). According to Mitrany:

> ...only by guiding material and technical resources into joint international activities and services could we possibly hope to meet the social needs and claims of the world's surging populations, with fair provision for all.
>
> (Mitrany1966, 19)

This statement shows that technical cooperation should not be conceived as only consisting of international treaties, but rather as being based on the existence or construction of material structures. For example, European integration was shaped, carried and flagged by both ideational or normative structures and material networks such as infrastructure, technical systems and artefacts (Misa and Schot 2005).

Considering the social constructivist insights (Adler 1997), it can be argued that Mitrany's technical cooperation or technical issues should be viewed from two perspectives, that is as either non-material or material structures. The non-material perspective looks at functional agreements, regulations, and rules, which address and facilitate both needs of ordinary people, elites, non-state actors, and states. The material perspective looks at transnational infrastructure, postal service, telecommunication cables, and natural resources, which shape society materially, address material issues or needs, and encourage state and non-state actors to cooperate as no single actor has the capacity to solve these issues or provide in these needs. The material perspective is helpful in thinking through the significance and the role of technical matters and material issues.

Mitrany admired the TVA, the ITU, and the UPU because they addressed human needs by dealing directly with the material and non-material aspects of a given problem. The ITU and UPU were the first administrative unions based around infrastructures. As one of the world's global service organizations, the UPU sets the rules, regulations, and agreements for specific material exchanges, including letters, mails, and parcels. However, while discussing the UPU or the TVA, the existing scholarship concentrates on rules, services and arrangements the UPU makes as an actor. In doing so, the literature neglects that the UPU offers global service to facilitate and address the material needs of people. In the same vein, the TVA designed the New Deal to address both non-material and material problems of the time by ignoring ideology or political differences, which existing scholarship does not fully appreciate. Therefore, it is necessary to understand the intertwined relationship between material and non-material needs and issues to fully appreciate the functioning of these unions.

Although the place of material need is apparent in classical functionalism, it has remained a marginal aspect within the literature. In light of this, the vocabulary of functionalist technical cooperation needs to be supplemented and modified via insights from social constructivism. It can be argued that the notion of a specific 'technical sector' can be interpreted as 'infrastructure' such as railways, roads, telecommunications, cables, and pipelines which transcend national boundaries, connect a number of different actors, bring new restrictions, and affect interaction capacities. Infrastructure is also self-determined, which means it fixes its own geographic scope, which actors are involved in it, its organizational structure, inherent nature, boundaries, and power. Particular infrastructure can have subtle and enduring functional importance for economic development, security, political, and societal interaction. The reason for this is that infrastructures have efficacy: they make a difference, produce effects, and alter the course of events through the advantages and disadvantages they offer. Infrastructure may facilitate movement, encourage cooperation, authorize new regulations, influence relationships, suggest new policies, and so on (Bennett and Patrick 2010). However, the influence infrastructure exerts often exceeds the deliberate intent of those who design it, as it can be more flexible and more unpredictable than its designers realize. For example, the way infrastructure reshapes landscapes and its capacity to promote or impede ways of living in particular places sometimes offers other actors an unforeseen purchase on power by providing unexpected means for them to act. Latour (2005) argues that infrastructure becomes 'strategic' because of the number of connections it makes possible in a highly contingent world. Therefore, infrastructure is much more than a power resource; it is the core medium of interaction for international actors (Herrera 2006).

Infrastructure has a number of functional aspects that need to be highlighted. First, cross-border infrastructure (e.g., gas or oil pipelines, fibre-optic cables, and railroads) forms material networks, and building those is beyond the economic, technical, political, and social capacities of most individual states, which may encourage governments to look for cooperation with other interested actors: other governments, companies, individuals, engineering communities, banks, and financial IGOs. Even large-scale domestic infrastructure projects often require international expertise, as was the case with the Yamal project in Russia. Also, in the case of China, whose government and state firms initiate huge infrastructural investments in Asia and Africa,

58 Revisiting functionalism

one needs to realize that their ability to do so is the result of opening up to the world economy. Its grown (perceived) power is not a unilateral achievement, but a result of giving up isolation. When the serious financial, political, environmental, and social risks that such projects often incur can be shared between multiple actors, the projects become much more viable. Meanwhile, these actors implicitly and explicitly decide who to connect to and who to bypass and how to design the infrastructure for economic, political and security-related purposes (Högselius, Van de Vleuten and Kaijser 2016). As explained by social constructivism, international organizations aim to spread, teach, and promote new norms and values (Finnemore and Sikkink 2001). Thus, international organizations look for ways and opportunities to do so. Facilitating the construction of infrastructure can offer international organizations, such as the World Bank, opportunities to spread their norms and values, because they can compel governments to comply with certain norms and rules (financial and ecological norms and rules for instance) by helping build infrastructure.

Second, infrastructure is an important component of economic activity. According to Nijkamp (1986) infrastructure is one of the tools for economic development. It can affect, directly or indirectly, a region's social-economic activities and other capacities, as well as influence its abilities to produce goods and services. According to Kuroda (2006), the president of Asian Development Bank, cross-border infrastructure may influence a country's prospects for economic growth, employment creation, poverty reduction, and social improvement. In the same vein, Martinkus and Lukasevicius (2008) consolidate that the infrastructural services and physical infrastructure are factors that affect the investment climate at the local level and increase the attractiveness of the region. An efficient infrastructure supports economic growth and improves the quality of life (Baldwin and Dixon 2009). This is one of the important reasons it gets the attention of both state and non-state elites. Clear examples of this are the ECSC and Euratom, which played a critical role as the centres at which the regulation of production and transport of raw materials across different borders was coordinated. They offered economic benefits and prosperity to their member states. In doing so, interest groups gradually promoted further cooperation, as they became aware of the benefits of so-called technical cooperation (Niemann 2009). However, the downside of infrastructural cooperation is that it is set up to exploit specific natural resources or places. In doing so, it may lead to the misuse of a given periphery rather than to its development. Infrastructure may unite or divide people and places through economic disparity, ecological issues, crises and wars (Herrera 2006). Transport, communication, and energy infrastructure may supply food, power, health products, and unprecedented wealth, but infrastructure capacities can also be utilized for waging war on scales hitherto unknown. Therefore, while discussing economic benefits, it is important to consider who is connected to whom, who is left out, and why?

Revisiting functionalism 59

Third, cross-border infrastructures such as railways or pipelines can enhance the regional and global capacity for interaction and connect land-locked countries to global networks. Mitrany favoured the ITU because from a material perspective, telecommunication infrastructure has provided links between different continents and effected global interconnectedness. Badenoch and Fickers (2010, 12) describe infrastructure as mediating interface, because it consists of structures 'in between' that allow things, people, and signs to travel across space by means of more or less standardized paths and protocols for conversion or translation. It is not enough to simply create regional institutions and coordinate tariffs and regulations at a regional level. Countries need to be connected by road, rail, electricity, and communications networks. In this sense, regional integration and/or cooperation requires both a coordinated set of rules across the region and physical interconnections such as road, rail, and electricity transmission lines, energy infrastructures between and within countries (Bond 2016).

According to social constructivism, there are several ways in which infrastructure can facilitate socialization among different actors (Finnemore and Sikkink 1998; Hurd 2008). Social constructivist usually relate socialization to international organizations, which will be discussed in detail in the next section. However, another way for socialization might take place is the construction of infrastructure, which offers different actors additional incentives to engage in joint action. If they wish to build infrastructure, governments need to build a shared consensus about bureaucratic regulations and overcome environmental, social, economic, political and technical obstacles (Bourguignon and Pleskovic 2008). In other words, to benefit from cross-border infrastructure, states need to relax their sovereignty concerns and create common rules, management strategies, and abide by common regulatory frameworks. To achieve this, they need to have regular meetings, joint studies and dialogue among politicians, experts, media, and citizens, which will help them to learn to appreciate the differences in their perspectives, share their risks, and deal with them accordingly. This regular interaction cutting across national borders might increase socialization among different state and private institutions and might lead to the creation of joint institutions to govern transnational infrastructures. Meanwhile, such material cooperation also requires social or institutional mediators, the institutions and individuals who work to govern and shape the way the finished infrastructure will be used (Badenoch and Fickers 2010, 12).

Finally, infrastructures can either be conflictual or cooperative. By using traditional interdependency theory, Oneal et al. (1996) argues that cross-border infrastructure can increase costs of conflict in the region, which would make international conflict less beneficial, less popular, and ultimately less feasible. Considering the high economic costs of the infrastructure, the foreign investment in it and the income it generates, states would think twice before starting a war with their neighbours (Oneal et al. 1996). Scholars going back to Adam Smith and Immanuel Kant have theorized about the

60 *Revisiting functionalism*

pacifying effects of economic interdependence. However, in the 21st century this argument is not fully applicable and too simplistic. As is mentioned by De Wilde (1991, 214), interdependency can be troublesome, but only when it is ignored. According to De Wilde (1991, Ch. 8), the basis for cooperation should not necessarily be the similarity of material resources and material needs or specific relational conditions, but rather the awareness of these conditions. In the absence of awareness of interdependency, even a high degree of material interdependency would not produce any particular progress toward either integration or cooperation (De Wilde 1991, Ch. 8 and Ch. 1). When actors are aware of their interdependency, they might coordinate their actions in order to enhance efficiency, or collaborate in order to find joint solutions to problems and challenges that are deemed relevant and important. When actors are not aware of their interdependency, or when they neglect or underestimate their importance, they will be confronted with unexpected crises. Therefore, cross-border infrastructures do not necessarily prevent conflict by themselves. Their interdependency conditions should also be understood and recognized by the actors involved.

Functionalist networks

In the previous section I discussed material networks, such as transnational infrastructure. However, another point that classical functionalism highlights but that is not explained systematically is the network of different agencies it advocates for, the so-called 'transnational networks.'[8]

According to Mitrany:

> ...the question will be asked, however, in what manner and to what degree the various functional agencies that may thus grow up would have to be linked to each other and articulated as parts of a more comprehensive organization. It should be clear that each agency could work by itself, but that does not exclude the possibility of some of them or all being bound in some way together, if it should be found needful or useful to do so. That indeed is the test. As the whole sense of this particular method is to let activities be organized as the need for joint action arises and is accepted, it would be out of place to lay down in advance some formal plan for the co-ordination of various functions.
>
> (Mitrany 1966, 73, 135)

This means that the coordination of several groups of functionalist agencies can provide different instruments (e.g., technical, administrative, economic) for broader functional application. The power of functional agencies rests in a large part on their access to the global donor and technical assistance networks that regional actors may not be able to reach (Mitrany 1966, 140–141). However, recent functionalist literature has paid surprisingly little attention

Revisiting functionalism 61

to analysing the role and structure of transnational networks. This oversight, however, has been addressed by social constructivism.

Social constructivists argue that the interaction of different actors is structured through networks (Checkel 1998; Keck and Sikkink 1998; Sikkink 2009). Considering the existing interconnected global arena, which has created complex economic, social, political, and environmental issues, social constructivists argue that strong transnational networking can play a number of roles, economic, political, cultural, and technical (Finnemore and Sikkink 2001). Networks include diverse actors, such as international organizations, private actors, scientists and illicit groups (Keck and Sikkink 1998). Along with nation states, international actors are actively involved in addressing specific new technical, political and economic challenges and have launched joint projects to bring different stakeholders together (Finnemore 1996; Sikkink 2009).

There are important ways in which transnational networks add value that need to be highlighted. The first way in which transnational networks add value is their capacity to draw the required resources from diverse sets of actors (Keck and Sikkink 1998). Given the complexity of modern cross-border or cross-sectorial problems (e.g., problems that have, for instance environmental, technical and economic dimensions), no state agency or public actor has the wherewithal to address issues single-handedly (Börzel and Heard-Laureote 2009). The result is an increasing reliance upon the cooperation and resources of outside private and non-private actors, who can bring to the table either material or non-material resources (e.g., information, empirical knowledge, specific technical expertise, financial means, and political clout and support), or both (Finnemore and Sikkink 2001). By using the networking power actors can facilitate valuable informal relations between private and public actors. Adler (1997) explains that they can formulate and shape new norms or rules (e.g., human rights and ecological sustainability), which can provide individuals and governments with direction and action. They can also balance the loss of some of economic, technological, and political powers by forging coalitions with other actors. In doing these things, networking participants bring different kinds of resources and expertise to the table by creating synergies. This coordination can create opportunities for each of those involved to address specific needs or issues while working towards a common goal.

The second way in which transnational networks add value is that they also have a socializing function, which is important in relation to the political, economic, and cultural diversity arising from organizational enlargement (Börzel and Heard-Laureote 2009; Finnemore 1996). In transnational networks, actors are often tied together in multiple ways, which is one way of generating continuous interaction because it invokes the image of connectedness amongst individuals, between different organizations and between private and public actors. Unlike realists and neoliberal institutionalists, who take identities and interests for granted, social constructivists recognize that

62   *Revisiting functionalism*

actors' behaviour, interests, self-understanding and identities are shaped by the social milieu in which they live (Adler 1997; Barnett and Finnemore 1999). The social constructivist literature argues that transnational corporations, NGOs or IGOs, are not only important for their economic, political and technical contributions, but also for their strong international networks, which might create informal interaction, new interests, and smooth negotiation among different actors. By using their networks, international organizations may link states in a network that allows for direct and indirect transmission of information about interests and intentions (Adler 1997; Finnemore 2001). Direct personal or organizational contacts may facilitate the creation of shared understanding of policy issues and measures to resolve them (Dorussen and Ward 2008; Gan 1993).

It is worth noting that when speaking of socialization, the literature expects norms, rules, interests or cooperation to arise on things that most of us would consider 'good', such as human rights and environmental cooperation. There is no reason for this misleading orientation because different actors perceive socialization under common issues differently and aim to achieve different goals (e.g., strengthening autocratic regime or crime syndicates). In this sense, social constructivism includes a set of pragmatic lenses through which it views all socially constructed 'good' and 'bad' reality (Adler 1997).

The third way in which transnational networks add value is through enhancing flexibility and adaptability (Cao 2009; Eilstrup-Sangiovanni 2017; Keck and Sikkink 1998; Sikkink 2009). This means the structure and composition of networks can be more easily modified to respond to changing needs. 'It is necessary to determine those activities which are common, where they are common and to the extent that they are common' as argued by Mitrany (1966, 115–116). Flexibility would also mean that different actors would be involved in the activities of any proposed cooperation while there would be no obligation to participate in all of the activities, or to stay out of any of them (Mitrany 1966, 205–210). The task itself can never be defined and limited in advance, but must remain continuously variable, reflecting the fact that situations may change. In this context, the informal nature of network ties allows different actors to collaborate on specific problems according to the nature of the problems rather than according to predetermined divisions of responsibility or jurisdiction (Podolny and Page 1998). This offers to even the weakest actor, either state or private, the assurance of non-domination and of equality of opportunity as working benefits of any functional activity in which it participates (Mitrany 1966, 205).

Economic leverage

While explaining the influence different kinds of agencies possess, Mitrany briefly mentions the particular leverage wielded by international actors. Mitrany explains this leverage with the example of a non-violent functional embargo as a means of restraining an aggressor. Mitrany proposed withdrawal of essential services, such as economic, technical, and administrative, by a number of functional organizations and actors as a deterrent to aggression and a means of ensuring compliance within a functional sector (Mitrany 1966, 76–77). According to Mitrany:

> …economic technical agencies, by their very nature, could be preventive in a way in which military agencies can never be. Just as it would be their function to give service wherever it was needed, so it would clearly be their duty to deny service where it was not obviously needed and might be abused; and they would have the means to do so without using force. A European railway authority, for example, would naturally and properly refuse to build railways which would have a strategic rather than an economic purpose, just as it could prevent the accumulation of rolling stock in a particular place in preparation for aggression.
>
> (Mitrany 1975, 183)

Mitrany never offered a detailed explanation for this aspect of transnational networks, however. Social constructivists on the other hand did explain how IGOs and NGOs seek to create, consolidate, or change and reformulate rules, norms, understandings, and interests by presenting the benefits that working with them would offer to states, such as technical assistance, financial grants, being spared from public shaming and set agendas (Adler 1997; Finnemore 2001). Having one of these kinds of benefits as leverage over a state plays a crucial role in attracting states, because states are no aware that when they join certain organizations they might give them certain rights to function in their territory, which states are inherently loath to do (Follesdal, Wessel and Wouters 2008). On the other hand, states are becoming aware that they need to comply with certain requirements in order to get help or support from international organizations. To do so, a state might need to break some of its old habits or adopt certain new habits. However, considering the number and functions of international organizations, states have the leeway to join one organization and ignore another. Because of this, states want to know what benefits an organization offers in cooperation.

One of the benefits that states look for is financial support or gains. According to Prange-Gstöhl (2009), states accept the requirements, norms, and values of international organizations because states envisage significant economic gains. For example, non-EU member countries like Georgia and Ukraine are willing to accept the EU norms and values because they want to access the EU's market and attract EU investors to their economies (Prange-Gstöhl 2009). Similarly, Schulze and Tosun (2013) argue that states are more willing to accept the requirements of international organizations if they can receive financial aid and developmental assistance from said international organizations. Offering assistance can help international organizations spread their norms and it can help states strengthen their institutional capacity and cover their certain costs.

64 *Revisiting functionalism*

Additionally, Karreth (2017) argues that IGOs with high economic leverage over states shape state behaviour during interstate disputes which substantially lowers the risk that such political disputes escalate to armed conflicts. Examples include the World Bank, the International Monetary Fund (IMF) and regional development banks. Their leverage derives from their ability to reliably and quickly impose penalties on states they are involved with that engage in violent conflict (Karreth 2017). The economic leverage these organizations have over states they are involved with includes the short-term or long-term loans they have provided, their ability to harmonize currencies and trade, and their ability to enhance market access, facilitate foreign investment, assist with and coordinate the production of goods, and facilitate the extraction, processing and sale of natural resources (Karreth 2017). IGOs with economic leverage can also facilitate the splitting of resources under dispute to prevent commitment problems arising from bargaining over resources that themselves will substantially alter the distribution of power.

Multilateral development banks lose some of their investments and loans when recipient states spend considerable resources on war and when military action causes damage in recipient countries. IGOs can convert, and have previously converted, such anticipated negative effects into costs for member states engaging in military conflict. When a member state chooses to go to war over an issue with another state, that member state can expect some form of negative ramification from the institution. This ramification may come in the suspension of benefits, or direct costs, such as sanctions or exclusion.

Economic benefits can be suspended on a number of time scales. They may be suspended immediately, as is the case when states go to war. Institutions that provide loans, projects, or information, such as the World Bank, typically 'step out during active conflict' (Karreth 2017, 8). In the medium term, states at war may be excluded from active institutional cooperation, such as the further liberalization of trade barriers in trade organizations. Similarly, IGOs may halt projects until states resume peaceful interactions. In the long term, warring states may gain the reputation of being unstable partners that tarnish the reputations of institutions they work with, which may then preclude them from extensions of current institutional arrangements. Altogether, going to war will create costs for the involved states, either directly or indirectly through the costs of the withdrawal of benefits (Karreth 2017).

Transnational corporations

The contribution of the idea of functional organizations to this research is to provide critical assumptions regarding the role of different intergovernmental and nongovernmental agencies. However, an oversight in functionalist assumption is the role of transnational corporations (TNCs) as functional agencies in international relations, to which very little attention has been paid. Although Mitrany worked as a policy adviser for Unilever and Lever

Brothers, Ltd. from 1944 until his retirement in 1960, which should have been enough to recognize the relevance of economic expertise in political enterprises, he paid scant attention to the role of transnational firms or corporations in terms of functionalism (De Wilde 1991). While the classical functionalists Haas and Lindberg later highlighted the contribution of non-governmental private elites to cooperation, recent scholarship on functionalism has overlooked this aspect of cooperation. Haas (1958, 312–313) in particular focused on the pressures exerted by non-governmental elites, such as business and professional associations, trade unions or other interest groups. In light of this, it can be argued that the role of TNCs did originate in the classical functionalist writings.

Considering the global economic, political, and technical developments, it can be argued that the category of functional actors should not be restricted to intergovernmental and non-governmental agencies only. Global developments are not fully dominated by states and institutions only, but also by private and semi-private firms and companies (Clapp 2005; Hall and Bierstekker 2002). Similar to international organizations, TNCs offer the resources, networks, and instruments that projects require but most states lack such as professional personnel, advanced technology, organizational capacity, access to the world market, support from their home countries, and financial power (Forsgren 2008). As a result, TNCs deliver specific functional services and products such as energy, security, agriculture, communication, financial, education and constriction to different projects (see e.g., Abdelal 2015, 2012; Hall and Bierstekker 2002; Nye 1974). Some TNCs can access certain regions easier and faster than certain international institutions.

In short, they do many of the things traditionally associated with the state. According to Hall and Bierstekker (2002, 6), TNCs can now set agendas, and establish boundaries or limits for action, and they offer rescue, guarantee contracts, and provide order and security. They act both in the domestic and in the international arenas simultaneously. These actors can challenge states while negotiating debt rescheduling, organizing external boycotts, or choosing new locations for production and employment (Hall and Bierstekker 2002; Nye 1974). From an economic perspective, they are financial powers to be reckoned with because their decisions to investment matter in particular communities and countries. By using their international reputation, TNCs can establish trust, socialization and financial connection between different actors. For example, certain financial institutions invest in different projects if there are well-known transnational corporations attached like BP, Huawei or Shell because it decreases project risk. It is worth noting that these functions are not only belong to TNCs. However, state firms (e.g., China National Petroleum), who internationally functions like TNCs, offer also these resources and functions. Their impact on their home governments is as big as the political influence of (Western) TNCs.

Meanwhile, the involvement of certain companies can influence the reputation of certain countries as being business-friendly place or not. In light of

66   *Revisiting functionalism*

this, it is important to link the principles of functional agencies to the possible role of transnational corporations like Shell, BP, Chevron, and Gazprom. Another reason this linkage is necessary that international affairs are growing more complex than ever and states cannot make decisions without considering international companies. Technical and economic challenges introduced by globalization are not manageable for institutions and states on their own.

Avoiding Utopic thinking: The ill-fitting European benchmark

While discussing classical functionalism (e.g., the spill-over assumption), the existing literature mostly argues that it is not applicable outside Europe. The reason for this misleading conclusion is that the existing scholarship expects to see integration that, although it takes place outside of Europe, is nonetheless similar to the integration that took place in Western Europe and produces strong organizations like the EU in other regions. More concretely, the relevant literature mainly focuses on endpoint rather than process. By using the EU benchmark, the relevant literature ignores that regions are socially constructed through different developments. In contrast to this, constructivists understand the relationship, both normative and material, between different regional structures. Constructivists argue that the concepts of cooperation, competition, norms and interests influence different actors differently (Checkel 2005, Finnemore and Sikkink 2001). Actors react differently for different reasons and can be influenced by geographical, economic, and social factors, for instance, which is important to understand the differences between regions, the most important of which are listed below.

First, integration by definition implies a giving up of sovereignty rights, either voluntarily or through pressure (Acharya 2012; Werner and De Wilde 2001). Therefore, the lens of cooperation is better suited to view non-Western regional cooperation through than the lens of integration. The reason for this is that, when considering the colonial history of other regions (e.g., the Middle East, Central Asia, Caucasus), it can be argued that when these regions create or join an organization, their end goal is to prevent external intervention and to preserve their autonomy, independence, and international recognition. Second, one may argue that the EU is a unique development and it is better to look for sector-specific developments rather than EU-style integration in other regions. Third, the classical functionalists like Mitrany did not claim that the end-point of functional cooperation should be a closed regional union like the EU. Instead, Mitrany advocated that regional organizations or unions need to recognize their global interdependency.

Finally, in expecting other regions to form institutions like the EU, the existing scholarship neglects one important dimension: time difference. Mitrany and Haas established the spill-over assumption in the 1950s, which saw the beginning of the Cold War and was a time of recovery for most countries. States were experiencing interconnection between different areas,

Revisiting functionalism 67

which hugely facilitated the spill-over process, for the first time. However, in 2019, the situation is different as states are aware of spill-over and countries outside the EU have seen the practice of spill-over cooperation, which makes them take further steps more cautiously and slowly. Also within the EU this has become manifest with features like the initial no-vote against the Maastricht Treaty by Denmark in 1992, the no-vote against the EU Constitution by France and the Netherlands in 2005 and most strongly by Brexit – in 2020. Considering this, it is important to explain why the decision-making system only occasionally succeeds in producing further cooperation. What is the time lag between spill-over occurring into the first and into the second spill-over area? And why does integration halt in some periods or parts? Functionalists continue to see national obstruction as a simple delay rather than as a fundamental variance with the theory that would require reflection. Functionalism leaves the question of spill-over's stop-and-go rhythm unanswered. Corbey (1995) proposed 'dialectic spill-over' to address these shortcomings of the theory, but it has been rarely mentioned since.

Dialectical spill-over does not expect the spill-over effect to produce integration straightforwardly. Instead, the hypothesis is that states protect sovereignty in those policy areas that are functionally linked to areas subject to integration. States only agree to integration when their mutual policy competition has turned into a lose-lose situation of them intervening in costly and dead-end ways. Dialectical spill-over facilitates an understanding of the stop-and-go in the spill-over process by proposing a number of assumptions.

According to dialectical spill-over, each spill-over round provokes resistance to further integration and decreases willingness to cooperate in adjacent areas. The first reason for this is that with each round of spill-over states become aware of the ongoing integration process and they know that to increase benefits they need to move to other areas and relinquish their autonomy over the spill-over areas. But they are unwilling to let go of the benefits they had hoped to reap from the policies subject to integration. Governments need room to manoeuvre and will thus safeguard functionally linked areas against further integration and thus prefer to safeguard their adjacent policy areas. The second reason for states' resistance to spill-over is that different interest groups are involved. Areas that are accessible to or covered by powerful interest groups are more liable objects of intervention than others when spill-over into these areas becomes likely. These interest groups can include companies and ministries, but this increase in intervention can also by caused more indirectly by structural limitations, because a country's economy, its demography, its legal tradition, or its administrative structure might also block integration. According to Schmitter (2005), governments may be constrained directly by agents, such as by lobby groups, opposition parties, the media or public pressure. Governments' restricted autonomy to act may prove disintegrative, especially when countries face strongly diverging domestic constraints. This may disrupt emerging

68 *Revisiting functionalism*

integrative outcomes, as domestic constraints of governments may lead to national vetoes or prevent policies from moving beyond the most easily defined shared interests.

In time, however, participants come to see this reaction as counter-productive. When state intervention (or policy rivalry) in neighbouring areas becomes counterproductive, policy preferences converge and further integration is demanded more and more by the member states. Stagnation and progress may thus be understood as regular stages in the process of integration. The spill-over effect seems to apply – but only much later than expected.

Conclusion

This chapter has argued that, despite what critics argue, classical functionalism still offers useful, alternative tools that promise to understand and explain contemporary developments. Although classical functionalism has been trapped and marginalized within European Studies, certain processes it describes, such as the role of multiple actors, the contribution of technical dialogue, spill-over, and socialization, are nonetheless insightful when analysing the cooperation potential in other regions. Benefitting from including the best of Mitrany's and Haas' original arguments, this chapter presented a revision of functionalism via social constructivism. Specifically, this chapter has illustrated that although there has not yet been systematic debate between functionalists and social constructivists, there are several promising avenues for cross-fertilization. This establishes a critical and innovative theoretical tool box as well as new areas for empirical investigation, which does not exist for realists and is overlooked by liberals.

First, by highlighting the importance of framing, the chapter has argued that Mitrany was wrong in distinguishing technical aspects from political aspects. In its place, the chapter has proposed that when something is framed as technical, cooperation is easier because it changes people's tendency to view something within a power political zero-sum framework. By (artificially) moving an issue or specific stakes from a political arena to a technocratic or bureaucratic arena there can be changes in the type of actors involved, their power relations and interests as well as their logical approaches to and modes of reasoning about the issues and stakes. In this sense, it is necessary to understand how the meaning, significance, role, and value of objects and issues are socially constructed and not fixed within a particular context. This also means that framing influences how people think about objects and issues and how people perceive and behave towards objects and issues; whether they are technical, (geo)political, economic, or social minded.

Second, the chapter has moved the discussion about functionalist cooperation beyond shared treaties, regulations, rules and policies by including the role of material artefacts and natural resources. Functionalist technical cooperation is argued to include both shared regulations and material

Revisiting functionalism 69

entities. This is because material objects influence and are influenced by actors' actions and interactions. In doing so, revised functionalism presents the potential benefits of completing infrastructural projects as one of the incentives for technical cooperation, which in effect means establishing policy coordination and the formation of administrative and regulatory bodies. These bodies do not infringe on sovereignty, but they help to create trans-governmental influences within the ministries and state-owned companies of the participating states. Therefore, it is necessary to understand correlations between technical artefacts and their bearing on social situations.

Third, considering the current global economic, technical and political developments, revised functionalism argues that it is necessary to include the contribution of transnational corporations in functional agencies, either directly as members, indirectly as powerful lobbying groups or as concrete stakeholders in the maintenance of infrastructures. They provide the neces-sary functional economic, technical, and administrative instruments that most states do not have. Combining the social constructivist insights, this chapter has highlighted that similar to NGOs and IGOs, transnational cor-porations socially construct alternatives, promote socialization, and help to create social reality. In contrast to neoliberal and realist works, which link them to transaction costs and grant limited roles to these actors, this chapter has explained that private actors as well as state firms do more than just levy transaction costs and are not just empty shells, as they can expand and constrain state interests.

Fourth, revised functionalism puts less emphasis on integration and more emphasis on the role of networking and coordination between different agencies, such as companies, IGOs, financial institutions, individuals, and NGOs. The interaction between diverse actors is structured in networks and aimed at achieving specific goals. Drawing insights from social con-structivism, this chapter has illustrated that networks of international and regional agencies establish, shape, articulate and transmit new norms, responsibilities, interests, and rules, which influence state practices and iden-tities. They help governments to overcome collective action dilemmas. In doing so, network of agencies, specifically regional networks, can become new sites for interaction, and they may help states, their elites or societies view themselves as part a region. The coordination of different agencies can provide opportunities for wider functional ends and access to global inves-tors and technical assistance that national regional actors may not be able to reach.

Related to this, revised functionalism highlights the economic and techni-cal leverages of international organizations, which can be used as a means of restraining aggressive policies and facilitating cooperation among different states. More specifically, the chapter has argued that states are more likely to accept the norms and values of international organizations if they can receive economic assistance in the form of grants, loans, credits, or access to other financial sources. This economic assistance can allow international

70 *Revisiting functionalism*

organizations to influence state behaviours and spread their norms, and it can help states to strengthen their institutional capacity and cover certain costs.

Finally, side lining the European benchmark, revised functionalism has highlighted that regions (both Western and non-Western) are socially constructed and can be redefined. In this sense, the ideas of cooperation, competition and conflict influence different regional structures differently. By understanding this difference, one can explain how and why complex dynamics change over time. By side lining Eurocentrism, this chapter has emphasized the idea of cooperation rather than that of integration. In this regard, revised functionalism does not expect Western Europe style cooperation or the establishment of dominant organizations like the EU in other regions. Rather, it seeks to understand and explain the process of cooperation. By using dialectical functionalism, this chapter has argued that the change necessary for cooperation happens in different areas according to perceived necessity and need. Often states only agree to cooperate when their mutual policy competition has turned into costly dead-end interventions.

Notes

1 For detailed information about Mitrany's life see Mitrany (1975, Ch1) and Hammarlund (2005, Ch 1).
2 In 1938 Mitrany was asked to work 'with an academic intelligence group (camouflaged as 'The Foreign Research and Press Service').' In 1941 he wrote two papers for this group that would culminate in the pamphlet. But, as the papers were badly received, he resigned from the Foreign Office in the meantime. His superiors were not interested in any post-war scenarios that included an active role for the Soviet-Union nor for Germany. According to Mitrany diplomats put too much emphasis on balance-of-power interests. But he published *A Working Peace System* as a book in 1943 (as cited in Mitrany (1975, 19–20)).
3 See: Haas (1958, Ch. 5 and 6); Lindberg (1963, Ch. 4) and engrenage has been defined on pp. 18–19.
4 Link for the journal: http://www.tandfonline.com/toc/rjpp20/12/2?nav=tocList.
5 With the country reeling from the Great Depression, President Roosevelt created his 'New Deal' to help America recover. The Tennessee Valley Authority was founded to help the hard-hit Tennessee Valley, where it was tasked with improving the quality of life in the region. See more at: https://www.tva.gov/About-TVA/Our-History#sthash.fQcNMkYS.dpuf.
6 For detailed information about this organization and its current members see: http://www.upu.int/en/the-upu/the-upu.html.
7 See the section 'Criticism' for an explanation of the positivist attitude.
8 There is diverse and growing literature on networking that explains the term from different perspectives such as economic, political, social, and technological. In this regard, the term network means different things to different scholars. One of these well-known interpretations is the Actor-Network-Theory (ANT) (Barry 2013a, 2013b; Chandler 2013; Coole 2013; Edward 2016; Latour 2005; Verbeek 2005). In contrast to ANT, this current work seeks to explain social and economic sides of a networking approach. While acknowledging the importance of the ANT, the contribution of this theory to this project is limited due to the abstract assumptions ANT is based on. Because of this, this work integrates only a few particular complements from the ANT.

Revisiting functionalism 71

Bibliography

Abdelal, Rawi. 2015. 'The multinational firm and geopolitics: Europe, Russian energy, and power.' *Business and Politics* 17 (3): 553–576.

Abdelal, Rawi. 2012. 'The profits of power: Commerce and realpolitik in Eurasia.' *Review of International Political Economy* 20 (3): 421–456.

Acharya, Amitav. 2016. 'Regionalism Beyond EU-Centrism.' In *The Oxford Handbook Of Comparative Regionalism*, by Tanja A Börzel and Thomas Risse-Kappen, 109–133. Oxford: Oxford University Press.

Acharya, Amitav. 2012. 'Comparative Regionalism: A Field Whose Time has Come?' *The International Spectator* 47 (1): 3–15.

Adler, Emanuel. 1997. 'Seizing the Middle Ground: Constructivism in World Politics.' *European Journal of International Relations* 3 (3): 319–363.

Alexandrescu, Mihai. 2007. 'David Mitrany: From Federalism to Functionalism.' *Transylvanian Review* 15 (1): 1–15.

Anderson, Dorothy. 1998. 'David Mitrany (1888–1975): An appreciation of his life and work.' *Review of International Studies* 24: 577–592.

Ashworth, Lucian. 2017. 'David Mitrany on the international anarchy: A lost work of classical realism.' *Journal of International Political Theory* 13 (3): 311–324.

Ashworth, Lucian. 2005. 'David Mitrany and South-East Europe: The Balkan Key to World Peace.' *The Historical Review* 3: 203–224.

Ashworth, Lucian. 1999. *Creating International Studies: Angell, Mitrany and the Liberal Tradition*. New York: Routledge.

Ashworth, Lucian, and David Long. 1999. *New Perspectives on International Functionalism*. London: Macmillan Press.

Badenoch, Alexander, and Andreas Fickers. 2010. *Materializing Europe*. New York: Palgrave Macmillan.

Baldwin, John, and Jay Dixon. 2009. 'Infrastructure Capital: What is it? Where is it? How Much of it is There?' *Canadian Productivity Review Research Paper* 16: 1–108

Barry, Andrew, and Evelina Gambino. 2019. 'Pipeline Geopolitics: Subaquatic Materials and the Tactical Point.' *Geopolitics* 25 (1): 1–35.

Barry, Andrew. 2013a. *Material Politics*. Sussex: Willey Blackwell.

Barry, Andrew. 2013b. 'The Translation Zone: Between Actor-Network Theory and International Relations.' *Journal of International Studies* 41 (34): 413–429.

Barnett, Michael, and Martha Finnemore. 1999. 'The Politics, Power, and Pathologies of International Organizations.' *International Organization* 53 (4): 699–732.

Bennett, Tony, and Patrick Joyce. 2010. *Material Powers*. London: Routledge.

Bijker, Wiebe E. 2001. 'Technology, Social Construction of.' In *International Encyclopedia of the Social and Behavioral Sciences*, 15522–15527. Oxford: Blackwell Publishing.

Blum, Douglas. 2002. 'Beyond Reciprocity: Governance and Cooperation around the Caspian Sea.' In *Environmental Peacemaking*, by Ken Conca and Geoffrey Dabelko, 161–190. Baltimore: The John Hopkins University Press.

Börzel, Tanja A. 2006. 'Mind the gap! European integration between level and scope.' *Journal of European Public Policy* 12 (2): 217–236.

Börzel, Tanja A. 2005. 'Preface.' *Journal of European Public Policy* 12 (2): 215–216.

Börzel, Tanja A, and Thomas Risse-Kappen. 2016. *The Oxford Handbook of Comparative Regionalism*. Oxford: Oxford University Press.

Börzel, Tanja A, and Karen Heard-Lauréote. 2009. 'Networks in EU Multi-level Governance: Concepts and Contributions.' *Journal of Public Policy* 29 (2): 135–151.

72 Revisiting functionalism

Bourguignon, François, and Boris Pleskovic. 2008. *Rethinking Infrastructure for Development*. Washington: World Bank Group.

Bond, James. 2016. 'Infrastructure in Africa.' *Global Journal of Emerging Market Economies* 8 (3): 309–333.

Breslin, Shaun, and Wilson D Jeffrey. 2014. 'Towards Asian Regional Functional Futures: Bringing Mitrany Back In?' *Australian Journal of International Affairs* 69 (2): 126–143.

Burr, Vivien. 2015. *Social Constructionism*. London: Routledge.

Cao, Xun. 2009. 'Networks of Intergovernmental Organizations and Convergence in Domestic Economic Policies.' *International Studies Quarterly* 53: 1095–1130.

Chandler, David. 2013. 'The World of Attachment? The Post-humanist Challenge to Freedom and Necessity.' *Millennium: Journal of International Studies* 41 (3): 517–534.

Checkel, Jeffrey. 2005. 'International Institutions and Socialization in Europe: Introduction and Framework.' *International Organization* 59 (4): 801–826.

Checkel, Jeffrey. 1998. 'The Constructivist Turn in International Relations Theory.' *World Politics* 50 (2): 324–348.

Coole, Diana. 2013. 'Agentic Capacities and Capacious Historical Materialism: Thinking with New Materialisms in the Political Sciences.' *Millennium: Journal of International Studies* 41 (3): 451–469.

Corbey, Dorette. 1995. 'Dialectical Functionalism: Stagnation as A Booster of European Integration.' *International Organization* 49 (2): 253–265.

Clapp, Jennifer. 2005. 'Transnational corporations and global environmental governance.' In *Handbook of Global Environmental Politics*, by Peter Dauvergne, 284–297. Northampton: Edward Elgar Publishing Limited.

De Wilde, Jaap. 1991. *Saved From Oblivion*. Aldershot: Dartmouth.

Diez, Thomas. 1999. 'Speaking "Europe": the politics of integration discourse.' *Journal of European Public Policy* 6 (4): 598–613.

Dorussen, Han, and Hugh Ward. 2008. 'Intergovernmental Organizations and Kantian Peace: A Network Perspective.' *Journal of Conflict Resolution* 52 (2): 189–212.

Edward, Mark. 2016. 'From actor network theory to modes of existence: Latour's ontologies.' *Global Discourse*, 6 (1–2):1–7.

Egbert, Jahn. 1979. 'The Revival of Functionalist Theory in East-West Cooperation.' *Bulletin of Peace Proposals* 10 (1): 73–78.

Eilstrup-Sangiovanni, Mette. 2017. 'Global Governance Networks.' In *The Oxford Handbook of Global Networks*, by Jennife Nicoll Victor, Alexander H Montgomery and Mark Lubell, 1–29. Oxford: Oxford University Press.

Farrell, Henry, and Héritier Adrienne. 2005. 'A Rationalist-Institutionalist Explanation of Endogenous Regional Integration.' *Journal of European Public Policy* 12 (2): 273–290.

Finnemore, Martha, and Kathryn Sikkink. 2001. 'The Constructivist Research Program in International Relations and Comparative Politics.' *Annual Reviews* 4: 391–496.

Finnemore, Martha, and Kathryn Sikkink. 1998. 'International Norm Dynamics and Political Change.' *International Organization* 52 (4): 887–917.

Forsgren, Mats. 2008. *Theories of the Multinational Firm*. Cheltenham: Edward Elgar.

Follesdal, Andreas, Ramses Wessel, and Jan Wouters. 2008. *Multilevel Regulation on the EU*. Boston: Martinus Nifhoff Publishers.

Gan, Lin. 1993. 'The making of the Global Environmental Facility.' *Global Environmental Change* 3 (3): 256–275.

Revisiting functionalism 73

Ghoshal, Sumantra, and Christopher Bartlett. 1990. 'The Multinational Corporation as an Interorganizational Network.' *Academy of Management* 15 (4): 603–625.

Groom, John A. 1994. 'Neofunctionalism: A case of mistaken identity'. In *The European Union*, by Nelsen Brent and Alexander Stubb, 111–123. London: Palgrave.

Groom, John A, and Taylor Paul. 1975. *Functionalism*. London: London Press.

Gulati, Ranjay. 1998. 'Alliances and Networks.' *Strategic Management Journal* 19: 293–317.

Gulati, Ranjay, Nitin Nohria, and Akbar Zaheer. 2000. 'Strategic Networks.' *Strategic Management Journal* 21: 203–215.

Guzzini, Stefano. 2000. 'A Reconstruction of Constructivisim in International Relations.' *European Journal of International Relations* 6 (2): 147–182.

Haas, Ernst B. 2004. *The Uniting Of Europe*. Notre Dame: University of Notre Dame Press.

Haas, Ernst B. 2001. 'Does Constructivism Subsume Neo-Functionalism?' In *The Social Construction of Europe*, by Thomas Christiansen, Knud Erik Jorgensen and Anje Wiener, 22–32. London: SAGE.

Haas, Ernst B. 1980. 'Why Collaborate? Issue-Linkage and International Regimes.' *World Politics* 32 (3): 357–405.

Haas, Ernst B. 1975. 'Is there a Hole in the Whole? Knowledge, Technology, Interdependence, and the Construction of International Regimes.' *International Organization* 29 (3): 827–876.

Haas, Ernst B. 1964. *Beyond The Nation State Functionalism and Internationalism*. California: Stanford University Press.

Haas, Ernst B. 1961. 'International Integration: The European and the Universal Process.' *International Organization* 366–392.

Haas, Ernst B. 1958. *The Uniting of Europe*. Indiana: University of Notre Dame Press.

Haas, Peter. 2016. 'Regional Environmental Governance.' In *The Oxford Handbook of Comparative Regionalism*, by Tanja Börzel and Thomas Risse, 1–39. Oxford: Oxford University Press.

Hall, Rodney, and Bierstekker Thomas. 2002. *The Emergency of Private Authority in Global Governance*. Cambridge: Cambridge University Press.

Hammarlund, Per. 2005. *Liberal Internationalism and the Decline of the State: The Thought of Richard Cobden, David Mitrany, and Kenichi Ohmae*. London: Palgrave Macmillan.

Henrich-Franke, Christian. 2016. 'Functionalistic Spill-over and Infrastructure Integration: The Telecommunication Sectors.' In *Linking Networks: The Formation of Common Standards and Visions for Infrastructure Development*, by Martin Schiefelbusch and Dienel Hans-Liudger, 85–110. New York: Routledge.

Herrera, Geoffrey. 2006. *Technology and International Transformation*. Albany: New York Press.

Hoffmann, Stanley. 1995. 'The crisis of liberal internationalism.' *Foreign Affairs* 98: 159–177.

Holland, Stuart. 1980. *Uncommon Market*. London: Macmillan.

Holthaus, Leonie. 2018. 'David Mitrany and the Purposes of Functional Pluralism.' In *Pluralist Democracy in International Relations*, by Leonie Holthaus, 179–208. New York: Palgrave Macmillan.

Holton, Robert J. 2011. *Globalization and the Nation State*. New York: Palgrave Macmillan.

74 Revisiting functionalism

Hooghe, Liesbet, and Gary Marks. *Multi-level Governance and European Integration*. New York: Rowman and Little Field Publisher.

Högselius, Per, Arne Kaijser, and Erik Van der Vleuten. 2016. *Europe's Infrastructure Transition*. New York: Palgrave Macmillan.

Hurd, Ian. 2008. 'Constructivism.' In *The Oxford Handbook of International Relations*, by Christian Reus-Smit and Duncan Snidal, 298–317. Oxford: Oxford University Press.

Imber, Mark F. 2002. 'Functionalism.' In *Governing Globalization*, by Anthony McGrew and David Held, 290–305. Cambridge: Blackwell Publishing.

Imber, Mark F. 1984. 'Re-Reading Mitrany: A Pragmatic Assessment of Sovereignty.' *Review of International Studies* 10 (2): 103–120.

International Labour Organization. 2019. 'About the ILO.' September 11. Accessed September 2019. http://www.ilo.org/global/about-the-ilo/lang-en/index.htm.

Jensen, Carsten. 2003. 'Neo-functionalism.' In *European Union Politics*, by Michelle Cini and Nieves Perez-Solorzano, 69–71. Oxford: Oxford University Press.

Karreth, Johannes. 2017. 'The Economic Leverage of International Organizations in Interstate Disputes.' *International Interaction* 44 (3): 1–29.

Keck, Margaret E, and Kathryn Sikkink. 1998. *Activists Beyond Borders. Advocacy Networks in International Politics*. Ithaca: Cornell University Press.

Kratochwil, Friedrich. 2000. 'Constructing a New Orthodoxy? Wendt's 'Social Theory of International Politics' and the Constructivist Challenge.' *Millennium: Journal of International Studies* 29 (1): 73–101.

Kuroda, Haruhiko. 2006. 'Infrastructure And Regional Cooperation.' Annual Bank Conference on Development Economics. World Bank Group. http://siteresources. worldbank.org/DEC/Resources/84797-1251813753820/6415739-1251814084145/Ha ruhiko_Kuroda_Infra.

Latour, Bruno. 2005. *Reassembling the Social*. Oxford: Oxford University Press.

Lindberg, Leon N, and Stuart A.Scheingold. 1970. *Europe's Would-be Polity: Patterns of Change in the European Community*. Englewood Cliffs: Prentice-Hall.

Lindberg, Leon N, and Stuart A.Scheingold. 1963. *The political dynamics of European economic integration*. Stanford: Stanford University Press.

Lelieveldt, Herman, and Sebastiaan Princen. 2015. *The Politics of the European Union*. Cambridge: Cambridge University Press.

Long, David. 1993. 'International Functionalism and the Politics of Forgetting.' *International Journal* 48 (2): 335–379.

Macmillan, Catherine. 2009. 'The Application of Neofunctionalism to The Enlargement Process: The Case Of Turkey.' *Journal of Common Market Studies* 47 (4): 789–809.

Macmullen, Andrew. 2004. 'Intergovernmental functionalism? The Council of Europe in European Integration.' *Journal of European Integration* 26 (4): 405–429.

March, James G, and Johen P Olsen. 2011. 'The logic of appropriateness.' In *The Oxford Handbook of Political Science*, by Robert E Goodin, 478–496. Oxford: Oxford University Press.

Mattli, Walter. 2005. 'Ernst Haas's Evolving Thinking on Comparative Regional Integration: of Virtues and Infelicities.' *Journal of European Public Policy* 12 (2): 327–348.

Martinkus, Bronislovas, and Lukosevicius Kazys. 2008. 'Investment environment of Lithuanian resorts: Researching national and local factors in the Palanga case.' *Transformations in Business and Economics* 7 (2): 67–83.

Revisiting functionalism 75

McGowan, Lee. 2007. 'Theorising European Integration: Revisiting Neo-Functionalism and Testing its Suitability for Explaining the Development of EC Competition Policy.' *European Integration Online Papers* 11 (3): 1–17.

Milward, Alan. 1992. *The European Rescue of the Nation-State.* London: Routledge.

Misa, Thomas J, and Johan Schot. 2005. 'Introduction to the special issue Inventing Europe.' *History and Technology* 21 (1): 1–19.

Mitrany, David. 1975. *The Functional Theory of Politics.* New York: St Martin's Press.

Mitrany, David. 1966. *A Working Peace System.* Chicago: Quadrangle Books.

Mitrany, David. 1965. 'The Prospect of Integration: Federal or Functional.' *Journal of Common Market Studies* 4 (2): 119–149.

Mitrany, David. 1948. 'The Functional Approach to World Organization.' *International Affairs* 24 (3): 350–363.

Molchanov, Mikhail. 2011. 'Extractive Technologies and Civic Networks' Fight for Sustainable Development.' *Bulletin of Science, Technology and Society* 31 (1): 55–67.

Moravcsik, Andrew. 2005. 'The European Constitutional Compromise and The Neofunctionalist Legacy.' *Journal of European Public Policy* 12 (2): 349–386.

Moravcsik, Andrew. 1993. 'Preferences and Power in the European Community: A Liberal Intergovernmentalist Approach.' *Journal of Common Market Studies* 31: 473–524.

Niemann, Arne. 2009. *Explaining Decisions in the European Union.* Cambridge: Cambridge University Press.

Niemann, Arne. 2006. *Explaining Decisions in the European Union.* Cambridge: Cambridge University Press.

Niemann, Arne. 1998. 'The PHARE Programme and the Concept of Spillover: Neofunctionalism In The Making.' *Journal of European Public Policy* 5 (3): 428–446.

Niemann, Arne, and Demosthenes Ioannou. 2015. 'European economic integration in times of crisis: a case of neofunctionalism?' *Journal of European Public Policy* 22 (2): 196–218.

Niemann, Arne, and Philippe Schmitter. 2009. *European Integration Theory.* Oxford: Oxford University Press.

Nijkamp, Peter. 1986. 'Infrastructure and regional development: A multidimensional policy analysis.' *Empirical Economics* 11 (1): 1–21.

Nye. Joseph S. 1974. 'Multinational Corporations in World Politics.' *Foreign Affairs* 53 (1): 153–175.

Oneal, John, Frances Oneal, Zeev Maoz, and Rusett Bruce. 1996. 'The Liberal Peace: Interdependence, Democracy, and International Conflict, 1950–85.' *Journal of Peace Researhc* 33 (1): 11–28.

Peltonen, Hannes. 2017. 'A tale of two cognitions: The Evolution of Social Constructivism in International Relations.' *Revista Brasileira de Política Internacional* 60 (1): 1–17.

Petersen, Alexandros. 2016. *Integration in Energy and Transport.* London: Lexington Books.

Podolny, Joel M, and Karen L. Page. 1998. 'Network forms of Organization.' *Annual Review of Sociology* 24: 57–76.

Prange-Gstöhl, Heiko. 2009. 'Enlarging the EU's internal energy market: Why would third countries accept EU rule export?' *Energy Policy* 37: 5296–5304.

Price, Richard, and Christian Reus-Smit. 1998. 'Dangerous Liaisons? Critical International Theory and Constructivisim.' *European Journal of International Relations* 4 (3): 259–294.

76 *Revisiting functionalism*

Risse-Kappen, Thomas. 2005. 'Neofunctionalism, European Identity, and the Puzzles Of European Integration.' *Journal of European Public Policy* 12 (2): 291–309.

Risse-Kappen, Thomas. 1996. 'Exploring the Nature of the Beast: International Relations Theory and Comparative Policy Analysis Meet the European Union.' *Journal of Common Market Studies* 34: 53–80.

Rosamond, Ben. 2005. 'The Uniting Of Europe And The Foundation Of EU Studies: Revisiting The Neofunctionalism Of Ernst B. Haas.' *Journal of European Public Policy* 12 (2): 237–254.

Rosamond, Ben. 2003. *Theories of European Integration.* New York: St. Martin's Press.

Rosenau, James. 2002. 'Governance in a New Global Orders.' In *Governing Globalization: Power, Authority and Global Governance,* by David Held and Anthony McGrew, 70–87. Cambridge: Polity Press.

Ruggie, John Gerard. 1998. 'What Makes the World Hang Together? Neo-Utilitarianism and the Social Constructivist Challenge.' *International Organization* 52 (4): 855–885.

Schmitter, Philippe C. 2005. 'Ernst B. Haas and The Legacy Of Neofunctionalism.' *Journal of European Public Policy* 12 (2): 255–272.

Schmitter, Philippe C. 1969. 'Three Neo-Functional Hypotheses about International Integration.' *International Organization* 23 (1): 161–175.

Schubert, James N. 1978. 'Toward a 'Working Peace System' In Asia: Organizational Growth And State Participation In Asian Regionalism.' *International Organization* 32 (2): 425–438.

Schulze, Kai, and Jale Tosun. 2013. 'External dimensions of European environmental policy: An analysis of environmental treaty ratification by third states.' *European Journal of Political Research* 52: 581–607.

Sewell, James Patrick. 2016. *Functionalism and World Politics.* Princeton: Princeton University Press.

Sikkink, Kathryn. 2009. 'The Power of Networks in International Politics.' In *Networked Politics: Agency, Power and Governance,* by Miles Kahler, 228–247. Cornell: Cornell University Press.

Sismondo, Sergio. 2009. *An Introduction to Science and Technology Studies.* London: Wiley-Blackwell Publishing.

Söderbaum, Fredrik. 2016. *Rethinking Regionalism.* London: Palgrave.

Steele, Brent. 2011. 'Revisiting classical functional theory: Towards a twenty first century micro politics.' *Journal of International Political Theory* 7 (11): 16–39.

Taylor, Paul. 1983. *The Limits of European Integration.* London: Croom Helms.

Thompson, Kenneth W. 1981. *Ethics, Functionalism, and Power in International Politics.* Baton Rouge, LA: Louisiana State University.

Tranholm Mikkelsen, Jeppe. 1991. 'Neo-functionalism: Obstinate or Obsolete? A Reappraisal in the Light of the New Dynamism of the EC.' *Journal of International Studies* 20 (1): 1–22.

Van der Vleuten, Erik. 2004. 'Infrastructures and Societal Change.' *Technology Analysis and Strategic Management* 16 (3): 395–414.

Verbeek, Peter-Paul. 2005. *What Things Do.* Pennsylvania: Pennsylvania State University Press.

Visoka, Gezim, and John Doyle. 2015. 'Neo-Functional Peace: The European Union Way Of Resolving Conflicts.' *Journal of Common Market Studies* 54 (4): 862–877.

Weiss, Thomas G, and Rorden Wilkinson. 2014. *International Organization and Global Governance.* New York: Routledge.

Wendt, Alexander. 1992. 'Anarchy is what States Make of it: The Social Construction of Power Politics.' *International Organization* 46 (2): 391–425.

Wendt, Alexander. 1999. *Social Theory of International Politics.* Cambridge: Cambridge University Press.

Werner, Wouter G, and Jaap de Wilde. 2001. 'The Endurance of Sovereignty.' *European Journal of International Relations* 7 (3): 283.

Zwolski, Kamil. 2018. 'Functionalism and Security without Boundaries.' In *European Security in Integration Theory*, by Kamil Zwolski, 101–133. Berlin: Springer.

3 Environmental issues

Conflict and cooperation potential for the Caspian Sea[1]

Introduction

Before a credible process of discussion can begin, it is crucial first to provide a brief account of the environmental problems that are being addressed by the CEP. The first of these environmental problems is the fluctuation of water levels, because it increases the risk of flooding. According to environmental studies, the fluctuation of sea levels is an important environmental issue in the Caspian Sea region (Firoozfar et al. 2012; Glantz and Zonn 1996; Nadim et al. 2006). Research has shown that sea levels fluctuate depending on changes in the temperature and amount of water flowing in from rivers (Chen et al. 2017). The water that flows into the Caspian Sea comes from three rivers, the Volga, the Ural, and the Kura, but it is not directly connected to the world's oceans, which makes it the largest landlocked body of water in the world (Firoozfar et al. 2012). The quantity and quality of water flowing in from these rivers play an important role in the fluctuation of the water level in the Caspian Sea (De Mora and Turner 2004). This is especially true of the water from the Volga as it constitutes 80 percent of the Caspian Sea's water inflow (Tehran Convention Secretariat 2010, 28–29). According to the Tehran Convention Secretariat (2010, 36) report, the sea's water level rose by about 24 cm per year between October 1992 and June 1995, but later it abruptly dropped. Currently, the water level is between 26 and 27 meters below oceanic sea levels (Tehran Convention Secretariat 2010). There is a risk of flooding in urban areas and damage to industrial infrastructure on land in Azerbaijan, Kazakhstan, and Dagestan (Chen et al. 2017).

Land degradation is the second environmental issue facing the littoral states. There are several factors that cause severe land degradation in the Caspian Sea, namely, significant droughts, salinity, population growth, fluctuation in sea level, and industrial developments (Ascher and Mirovitskaya 2000; Villa 2014). Turkmenistan and Kazakhstan face the highest risk of desertification due to the high salinity of their soil, their irrigation system and their oil and gas industries (Akiner 2004).

Another environmental problem is the loss of marine biodiversity, which has serious economic consequences for the coastal areas, where fishing is the

DOI: 10.4324/9781003189626-4

Environmental issues 79

only source of income (Shadrina 2007). The loss of marine biodiversity is the result of overfishing and water pollution (Van Uhm and Siegel 2016). Due to its isolation and its climatological as well as geographical characteristics (such as the salinity of its soil), the Caspian Sea has a unique ecological system, which comprises of approximately 400 different species of flora and fauna (Nadim et al. 2006). There are about 40 species of fish that are important to the local fishing industry, of which six are valuable sturgeon fish that have produced between 80 and 90 percent of the world's caviar in the past (Tehran Convention Secretariat 2010). However, because of water pollution and overexploitation, the breeding-stock of Caspian Sea sturgeon has declined significantly since the dissolution of the Soviet Union (Van Uhm and Siegel 2016; Zonn 2001).

Apart from leading to a loss of biodiversity, water pollution is an ecological issue in itself (Blum 2002). Scholars have argued that there are several causes for water pollution, such as industrial development, demographic growth, and coastal cities (Karataeva 2014; Villa 2014; Yablokov 2010). Furthermore, this pollution has intensified due to the increase of extraction and transportation of oil and natural resources, and the accompanying increase in industrial incidents, such as oil spills, in the Caspian Sea region (Karataeva 2014). Because of the scope and interconnectedness of these ecological issues, they are mostly beyond the economic, technical, political, and social capacities of a single state and cannot be addressed adequately by individual state efforts.

In order to address the common ecological issues and to facilitate sustainable cooperation, the CEP was established as a regional umbrella program by the governments of the littoral states specifically by their Ministries of Environment and Natural Resources and Ministries of Foreign Affairs. It was established with support from international agencies (e.g., the United Nations Environmental Program, the Global Environment Facility, the United Nations Development Program, and the World Bank) in 1998. The program has developed common regional and national measures to address the ecological issues and to promote environmental agreement among the littoral states. In 2003, the CEP was given more gravity as the littoral states signed the first ecological and legally binding agreement: the Tehran Convention.

The Tehran Convention serves as an overarching framework laying down the general requirements and the institutional mechanism for the protection of the marine environment of the Caspian Sea (Tehran Convention Secretariat 2010, 8). Through it, four concrete ecological protocols have been developed, which have all been signed by the littoral governments. On 20 July 2018, the governments of the littoral states organized an extraordinary meeting in Moscow, which ended with the signing of the fourth protocol (Trend 2018). One month after this event, the governments of the Caspian littoral states met in Aktau for signing the Legal Status Convention, which includes agreements about the legal division, naval security and

80 *Environmental issues*

environmental protection of the Caspian Sea, and the division of fishing and natural resource extraction and transportation rights among the littoral states.

Previous scholarship on the CEP has tended to emphasize its scientific aspects and environmental effectiveness over the program's efficacy in addressing implicit non-environmental issues. By incorporating the scientific aspects of the study in a functionalist perspective, this chapter will show that the technical environmental cooperation has helped create suitable conditions for finding mutually beneficial interests among the littoral governments. In other words, this chapter aims to show that the shared environmental resources are one of the starting points for the current cooperation in the Caspian Sea.

This chapter highlights three aspects of environmental cooperation in the Caspian Sea that have so far been omitted from research. First, this chapter illustrates the first attempt of the governments at technical, pragmatic and issue-specific cooperation. More concretely, it shows how common environmental issues challenged the individual littoral states and brought their respective governments under the CEP umbrella in 1998. In doing so, the chapter illustrates how issue-specific and technical environmental cooperation in the Caspian Sea has reduced the frequency and severity of regional conflicts and has built a feeling of security in the region.

Second, this chapter shows who is behind this dynamic and what do they discuss. This helps to show and highlight the key actors besides states involved in shaping the Caspian Sea politics and how their preferences both political and economic, and networks affect the capacity, opportunity, and will of governments (e.g., ministries, parliaments, presidents etc.) to cooperate. Third, this chapter explains the link between low environmental politics and other issues such as the uncertain legal status of the Caspian Sea. In doing so, the chapter shows that the CEP is subject to a spill-over effect in that it causes changes beyond its original scope. More concretely, it illustrates whether and how issue-specific environmental cooperation has created suitable conditions for signing the Legal Status Convention.

The chapter proceeds as follows. Following the introduction, the second section gives a descriptive account of the evolution of the CEP and the Legal Status Convention. The third section outlines the New Great Game views on the uncertain legal status of the Caspian Sea and environmental issues in the region. The fourth section analyses the CEP and its relation to the Legal Status Convention from the functionalist perspective. The conclusion presents the chapter's findings.

The Caspian Environmental Program and the Legal Status Convention

Environmental cooperation

The early 1990s were not the best time for the newly independent Caspian Sea states because aside from having to contend with ecological issues, the

Environmental issues 81

littoral states were at varying stages of economic hardship, political instability, regional conflicts (e.g., Nagorno-Karabakh), and socio-economic transition. The littoral states, in particular Azerbaijan, Kazakhstan, and Turkmenistan were limited in their ability to tackle (costly) environmental issues because of the economic hardships (The World Bank 2019). This difficult situation was also reinforced by disagreement over the legal division of the Caspian Sea and the exploitation of its undersea natural resources. However, considering the high cost of addressing ecological issues, insufficient technical capacities and bureaucratic difficulties, the governments (mostly the Ministries of Natural Resources and Environment and the Ministries of Foreign Affairs) realized that the ecological problems could not be solved in any other way than through joint efforts. In other words, the leaders of the Caspian Sea states recognized the necessity of environmental cooperation as a starting point for further regional collaboration.

Iran undertook the first formal initiative in 1992 by proposing a regional organization among the Caspian countries for environmental protection (Blum 2002, 166). Several proposed frameworks followed from this initiative, but the idea of ecological cooperation did not move beyond an abstract discussion phase until 1994 because of two reasons. First, the environmental discussion was forestalled by the desire to extract oil and natural gas (Blum 2002, 166–167). That is to say, accessing oil and natural gas wealth had a higher priority for Azerbaijan, Kazakhstan, and Turkmenistan. Second, the governments of the littoral states did not have the financial means, advanced technical equipment, knowledge, or institutions necessary for addressing ecological issues. Because of this, negotiations were slow, as ecological issues did not form the highest priority for the five states. To address these issues, the littoral states sought the help of a number of international organizations. By adopting the *Almaty Declaration* in 1994, the littoral states expressed their willingness to cooperate on environmental issues and sought financial and technical aid from the international community (Global Environment Facility 1998, 16).

Following this, the struggle for regional environmental cooperation began to decrease by a joint response from the UNDP, the UNEP, the World Bank, and the GEF in 1995 (Global Environment Facility 1998, 15). The specific role of these actors will be discussed in detail in the following sections. During a joint mission, the international actors and the governments of the littoral states agreed upon at the draft of the CEP (Global Environment Facility 1998, 16). Three years later, in May 1998, the CEP was officially launched in Ramsar, Iran. Figure 3.1 details the timeline of the environmental cooperation from 1994 until 2018.

The CEP is an issue-specific program, designed to deal with shared ecological issues and create the necessary circumstances for environmentally sustainable development. It has brought a number of the Caspian Sea governments together under its umbrella, such as the Ministries of Ecology and Natural Resources and the Ministries of Foreign Affairs. The CEP has

82 *Environmental issues*

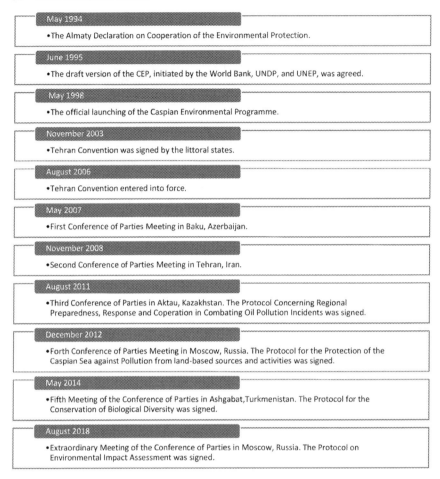

Figure 3.1 Timeline of the Caspian Environmental Program and the Tehran Convention from 1994 until 2018. It shows important meetings, agreements and the date of decisions.
Source: Author's own compilation.

received support from the EU's Technical Assistance for the Commonwealth of Independent States (TACIS) program and other organizations such as the International Maritime Organization (Blum 2002, 167). Besides these intergovernmental organizations, British Petroleum (BP) has supported the CEP as a private actor. An important example of this support is that BP provided a grant of USD 150,000 for the establishment of the Caspian Environment Information Centre (CEIC) (Bernstein 2015). Besides financial support, BP and other partners shared a range of offshore and near-shore environmental data with the Caspian countries helping to establish the CEIC.

The UNECE Environmental Performance Review (2004, 30) mentions that the policy, the legal and institutional framework, and the technical capacities left in place after the dissolution of the Soviet Union were not designed to address shared environmental issues. By the late 1990s, the governments of the littoral states still had outdated national data centres, poor national environmental programmes, weak national legislation mechanisms and regulation, and old-fashioned monitoring equipment and laboratories according to the Global Environment Facility report (1998, 6–7). To address this the CEP assigned particular Thematic Centres to each of the littoral states so that each state can tackle specific material and non-material issues regarding natural resource protection and determine action plans addressing pollution, data management, biodiversity, and water level fluctuations. In 1998, a Program Coordinating Unit was established in Baku to oversee communication and policy development among the different governments. To show their support, the littoral governments have issued several statements to endorse the CEP and complied with its agenda (Blum 2002, 169). Figure 3.2 enumerates the actors involved in the program.

To structuralize the cooperation and in order to be able to address the ecological issues systematically, the CEP launched three phases. Its first phase was launched in 1998 and lasted until 2002. It helped the littoral governments to establish suitable ecological mechanisms. This included: (a) developing a regional coordination mechanism, (b) completing a Transboundary Diagnostic Analysis (TDA) of the priority of environmental issues, (c) formulating and endorsing the Strategic Action Programme (SAP), and (d) adopting the National Caspian Action Plans (NCAPs) (the UNECE Environmental Performance Review 2004, 102). To implement these ecological plans, the CEP launched its second phase in 2003, which finished in 2007. This phase aimed to strengthen the governments' legal and policy-related

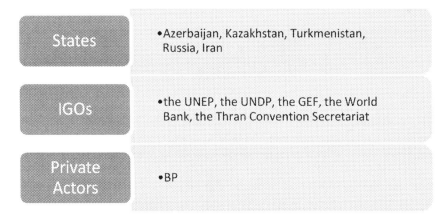

Figure 3.2 List of actors involved in the Caspian Environmental Program and the Tehran Convention
Source: Author's own compilation.

84 *Environmental issues*

mechanisms and foster the discussions and adaptation of environmental documents of the first phase.

The second phase thus led to the adaptation of the action plans, which created a clear pathway to the first legally binding framework in the CEP. In 2003, the governments of littoral states signed *the Framework Convention for the Protection of the Marine Environment of the Caspian Sea* (referred to as the Tehran Convention) after a complex and politically sensitive bargaining process. It entered into force in 2006 after being ratified by the five littoral states. The Tehran Convention is an important success because the environmental programme became the first regional and legally binding agreement between the littoral states. The Convention sets out to the basic principles and rules of international environmental law relating to the protection of the environment, including provisions concerning prevention, reduction and regulation of pollution, as well as protection, preservation and restoration of the marine environment (Janusz-Pawletta 2015, 2005).

Besides the general ecological duties, the Tehran Convention includes four concrete environmental protocols. These are (1) the Protocol on the Conservation of Biological Diversity; (2) the Protocol on the Protection of the Caspian Sea against Pollution from Land based Sources and Activities; (3) the Protocol concerning Regional Preparedness, Response and Co-operation in Combatting Oil Pollution Incidents; and (4) the Protocol on Environmental Impact Assessment in a Trans-Boundary Context (Tehran Convention Secretariat 2010). The Secretariat and Conference of Parties (COP) were established under the Tehran Convention to further the environmental discussions, protocols and national action plans. They have become the main supervisory bodies of the Convention. The key purpose of the COPs is to continue ordinary meetings at regular intervals. Experts from different governments regularly meet outside of COP meetings to discuss the technical aspects, specific issues and find common points. In this sense, COP always oversees the final meeting which governments officials attend to sign final documents. To implement these ecological plans, the CEP launched its third phase in 2008, which concluded in 2012.

Since 2006, the CEP has organized six successful COPs (see Figure 3.1), with the seventh to take place in 2019 in Baku, Azerbaijan. Throughout this time, the littoral governments have discussed and signed the four protocols of the Tehran Convention as they were required to by the IGOs. The last protocol was signed in July 2018 one month earlier than the signing of the Legal Status Convention. Currently, the littoral governments and the IGOs are busy with the ratification and implementation of the protocols. The following section will describe the history of the legal status of the Caspian Sea.

The long journey to the Legal Status Convention

During the Cold War, the Caspian Sea was legally divided among two littoral states: the Soviet Union and Iran, and this division was based on a series of bilateral agreements. For example, Iran and the Soviet Union signed a Treaty of Friendship on 26 February 1921, which guaranteed the right to fish and the freedom of navigation in the Caspian Sea for ships flying under the flag of either of these states (Janusz-Pawletta 2015). On 25 March 1940, Russia and Iran signed a Navigation Agreement, which consolidated their rights and obligations regarding navigation, for military purposes as well as for fishing, in the Caspian Sea as it eliminated extra fees and offered the equal treatment of all vessels operating under the flag of either state (Zonn 2001).

Following the dissolution of the Soviet Union, the newly independent states Azerbaijan, Kazakhstan, and Turkmenistan explicitly reaffirmed the validity of the treaties of 1921 and 1940 by signing the founding treaty of the Commonwealth of Independent States (CIS). They reiterated their adherence to these treaties on 20 December 1991 by signing the Alma-Ata Declaration (Janusz-Pawletta 2015). However, Azerbaijan, Kazakhstan, and Turkmenistan also questioned their legality because the treaties did not include the rights and interests of the newly independent states, nor did they provide clear norms to regulate the division and extraction of mineral resources. Therefore, they argued that the Caspian Sea needs a new legal agreement that divides the rights, including the rights to natural resources, and obligations pertaining to the sea among the five littoral states. In light of this, the governments of the littoral states started bilateral and multilateral negotiations to decide whether it should be divided as a lake, a sea, or a condominium.

Azerbaijan supported the idea of treating the Caspian as a border lake (Garibov 2018). In this conception, the Caspian Sea would be divided into national sectors along the median line principle, which implies that all coastal states would have sovereignty over the biological resources, seabed, navigation, water column, and surface of the Caspian Sea (Janusz-Pawletta 2015). Kazakhstan's position was similar to Azerbaijan's position but favoured defining the Caspian as an enclosed sea detailed in the *United Nations Convention on the Law of the Sea* (UNICLOS). This would mean that only the seabed and its resources would be divided among the littoral states along the middle line. However, Russia and Iran held the view that the Caspian Sea should be understood as a condominium (Liakopoulou 2018). Turkmenistan initially supported this view but its position changed over time due to internal political changes. Under the condominium status, a border sea can be under the joint political authority of all coastal states, which are equally sovereign in the sea (Janusz-Pawletta 2015, 2005). This means that the littoral states would not be able to undertake individual action in managing their own natural resources. In other words, the condominium status would enable Russia and Iran to preserve their position of dominance in managing and exporting resources from the Caspian Sea.

In order to end the uncertain legal status of the Caspian Sea to everyone's satisfaction, the littoral states started negotiations in 1992. From 1992 to 1996 the states held five meetings with the deputy foreign ministers of the states, three expert meetings and a number of bilateral and trilateral

86 *Environmental issues*

meetings, where they discussed issues specific to the two or three countries in attendance (Janusz-Pawletta 2015). As a result of one of the Meeting of Ministers of Foreign Affairs of the Littoral States, held in Ashgabat in November 1996, the parties established an *ad hoc* working group tasked with developing the Legal Status Convention (Ministry of Foreign Affairs Kazakhstan, 2018). The governments of the littoral states organized more than 50 meetings of the *ad hoc* working group. In order to find common position, the Caspian states held consultations on a regular basis in various formats. Figure 3.3 shows the timeline of legal status discussion from 1992 until 2018 which can be conferred with the outline of the negotiation process for the CEP in Figure 3.1.

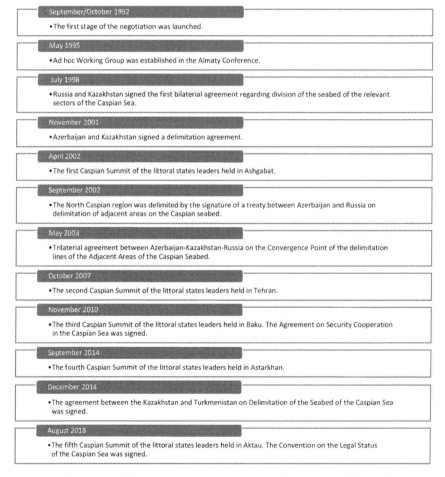

Figure 3.3 Timeline of the Convention on the Legal Status from 1992 until 2018. It shows important meetings, agreements and the date of decisions.
Source: Author's own compilation

Environmental issues 87

As illustrated by Table 3.3, a number of bilateral and trilateral agreements and protocols were signed between Azerbaijan, Kazakhstan and Russia for delimitation of the Northern part of the Caspian Sea between 1998 and 2004. It is argued that internal political changes in Russia, the firm position held by Azerbaijan and Kazakhstan and the investments of international energy companies were the main factors that moved Moscow to change its position in the early 2000s (Liakopoulou 2018). Because of this, Russia signed bilateral and then trilateral agreements both with Azerbaijan and Kazakhstan between 1998 and 2003. However, these agreements were protested and not recognized by Iran and Turkmenistan.

The Presidents of the five Caspian littoral states met for the first time in 2002 in Ashgabat, Turkmenistan. During this First Caspian Summit, the littoral states agreed not to use force to solve the legal issue. However, the meeting ended without a joint communique, and the leaders did not make any decision on the regulation of natural resources (Radio Free Europe 2002). Five years later, the Second Caspian Summit took place in Tehran, Iran, which led to the signing of a joint declaration (Pritchin 2019). The declaration acknowledged the sovereign rights of the littoral states in relation to the Caspian Sea and natural resources, and it asserted that only the littoral states can station their military vessels in the sea (Ministry of Foreign Affairs Kazakhstan 2018). In 2010, the Caspian Sea leaders met at the Third Caspian Summit, which was held in Baku, Azerbaijan. The summit was successful as the Presidents signed a joint statement and the Agreement on Security Cooperation in the Caspian Sea (Kremlin 2010). It was the second shared agreement that was signed after the Tehran Convention. Garibov (2018) argues that the littoral states moved one step forward because Iran softened its position to some extent. According to Garibov (2018) Iran became inclined to pursue a more amicable relationship with the other littoral states and softened its position due to US sanctions, international isolation and Hasan Rouhani's election as president of Iran in 2013.

Four years later, the five leaders of the littoral states met in Astrakhan, where they signed another joint statement. More specifically, at the Fourth Caspian Summit, the parties also signed the Agreement on Conservation and Rational Use of the Aquatic Biological Resources of the Caspian Sea, the Agreement on Cooperation in Emergency Prevention and Response in the Caspian Sea and the Agreement on Cooperation in the Field of Hydrometeorology of the Caspian Sea (Kremlin 2014). The five leaders also agreed to the creation of exclusive economic zones of 25 square miles, subject to exclusive sovereign rights. In the same year, Kazakhstan and Turkmenistan signed a bilateral agreement on the delimitation of the bottom of the Caspian Sea, which is similar to the previous trilateral agreement between Azerbaijan, Kazakhstan and Russia (Ministry of Foreign Affairs Kazakhstan 2019). On 20 May 2018, the 52nd meeting of the ad-hoc working group took place in Astana, where a draft of the final document was agreed upon. Three months later, the leaders of the littoral states signed the Legal Status

88 *Environmental issues*

Convention at the Fifth Caspian Summit in Aktau, Kazakhstan, on 12 August 2018 (Kremlin 2018). It is the third agreement that has been signed by all the littoral states after 22 years of negotiations.

The Legal Status Convention includes the previous documents signed by the littoral states, such as the Tehran Convention's protocols and the Agreement on Security Cooperation. More concretely, if the littoral states would want to construct an undersea pipeline, they would need to meet the requirements of the Tehran Convention (Article 14). Additionally, no naval forces other than those belonging to the littoral states are allowed in the Caspian Sea (Article 3). The agreement does not clarify whether it is a sea or lake, however, nor does it include a delimitation of the seabed, which still requires additional negotiations between the littoral states (Article 8 of the Convention).[2]

The New Great Game explanation for the Caspian environmental cooperation and the Legal Status Convention

Chapter 1 introduced the general picture and arguments of a New Great Game. However, to make the discussion more concrete and easy-to-follow, it is necessary to introduce specific arguments of the New Great Game literature with regard to the uncertain legal status of the sea and the ecological issues. This section therefore illustrates whether and how the New Great Game literature mentions and explains the above-mentioned environmental issues, the process of cooperation and the signing of the Legal Status Convention. This will also help to contrast the functionalist perspective with the arguments of the New Great Game literature.

According to the relevant scholarship, the essence of the competition is the West's attempt to create an uninterrupted flow of natural resources from the Caspian Sea to the Western energy markets by eliminating Russian and Iranian monopoly over transportation routes (Alam 2002; Karasac 2002; Kubicek 2013; Labban 2009; Monshipouri 2016; Uddin 1997). In light of this, the literature has depicted both the environmental issues and the uncertain legal status as important tools for Russia and Iran to prevent transportation of natural resources.

The relevant academic works from the early 2000s argued that the uncertain legal status of the sea is one of the main reasons for the military advancement in the region and naval competition between the littoral states (Alam 2002; Cohen 2002; Haghayeghi 2003; Lelyveld 2001). In July 2001, for example, an Iranian naval vessel forced two British owned oil exploration ships (BP-Amaco), that were jointly run by Azerbaijan, away from a disputed area in the Caspian Sea. At the time, local and international experts argued that this dispute between Azerbaijan and Iran may reach the point of employing military means (Alam 2002; Cohen 2002; Haghayeghi 2003; Lelyveld 2001; Yusin 2005).

A year later, the littoral states met in Ashgabat for the First Caspian Summit in 2002. The relevant scholarship interpreted this summit as a failure

Environmental issues 89

since Russia announced military exercises in the Caspian Sea after the summit (Cohen 2002). It was argued that the military exercises were designed to show Russia's muscle and to put pressure on Iran (Cohen 2002; Torbakov 2002). A few months later, Azerbaijan and Russia signed a bilateral agreement on the delimitation of the North Caspian Sea, which was criticized and rejected by Iran (Feifer 2002). Similarly, Alam (2002, 22) argued that 'there are two burning issues in the Caspian Sea Basin—the legal status of the Caspian Sea and the ethnic conflicts (e.g., Nagorno-Karabakh). These two sensitive issues can at any time jeopardize the security of the region. Thus, these issues should be properly and carefully resolved.' In the same vein, Haghayeghi (2003, 36) claimed 'Azerbaijan, Turkmenistan and Kazakhstan have small naval forces but are increasing them as the legal status of the Caspian continues to be contested.' Overall, due to these geopolitical issues, bilateral and trilateral agreements, the relevant literature has depicted the uncertain legal status of the sea as a threat to the regional stability and transportation of natural resources in the Caspian Sea region.

Similar to the uncertain legal status of the Caspian Sea, it has been argued that ecological issues are an important pressure tool for Iran and Russia to obstruct the potential exploration of oil and natural gas fields in the Caspian Sea (Anceschi 2019; Garibov 2018; Gurbanov 2017; Ismayilov 2019; Ismail-zade 2006; Pritchin 2019). For example, Nuriyev (2015) argues that Iran and Russia use the existing environmental concerns to block or hinder crude oil shipping and the construction of pipelines between Azerbaijan, Kazakhstan, and Turkmenistan.

Although the littoral states signed the Legal Status Convention on 12 August 2018, the (neo)realist line of argumentation has not been changed. Considering the recent legal agreement, a number of scholars have argued that Russia and Iran have intentionally included environmental articles (see Articles 3, 11, 14) in the agreement to be able to veto and/or disrupt the possible natural gas pipeline connection between Azerbaijan and Turkmenistan (Anceschi 2019; Garibov 2018; Gurbanov 2018). According to Garibov (2018, 193), Russia and Iran have used environmental concerns to halt the construction of the Trans Caspian Pipeline (TCP) for about two decades and the wording of the convention seems to leave room for debate about the 'requirements and standards for the pipeline.' This view is shared by Anceschi (2019) who argues that the convention does not satisfy environmental conditions for the construction of the TCP project. The convention provides Russia and Iran with extensive environmental monitoring powers, which they use to influence the construction of any transport infrastructure side lining Russia or Iran (Anceschi 2019). In the same vein, Ismayilov (2019, 9), claims that 'Russia and Iran have used environmental requirements in the past and could use them to oppose the TCP in the future.'

As mentioned at the beginning of this chapter, caviar has been an important source of income for the Caspian Sea states. It has been claimed that 'sturgeon of the Caspian Sea produce has been the source of most of the

90 *Environmental issues*

caviar in global trade from wild stocks historically' (TRAFFIC Report 2018, 13). Russia and Iran are still the largest caviar producers and exporters among the Caspian Sea states (Van Uhm and Siegel 2016). Considering the current biodiversity issues, it is also claimed that there is a real possibility that popular anger over accumulating environmental problems and disasters might turn into a significant channel for the expression of political discontent. By exaggerating the ecological issues, it is even claimed that they might lead to a Great Caviar Game in the Caspian Sea. According to Shadrina,

> ...we can clearly trace a link between regional security and the exploitation of aquatic bio-resources. The struggle over these resources could escalate into a conflict between the countries of the Caspian region or could evolve into a sturgeon war.
>
> (Shadrina 2007, 56)

Considering these arguments, it can be seen that the relevant literature does not recognize the difference between the uncertain legal status of the Caspian Sea and the signing of the legal agreement, because Russia and Iran are depicted as the only ones to profit from both situations. Additionally, the relevant literature does not show an awareness of the history of environmental protocols leading up to the signing of the legal agreement (see Table 3.3). There are two possible explanations for this ignorance. First, the scholarship is not aware of the CEP and the Tehran Convention and does not recognize their added value in high politics. Because of this, the role of ecological issues and protocols are underestimated in the relevant debate. Second, the environmental issues also include politics because they might affect the exploration of natural resources, therefore the New Great Game literature does not expect environmental cooperation and/or their institutionalization. Since the literature does not recognize the evolution of the Tehran Convention and the CEP, it fails to explain when, why and how Azerbaijan, Kazakhstan and Turkmenistan agreed with the environmental protocols. It also fails to explain if ecology is a tool for Russia and Iran, why the three littoral states have signed the legal agreement. As a result, the literature produces a redundant picture of the Caspian Sea.

Economic leverage, networking and technical expertise

This section analyses the three core aspects of the CEP. First, in contrast to insights derived from a geopolitical literature, this section shows that cooperation on environmental issues has functionalist characteristics for many of the actors involved (e.g., governments, private actors, intergovernmental, and non-governmental organizations), which enables them to achieve their diverse and interconnected purposes. In this sense, this section explains and highlights the various actors' significant contributions, such as economic leverage, networks, and technical expertise, and how these have influenced the process of cooperation in detail. Second, this section shows that despite geopolitical uncertainty, the environmental cooperation has created suitable conditions for finding common interests and for constructing new ways of working together between the governments of the littoral states, such as the Ministries of Foreign Affairs and the Ministries of Ecology and Natural Resources. Finally, this section illustrates that the CEP has encouraged the governments of the littoral states to establish cooperation on other common issues namely, the legal status of the Caspian Sea. More concretely, it shows complex interconnection between the CEP and the Legal Status Convention.

Economic leverage

The first important point that needs to be highlighted is economic contributions of the UNEP, UNDP, GEF, and the World Bank made to the governments because of the CEP. As argued in revised functionalism, international organizations offer the government of a target states positive incentives (e.g., financial support) on the condition that the government accepts and complies with their requirements (Delmas and Young 2009; Finnemore and Sikkink 2001). In the 1990s, it was not in the interest of the all littoral states to address the shared environmental issues because of the uncertain geopolitical situation and internal political and economic transitions. However, with the strong financial help of the intergovernmental organizations, it was possible to start with solving the technical ecological problems impeding cooperation. More specifically, the economic assistance and benefit of participating in the CEP brought the governments to the bargaining table.

As mentioned above the GEF, the UNEP, the UNDP, and the World Bank were the key actors that accepted the invitation of the littoral states. In June 1995 they presented the draft of the CEP, which includes a comprehensive environmental reform package (Global Environment Facility 1998, 16). In order to receive the financial and technical support, the littoral states accepted the reform package and restated their invitation in Tehran (Global Environment Facility 1998, 16). Three years later, the CEP was officially established. The GEF, the UNEP, the UNDP, and the World Bank have invested more than USD 20 million over the three phases of the CEP (Lenoci 2012). This financial support enabled these actors to put pressure on the governments of the littoral states to discuss and sign the regional environmental policies, which the governments of the littoral states complied. For example, the Caspian Sea governments accepted a new environmental framework, such as the National Environmental Action Plan (NEAP) and the Strategic Action Plan (SAP). Later, the NEAP guided institutional changes in Azerbaijan, which led to the establishment its new Ministry of Ecology and Natural Resources in 2001 (Lenoci 2012).

Another important consequence of the economic support is the Tehran Convention, which was signed in November 2003 as a result of a complex

92 *Environmental issues*

and politically sensitive bargaining process. It was a remarkable achievement because in July 2001 a dispute had arisen between the Iran military vessel and BP Azerbaijan over the exploration of natural resources. A year later, Russia held a military exercise in the Caspian Sea. In May 2003, Azerbaijan, Kazakhstan, and Russia signed a trilateral agreement on the Caspian seabed, which was protested by Iran and Turkmenistan (Janusz-Pawletta 2015). Despite the complex geopolitical obstacles, the five littoral states signed the first legally binding common agreement, namely the Tehran Convention. The signing of the Tehran Convention was successful because it created conditions for the governments of the littoral states to continue to work together in addressing their common problems. According to an expert from the CEP:

> ...in the early 2000s it created hope because even Turkmenistan, which is known for its isolationist policy and disagreement with Azerbaijan, signed one week after the convention. Turkmenistan waited and sent the Minister of the Environment a week later to sign the agreement after the four other Caspian Sea states signed.
>
> (Interview, October 16, 2017)

To keep the five governments in the negotiations, the international actors have continued to finance the environmental projects. By 2006, the Caspian littoral states ratified the Convention and it entered into force on 12 August 2006, which was the most significant step for the CEP (Villa 2014). The fast ratification of the Convention confirmed that there was willingness and commitment among the governments of the littoral states to work together and to include environmental concerns in their planning of future development.

By financing the CEP projects, the international community aimed to persuade the governments of the littoral states to sign and ratify the four protocols of the Tehran Convention. Because of this, the littoral governments have signed the four protocols and ratified one of them (the Aktau Protocol) and signed a number of crucial documents, such as the Strategic Convention Action Plan (SCAP) since 2003. According to Kvitsinskaia (2009), the approval of the SCAP allowed the COP-2 to launch an important tool to help achieve the national and regional goals of the Tehran Convention for a period of ten years. According to a former expert from the CEP:

> ...as long as the money is paid by someone else, they are willing to work together to address the ecological issues. Therefore, financial support from international organizations was one of the incentives that encouraged the governments to talk to each other and cooperate.
>
> (Interview, October 16, 2017)

The governments of the Caspian littoral states know that if they stop cooperating, the economic support and benefits will likely be suspended

Environmental issues 93

(Bernstein 2015). Since the governments of the littoral states accepted the financial contributions from the World Bank, the UNEP, the UNDP, and the GEF, they are required to comply with environmental reform packages, sign environmental protocols, policies, and action plans, and need to work together in order to receive these contributions (Lenoci 2012). This is the case because if the decision-making is blocked or suspended by the governments, these organizations will not see any reason to keep investing their economic resources for further developments. In this regard, it can be argued that the CEP has facilitated suitable conditions for stabilizing the relations among the governments because these international organizations have made stable cooperation a prerequisite for providing essential services (economic, technical, and administrative).

By using financial grants international organizations have pushed the governments of the littoral states to work together to address their ecological issues. More specifically, these actors used their economic leverage to ensure the compliance of the governments with the Tehran Convention. For example, while the main discussants are the representatives of the governments, these meetings have been organized, monitored and guided through the systematic support of the UNEP (Villa 2014). One interviewee said that:

> ...if UNEP had not been in a position to support the (Interim) Secretariat, the governments would not have come to the table. These days it is even difficult to bring together local institutions within a country. But the UNEP has managed to bring different governments from five Caspian Sea states together.
>
> (Interview, August 22, 2018)

However, following the third phase of the CEP, the IGOs started to decrease their financial support as the littoral states had started to generate significant financial income from their natural resources (Bernstein 2015). Additionally, two of the Caspian littoral states (Iran and Russia) are under constant international sanctions, which also implicitly influenced the decision of international financial organizations. An expert from one of the sponsor organizations highlighted that 'direct sanctions against two of the Caspian Sea states make it difficult to find financial sponsors or receive international grants' (Interview, October 6, 2017). Third, there are also bureaucratic difficulties. According to an expert from the Ministry of Natural Resources of Iran:

> ...to increase the budget of this program each government needs to propose this issue to their Ministry of Finance and then to their Parliament, which is a long process. Due to this issue, the Ministry of the Environment and Natural Resources of the Caspian Sea states are reluctant to do this.

This means that when evaluating the CEP and/or the actions of the governments of the Caspian littoral states, it is necessary to include local, global,

94 *Environmental issues*

and regional dimensions and their interrelatedness in the broader discussion because they mutually influence each other.

Networking and socialization under the CEP

Besides economic benefits, another contribution of the CEP is the facilitation of international and regional networking among diverse interest groups. In doing so, it has created suitable conditions for socialization amongst the government officials and experts involved, which improved chances of success.

First, after getting involved in the programme, the UNEP, the UNDP, and the World Bank utilized their strong networks and lobbing capabilities to attract more financial support and mitigate economic risks (Global Environment Facility 1998, 1–2). For example, the World Bank received start-up funding for the CEP from the Japanese government and the EU/TACIS program in 1998 (Blum 2002, 167). Additionally, the UNEP, the UNDP, and the World Bank have used their privileged international positions, lobbying power, and political capacity to gain support from different groups, such as the Food and Agriculture Organization (FAO), the International Atomic Energy Agency (IAEA), and the private sector (e.g., BP) (Lenoci 2012, 34). In this way, the organizations have brought different kinds of necessary resources and expertise to the table. Along with the governments of the littoral states, they have been actively involved in addressing technical, political, and economic problems and they have conducted joint projects to facilitate the work of different stakeholders. For example, the CEIC was developed by GRID-Arendal with the financial support of BP in 2012 (Bernstein 2015). The CEIC is based on a network of collaborating institutions in Caspian littoral states, most importantly governments, ecological monitoring stations, actors from the private sector, and NGOs. It provides these parties with an online collaborative information-sharing tool, making it easier to collaborate on environmental issues and to share information. It was recognized as an important collaborative tool by the governments of the littoral states at the COP5 meeting Ashgabat in 2014 (Tehran Convention Secretariat 2018a, 1).

Second, the UNEP has helped the Secretariat to organize the six COPs, regional projects (e.g., CASPECO) and the regular meetings of experts from different governmental, non-governmental and private institutions (Bernstein 2015, 65). The aim of these meetings and projects is to bring a range of experts into frequent contact with each other, facilitate their networking, and allow for the discussion of the four protocols and national as well as regional action plans. A quick glance at the attendance list of the six COPs reveals the systematic presence of diverse expert groups from the Ministries of Ecology and Natural Resources, the Ministries of Foreign Affairs, BP, scientists, and representatives of the UNEP, the UNDP and the World Bank (Tehran Convention Secretariat 2012). Considering the uncertain geopolitical situation of the early 2000s, it can be argued that the CEP has provided the governments

Environmental issues 95

of the littoral states with a suitable place to learn to share their different perspectives, concerns and arrange them accordingly. For example, an expert from the Ministry of Ecology and Natural Resources of Azerbaijan mentioned that:

> …in the early 2000s, the first meeting of different experts from the governments was very cold and official. The early 2000s was not the best time for the governments due to several political, economic and legal disagreements. However, due to this program we started to have regular meetings, which helped us to establish informal relations, trust and even friendship. Now, it is easy to foster consensus formation amongst different agents of the Caspian governments.
>
> (Interview, August 22, 2018)

Additionally, the regular meetings have played a socializing function as they have facilitated the development of shared meanings and values which evolve through the use of a common language to deliberate on particular problems or issue areas. While preserving their national governments positions, officials in this programme tend to socially construct a sense of collective identity and shared meaning due to regular meetings. For example, an expert from the Ministry of Ecology and Natural Resources of Iran mentioned that:

> …these regular meetings among the government experts help to build certain connections, trust and consensus. I would call us Caspian Family because of these meetings. Everyone knows each other, familiar faces and experts attend every meeting. Since we meet regularly to discuss the same subject, we also prefer same experts rather than outsiders because this makes it easier to discuss and find a common point.
>
> (Interview, August 3, 2018)

While checking the attendance list of the COPs and other meetings, one can see that since the beginning of the CEP, the same experts have been attending all the meetings and training programmes. Although the Minister of Ecology and Natural Resources of Azerbaijan has been changed a few times, the CEP contact person within the Ministry has stayed same. This makes it easy to establish and maintain informal relations between experts, which can ease the negotiation process. The successful signing of the Tehran Convention, its ratification, and the signing of the four environmental protocols and the environmental action plans illustrate the success of the regular meetings under the CEP. Considering this, it can be argued that the CEP has offered a space of cooperation where the expectations and visions of the governments of the littoral states can be freely stated, redefined and exchanged.

It is worth mentioning that each of actors has their own specific function and purpose within the networking meetings. One interviewee from BP mentioned that 'BP attends these meetings to observe the discussion because

96 *Environmental issues*

environmental decisions directly impact on BP's work' (Interview, October 25, 2017). In the same vein, different experts from the Ministries of Foreign Affairs of the littoral states participate in the discussion and decision-making every year. An expert from the Ministry of Ecology and Natural resources of Azerbaijan stated that

> ...the reason for this is to observe the environmental experts' discussion and prevent them from making wrong political statements by accident. These environmental experts do not know too much about the ecological issues, but their purpose is to observe our discussion because we are also not expert on foreign policy or legal treaties.
>
> (Interview, October 28, 2017)

This aspect of the CEP came to the fore in the interviews I conducted with the employees from the different governments. When I asked an employee of the Ministry of Natural Resources and Ecology in Azerbaijan questions about foreign policy, the employee said that 'they could not comment that much on foreign relations or political aspects' (Interview, November 28, 2017). In the same vein, when I asked an expert from a Ministry of Foreign Affairs a question pertaining to environmental security, that person also said that they could not 'comment on ecological security.' Another participant from the UNEP mentioned that they 'try to keep politics and political issues away from the discussion, but [they] also need the experts from Ministries of Foreign Affairs because of their internal influence' (Interview, October 16, 2017). However, the COPs and other meetings have provided the governments with a non-political platform to discuss specific issues. Several experts mentioned that during non-political or technical meetings, the representatives of the governments surreptitiously discuss political, economic, or legal disagreements, which eases their further negotiations.

Overall, these examples illustrate that despite the complex geopolitical developments, the CEP succeeded in facilitating a dialogue among the five governments and created a sense of Caspian community. Since the early 2000s, the CEP has, with the support of the UNEP and under its authority, offered the five governments a functional platform for dialogue and of the coordination of solutions to shared ecological issues. By implementing regular, long-term training programs (e.g., CASPECO), the CEP has increased the likelihood of socialization occurring amongst national civil servants by grouping experts together in specific activities according to interests and acceptability.

Technical expertise and construction of environmental protocols

Besides economic incentive and socialization, the CEP has brought advanced technical equipment and knowledge to the region, and it has kept the discussion within the technical framework by avoiding politics.

Environmental issues 97

First, with their expertise the World Bank, the UNEP, the UNDP, and the GEF have assisted the governments of the littoral states in improving their bureaucratic, technical and policy making skills, and in establishing a new set of ecological norms and understandings (Villa 2014). More specifically, the UNEP and the UNDP have formulated the National, Regional, and Strategic Environmental Action Plans, the Tehran Convention, its four protocols, policy documents, regulations, and creating the concept papers under the CEP on behalf of the governments (Bernstein 2015). The World Bank has managed the CEP's funding and investment projects (Bernstein 2015). According to an expert from the CEP, 'the governments usually check draft version of these documents, give their feedback and then these intergovernmental organizations finalize the documents' (Interview, September 21, 2018). This is because the governments of the littoral states lacked technical expertise and ecological knowledge needed to introduce new regulations and existing regulations were based on Soviet regulations, which were not relevant anymore (Global Environment Facility 1998; UNECE Environmental Performance Review 2004, 2011).

Second, the CEP has sought to highlight the best technical ways of achieving its goals without implying a balance of power. The CEP started from scratch and aimed to construct a new ecological base that the governments of the littoral states needed. When reviewing the language of the CEP documents, it can be seen that they emphasize the idea of shared environmental issues rather than focusing on environmental issues facing individual states because these documents influence the way governments perceive ecological problems and thus their solutions. Considering the perspectives of revised functionalism (see chapter 2), it can be argued that these environmental norms and rules socially influence or cause governments to do the things they do, and they provide the governments with new direction, obligations, regulations and goals for action. According to an expert from the UNEP:

> In the early 1990s, there was a lack of common documents to refer while discussing the Caspian Sea ecological issues. Most of the documents were signed between the Soviet Union and Iran and did not include the new littoral states. In this regard, these environmental protocols and agreements offer common base for the governments and they can refer to these documents while discussing the Caspian Sea.
>
> (Interview, October 6, 2017)

These protocols and scientific documents facilitate the littoral states' negotiations with each other as there are common documents that they can cite or use as examples (Bernstein 2015). After signing four new protocols, the governments can refer to shared documents (Janusz-Pawletta 2015).

Third, when reviewing the language of the four protocols, one can also see that they were written with an awareness of the inter-wovenness of ecological

98 *Environmental issues*

issues with other areas (e.g., natural resources). This means that these protocols directly influence exploration and transportation of natural resources in the Caspian Sea. For example, Aktau includes the principle of 'the polluter pays', by virtue of which the polluter bears the costs of the pollution, including its prevention, control and reduction (see Article 4 of the Aktau Protocol). The governments of the littoral states (Azerbaijan and Kazakhstan) are thereby encouraged to be more cautious in their behaviour and to enhance their measures against spilling any fossil fuels.

In the same vein, the Environmental Impact Assessment (EIA) protocol explicitly regulates the construction of underwater pipelines and the ecological impact they may have on the Caspian Sea (see annex I of the protocol). Before the signing of the last protocol, one interviewee from the Ministry of Ecology and Natural Resources of Azerbaijan mentioned that 'Azerbaijan and Kazakhstan currently want to change the language of the next protocol because it brings restrictions to their natural resource production and transportation' (Interview, November 26, 2017). According to the protocol, the littoral states need to inform each other when they plan on undertaking any of the activities listed in annex I, which include the construction of large diameter pipelines and production of natural resources. When reviewing the documents it becomes apparent that Turkmenistan suggested to take out the word 'large diameter' and add the word 'exploration' after 'production' (see Annex I, list of activities 9 and 16). Iran and Russia supported these suggestions, but Azerbaijan and Kazakhstan were against them because the changes would restrict construction of all pipelines, large and small, as well as exploration activities. Because of this it took several years to agree upon its principles. When reviewing the documents of preparatory meetings (e.g., Tehran Convention Secretariat 2014), one can see that Azerbaijan and Kazakhstan opposed the protocol. To solve this disagreement, the CEP sent a letter to the Secretariat of the Espoo Convention, asking whether the protocol contradicted the Espoo Convention or limits its scope (see Tehran Convention Secretariat 2015). Per the letter of 15 October 2015, the Secretariat of the Espoo Convention replied that the protocol does not limit the bilateral or multilateral activities of the littoral states. However, the letter could not solve the issue and in the end Turkmenistan's suggestions were not accepted (Tehran Convention Secretariat 2018b).

In contrast to the New Great Game arguments, the disagreement illustrates that the ecological protocols have gone through systematic discussion process and each round of cooperation might incur resistance since the governments are now aware of upcoming obligations and restrictions. Unlike the geopolitical arguments, it is also good to emphasize that it was Turkmenistan, not Iran or Russia, who suggested these changes. In the end, Azerbaijan and Kazakhstan were able to reject the changes despite the support of Russia, Iran, and Turkmenistan. They preferred to safeguard envisioned projects in adjacent areas to keep their autonomy and room to manoeuvre. What this situation also shows is that the language of every document is very important and that each country weighs every word because these documents can influence the littoral states' ability to extract natural resources.

Another important aspect of the CEP is the way in which it side-lines general political attitudes during the negotiation process. As mentioned above, in 2003, the GEF, GRID-Arendal, the UNDP, and the World Bank helped to establish the Secretariat under the Tehran Convention. However, the governments of the littoral states could not agree on the location of the Secretariat and therefore the UNEP has carried out the functions of the Secretariat, such as organizing meetings and drawing up documents and treaties (Bernstein 2015). One expert even said that 'under the arrangement with the UNEP the staff of the interim Secretariat is employed through GRID-Arendal' (Interview, July 23, 2018). The organization has provided financial, technical and administrative support for the Secretariat. According to an expert from the UNEP:

> ...in 2003 the governments offered their own capitals as the place for the Secretariat. However, they could not agree on a place because of economic, administrative and political reasons. As a result, the UNEP intervened and temporarily took the responsibility.
>
> (Interview, October 6, 2017)

In 2012, the governments finally decided to move the place of the Secretariat from Geneva to Baku and to change it every four years, but this has not yet been done due to political and economic disagreements. An expert from the Ministry of Natural Resources of Azerbaijan said that 'the UNEP did its best to prevent this delay and these political issues, and decided to continue the secretariat responsibilities' (Interview, October 6, 2017). As a result of this, sensitive questions have been deconstructed into acceptable piecemeal agreements during the CEP discussions, which has paved the way for broadly supported solutions. This example therefore shows that within the CEP, the preferable mode of problem solving is to find a way around general political attitudes of animosity and distrust between the governments.

Overall, the CEP encompasses a vast and far-reaching network of actors, all of whom have their own motivation, policy goals, professional staff and preferences. Since the early 1990s, these actors have served to initiate, acquire funding for, facilitate, and extend the smooth communication, cooperation, and information exchange among the governments of the five Caspian Sea states, and have tried to prevent direct regional competition between the state and misunderstanding while discussing protocols. In this regard, this environmental cooperation would never have been possible without systematic support of the UNEP, the UNDP, the GEF, and the World Bank. Additionally, despite serious geopolitical issues and disagreements among the littoral states, the environmental cooperation has continued and become institutionalised under the CEP umbrella, which has produced politically relevant treaties, norms and regulations.

100 *Environmental issues*

From environmental cooperation to the Legal Status Convention

When considering the dialogue, environmental cooperation, and socialization that took place as part of the CEP, one may ask whether these experiences have created suitable conditions for cooperating in other areas, such as on political, economic, legal and security related issues. What is the transferability of lessons learned in environmental cooperation to solving the legal status of the Caspian Sea?

The Legal Status Convention is a comprehensive agreement, which covers diverse, interconnected areas, namely security, the environment, navigation, fishing rights and the construction of pipelines. In order to achieve this comprehensive legal agreement, the governments of the littoral states started to negotiate each issue step-by-step. In this sense, the CEP was the first step, which facilitated suitable conditions for the five governments of the littoral states to sign the first shared legal agreement among the five littoral states, namely the Tehran Convention. When one reviews Table 3.1 above, it becomes clear that the governments of the littoral states gradually moved from discussing ecological issues to discussing issues in the field of regional security, which is another component of the Legal Status Convention. In 2010, the littoral states signed the Caspian Security Agreement in Baku, Azerbaijan (Kremlin 2010). It is the second agreement among all the littoral states, which brought the Legal Status Convention one step closer. The Legal Status Convention itself was finally signed in 2018. In this sense, the cooperation has gradually moved forward despite the geopolitical developments complicating it. However, while discussing the Legal Status Convention, the literature on the Caspian Sea region focusing on geopolitical influences neglects the complex interconnection between the three agreements.

Although it is not explicitly mentioned in the CEP's aims, the program offers an institutional framework for the negotiation of shared interests, mutual gains and common issues. While discussing the legal status, the governments of the littoral states highlighted the example of the Tehran Convention to show that they might pursue a similar line of agreement. More specifically, the CEP has been proposed by the governments of the littoral states as an important example of mutual cooperation (Ministry of Foreign Affairs of Azerbaijan 2017). Several interviewees highlighted that unlike the environmental meetings, the legal status discussions are closed meetings. Because of this, it is difficult to say anything about how the legal status discussions are carried out but these environmental agreements play an indirect facilitative role.

In 2010, at the Third Caspian Summit in Baku, the heads of the Caspian Sea states issued several statements to endorse the CEP and reiterate the urgency to sign and ratify the four environmental protocols (Kremlin 2010). During this summit, the heads of state highlighted the importance of the environmental protocols as part of the legal status discussion. In the press statement, President Medvedev of Russia highlighted that they 'agreed on the

Protocols to the Framework Convention for the Protection of the Marine Environment of the Caspian Sea, and soon they all will be signed by our colleagues' (Kremlin 2010). Following the Third Summit, the CEP organized three COP meetings between 2011 and 2014, during which it achieved the signing of the three environmental protocols. One of the signed protocols (Aktau protocol) was ratified by the governments of the littoral states in 2012. The fifth COP took place in May 2014, and it led to the signing of the Ashgabat Protocol. A few months later in September, the fourth summit of the heads of the Caspian states took place in Astrakhan. During the summit, the ratification and implementation of the two other protocols (those of Moscow and Ashgabat) were emphasized by the littoral states' presidents (Kremlin 2014; President 2014). A similar parallel development occurred in 2018 as the last protocol of the Tehran Convention was signed one month before the Legal Status Convention was signed.

These developments illustrate the explicit interconnection between the environmental cooperation and legal discussion. Because of this interconnection, environmental cooperation is not just standalone cooperation but it is one of the driving forces and conditions. Several interviewees mentioned that sometimes during the discussion of legal status, government officials mentioned minor issues that need to be agreed upon. On occasion, these minor issues are also related to the CEP and then the experts of the littoral states would work together to find a common solution and/or agreement. According to an expert from the Ministry of Natural Resources of Iran, 'cannot say that the last protocol is directly linked to the legal status discussion, but the heads of the littoral states mentioned this protocol at their previous meetings and it can therefore be said that this protocol has indirectly helped the discussion of the Caspian leaders in August along' (Interview, August 3, 2018).

When reviewing the Legal Status Convention document, one finds that articles 1, 3, 14, and 15 explicitly refer to ecological concerns and article 3 refers directly to the four environmental protocols of the Framework Convention for the Protection of the Marine Environment and highlights their importance. It states that:

> ...the parties may lay trunk submarine pipelines on the bed of the Caspian Sea, on the condition that their projects comply with environmental standards and requirements embodied in the international agreements to which they are parties, including the Framework Convention for the Protection of the Marine Environment of the Caspian Sea and its relevant protocols.
> (as cited in the Convention on the Legal Status of the Caspian Sea 2018)

This shows first, the (legal) importance of the environmental protocols as the governments need to consider them when they want to build a pipeline. This also shows the interdependent relationship between environmental protocols

102 *Environmental issues*

and pipelines. The Legal Status Convention should be seen as a comprehensive agreement and the Tehran Convention should be seen as one of the parts of the big picture that comprehensive agreement paints. Contrary to the conclusions in the realist line of literature, this shows that the CEP is not just a standalone or unrelated cooperation. Rather, it has strong cooperative autonomy in the face of geopolitics because if this environmental cooperation had failed, that would have meant that one of the requirements in the Legal Status Convention would not have been fulfilled. These protocols set boundaries and limitations for future pipeline construction. In this regard, it is necessary to consider the low environmental cooperation in order to understand the complex dynamics of the Caspian Sea. However, while discussing this program, a UNEP expert mentioned that:

> ...it is important to be realistic because one should not compare this environmental cooperation with the EU or European style integration. This program will not lead to a new EU or the UN. However, it can be also argued that if there was no environmental program, the situation in the Caspian Sea could never have been as good as this. This environmental program is not perfect but it provides the place to talk, socialize, negotiate and increase trust.
>
> (Interview, October 16, 2017)

This is a remarkable point because there is a tendency among the relevant scholars to mistakenly expect European style integration in the Caspian Sea region (Blum 2002, 171–172; Petersen 2016, 151). In doing so, these scholars ignore the fact that regional cooperation in other parts of the world is driven by different functional pursuits than it is in Western Europe and that these other parts of the world have their own functional objectives and approaches to cooperation or impulses peculiar to them. As argued in revised functionalism, international norms (e.g., solving ecological issues) influence different actors and regions differently, but this is either misunderstood or ignored in the relevant literature (Finnemore and Sikkink 2001). Considering this, it can be argued that the CEP should be seen and interpreted through the lens of cooperation rather than integration. As it is also put forth in revised functionalism, integration by definition implies loss of sovereignty, voluntarily, or through pressure (Acharya 2016). Taking into account the colonial history of Azerbaijan, Kazakhstan, and Turkmenistan, it can be argued that environmental cooperation is functional for them because it helps to preserve their autonomy and independence while establishing dialogue, trust, and a habit of cooperation.

Conclusion

I have analysed the CEP and its relation with the Legal Status Convention in this chapter. In doing so, I have identified three core aspects, which reveal a comprehensive picture of the Caspian Sea and distort the erroneous explanations of the New Great Game literature.

The first core aspect of the CEP is that it acts issue-specific and on the basis of technical cooperation. Because the environmental problems in the region had (geo)political dimensions, as the legal issue on the uncertain status of the seabed did, the New Great Game literature did not expect environmental cooperation to be easily reached, institutionalized and effective. However, the relevant ecological issues have been framed as issue-specific and technical under the CEP umbrella. Despite the complex geopolitical developments, the technical formulation has made the ecological issues relatively easy to cooperate on in the Caspian Sea region. Through these measures the CEP has created suitable conditions for the governments of the littoral states to sign the first common agreement (the Tehran Convention), construct new norms, draw up regulations, form regional identities and interests, and to operationalize routine communication. In contrast to the New Great Game literature, which has depicted the ecological protocols of the recent legal agreement as a political tool used by Russia and Iran, this chapter has showed that the governments of the littoral states have been working on the four environmental protocols and other regulations freely and autonomously since the late 1990s. By addressing shared technical and ecological issues, the CEP has offered the governments of the littoral states an indirect and apolitical starting point for establishing the habit of cooperation, a regional dialogue, socialization, and for building trust. Additionally, it has created a channel for regular communication between the governments of the littoral states. In doing so, it has managed to mobilize respective actors successfully by avoiding power politics, nationalism and ideological differences.

The second aspect of the CEP highlighted in this chapter is a catalytic advantage; lessons learned from environmental cooperation have spilled over into the discussion on the uncertain legal status of the Caspian seabed. In contrast to the conclusion offered in the New Great Game literature, this chapter has shown that there is a parallel and complex interconnection between the agreement reached on the environmental protocols and the agreement reached on the legal status of the seabed. The agreement is very comprehensive, as it includes consensus on security, navigation, fishing rights, and ecological rules. To reach such a comprehensive agreement, the governments of the littoral states first started negotiating the ecological norms under the CEP umbrella. This culminated in the signing of the Tehran Convention, its four environmental protocols, and additional regulations. Later, the successful cooperation on ecological issues spilled over into cooperation on regional security. More specifically, the governments of the littoral states took the ecological cooperation one step further by signing the Caspian Security Agreement in November 2010, which is the second document signed by all five littoral states. In this regard, the governments of the littoral states have built the legal agreement step by step. The signing of ecological and

104 *Environmental issues*

security agreements has created suitable conditions for enhancing cooperation by signing the Legal Status Convention. In this regard, the Legal Status Convention cannot be explained without reference to how the environmental interests of the Caspian Sea governments were expressed and worked on under the CEP and later the Tehran Convention during the early 2000s.

However, it is important to note that the relevant studies should not expect European style cooperation in the Caspian Sea. Unlike European integration, the purpose of the Caspian Sea cooperation is to ensure autonomy and independence from colonial rule and limit the intervention of outside powers in regional affairs. In relation to this, this chapter has showed that the Caspian Sea has its own peculiar impulses, which should be considered by the existing scholars.

The third salient aspect of the CEP is that, despite the diplomatic role of the governments, the ecological cooperation among them is orchestrated by multiple international agencies like the UNDP, the UNEP, the World Bank, and the GEF, which have offered the required resources and instruments that the governments did not have or could not afford. By using their economic, technical and networking advantages, these actors have kept the governments of the littoral states in the negotiations and pushed them to comply with the CEP requirements. More concretely, the economic leverage these actors possess is one of the key reasons that pushed the governments of the littoral states, in particular the Ministries of Foreign Affairs and the Ministries of Environment and Natural Resources towards trans-boundary cooperation. Environmental cooperation has brought them direct and indirect economic profit and development. This shows that unlike what is assumed in the New Great Game literature, states are not the only actors in the Caspian Sea region, but there are a number of private, non-governmental, intergovernmental and semi-governmental actors, who play key facilitating roles. Therefore, when one discusses the recent political achievements of the governments of the Caspian littoral states, one has to consider the complex network of international actors around them.

These three aspects also illustrate that the New Great Game literature not only presents an inaccurate but a false picture of the Caspian Sea region. While the CEP does include low politics, it is necessary to understand and explain the environmental cooperation of the governments of the littoral states in order to understand the complex picture of the Caspian Sea region.

Notes

1 Some parts of this chapter (e.g., Table 3.1 and Table 3.2,) were published in *the Caucasus Analytical Digest* in 2019.
2 This chapter does not provide the legal explanation of the agreement but there are a number of works in existence that comprehensively address the legal status of the Caspian Sea (e.g., Janusz-Pawletta 2015; Zimnitskaya and Geldern 2011).

Bibliography

Acharya, Amitav. 2016. 'Regionalism Beyond EU-Centrism.' In *The Oxford Handbook Of Comparative Regionalism*, by Tanja A Börzel and Thomas Risse-Kappen, 109–133. Oxford: Oxford University Press.

Akiner, Shirin. 2004. 'Environmental security in the Caspian Sea.' In *The Caspian: Politics, Energy and Security*, 342–362. London: Routledge.

Alam, Shah. 2002. 'Pipeline politics in the Caspian Sea Basin.' *Strategic Analysis* 26 (1): 5–26.

Anceschi, Luca. 2019. 'Caspian Energy in the Aftermath of the 2018 Convention: The View from Kazakhstan and Turkmenistan.' *Russian Analytical Digest* 235: 6–9.

Ascher, William, and Natalia Mirovitskaya. 2000. *The Caspian Sea: A Quest for Environmental Security*. Berlin: Springer.

Bayramov, Agha. 2021. 'Conflict, cooperation or competition in the Caspian Sea region: A critical review of the New Great Game paradigm.' *Caucasus Survey* 9 (1): 1–20.

Bayramov, Agha. 2020. 'The reality of environmental cooperation and the Convention on the Legal Status of the Caspian Sea.' *Central Asian Survey* 39 (4): 500–519.

Bernstein, Johannah. 2015. *Terminal Evaluation of the UNEP Project (Interm) Secretariat Services to the Framework Convention for the Protection of the Marine Environment of the Caspian Sea*. Geneva: UNEP.

Blum, Douglas. 2002. 'Beyond Reciprocity: Governance and Cooperation around the Caspian Sea.' In *Environmental Peacemaking*, by Ken Conca and Geoffrey Dabelko, 161–190. Baltimore: John Hopkins University Press.

Caspian Environment Program. 2007. 'Caspian Strategic Action Programme Implementation: A Regional Review and Assessment.' CEP Secretariat.

Caspian Environment Program. 2007. 'Transboundary Diagnostic Analysis Revisit.' CEP Secretariat.

Chen, Jianli, Tatyana Pekker, Clark R Wilson, Byron D Tapley, Andrey Kostianoy, Jean-François Cretaux, and Elnur Safarov. 2017. 'Long-term Caspian Sea level change.' *Geophysical Research Letters* 44 (13): 6993–7001. doi:10.1002/2017GL073958.

Cohen, Ariel. 2002. *Iran's Calims over Caspian Sea Resources Threaten Energy Security*. Washington: The Heritage Foundation.

De Mora, Stephen, and Tim Turner. 2004. 'The Caspian Sea: A Microcosm for Environmental Science and International Cooperation.' *Marine Pollution Bulletin* 48: 26–29.

Delmas, Magali A, and Oran Young. 2009. *Governance for the Environment*. Cambridge: Cambridge University Press.

Dunlap, Ben. 2004. 'Divide and conquer? The Russian plan for ownership for the Caspian Sea.' *Boston College International Comparative Law Review* 27 (1): 115–130.

Feifer, Gregory. 2002. 'Caspian: Russia, Azerbaijan Sign Agreement On Sea Boundaries.' September 24. Accessed September 10, 2018. https://www.rferl.org/a/1100881.html.

Firoozfar, Alireza, Edward N Bromhead, and Alan P Dykes. 2012. 'Caspian sea level change impacts regional seismicity.' *Journal of Great Lakes Research* 38: 667–672.

Finnemore, Martha, and Kathryn Sikkink. 2001. 'The Constructivist Research Program in International Relations and Comparative Politics.' *Annual Reviews* 4: 391–496.

Finnemore, Martha, and Kathryn Sikkink. 1998. 'International Norm Dynamics and Political Change.' *International Organization* 52 (4): 887–917.

Garibov, Azad. 2018. 'Legal Status of the Caspian Sea is Finally Defined What is Next?' *Caucasus International* 8 (2): 179–195.

106 *Environmental issues*

Glantz, Michel H, and Igor Zonn. 1996. *Scientific, Environmental, and Political Issues in the Circum-Caspian Region*. Berlin: Springer.

Global Environment Facility. 2016. 'Towards a Convention and Action Programme for the Protection of the Caspian Sea Environment.' Accessed March 4, 2016. http s://www.thegef.org/project/towards-convention-and-action-programme-protection-c aspian-sea-environment.

Global Environment Facility. 1998. 'Addressing Transboundary Environmental Issues in the Caspian Environment Programme.' Project Brief, Washington: Global Environment Facility.

Gurbanov, Ilgar. 2017. 'Propaganda Against Trans-Adriatic Pipeline Continues Under "Environmental Concerns".' April 26. Accessed May 20, 2017. https://jamestown. org/program/propaganda-trans-adriatic-pipeline-continues-environmental-concerns/.

Haghayeghi, Mehrdad. 2003. 'The Coming of Conflict to the Caspian Sea.' *Problems of Post-Communism* 50 (3): 32–41.

Ismayilov, Murad. 2019. 'Azerbaijan and Russia: Towards a Renewed Alliance, for a New Era.' *Russian Analytical Digest* 232: 5–10.

Ismailzade, Fariz. 2006. *Russia's Energy Interests in Azerbaijan*. London: GMB Publishing Ltd.

İşeri, Emre. 2009. 'The US Grand Strategy and the Eurasian Heartland in the Twenty-First Century.' *Geopolitics* 14 (1): 26–46.

Interm Secretariat of the CEP. 2010. 'Caspian Sea: State of the Environment.' Grid Arendal.

Janusz-Pawletta, Barbara. 2015. *The Legal Status of the Caspian Sea*. Berlin: Springer.

Janusz-Pawletta, Barbara. 2005. 'The Framework Convention for the Protection of the Marine Environment of the Caspian Sea.' *Chinese Journal of International Law* 4 (1): 257–270.

Karataeva, Elena. 2014. 'Can the Caspian Sea Survive its Own Oil? Environmental Regulation of the Offshore Oil and Gas Industry in the Caspian Sea.' *The International Journal of Marine and Coastal Law* 29: 415–456.

Karasac, Hasene. 2002. 'Actors of the New Great Game Caspian Oil Politics.' *Journal of Southern Europe and the Balkans Online* 4 (1): 15–27.

Kremlin. 2018. 'Convention on the Legal Status of the Caspian Sea.' August 12. Accessed August 13, 2018. http://en.kremlin.ru/supplement/5328.

Kremlin. 2014. 'The Fourth Caspian Summit has taken place in Astrakhan.' September 29. Accessed September 29. http://en.kremlin.ru/events/president/news/46686.

Kremlin. 2010. 'The Third Caspian Summit.' November 18. Accessed September 10, 2018. http://en.kremlin.ru/events/president/news/9543.

Kubicek, Paul. 2013. 'Energy politics and geopolitical competition in the Caspian Basin.' *Journal of Eurasian Studies* 4: 171–180.

Kvitsinskaia, Elena. 2009. 'Protecting the Marine Environment of the Caspian Sea.' *Environmental Policy and Law* 39 (1): 63–74.

Labban, Mazen. 2009. 'The Struggle for the Heartland: Hybrid Geopolitics in the Transcaspian.' *Geopolitics* 14 (1): 1–25.

Laruelle, Marlène, and Sébastien Peyrouse. 2009. 'The Militarization of the Caspian Sea:'Great Games' and 'Small Games' Over the Caspian Fleets.' *China and Eurasia Forum Quarterly* 7 (2): 17–35.

Lelyveld, Michael. 2001. 'Caspian: Tempers Flare In Iran-Azerbaijan Border Incident.' July 25. Accessed March 21, 2018. https://www.rferl.org/a/1097012.html.

Environmental issues 107

Lenoci, James. 2012. *The Caspian Sea: Restoring Depleted Fisheries and Consolidation of a Permanent Regional Environmental Governance Framework 'CaspEco'*. Geneva: UNDP.

Liakopoulou, Mariana. 2018. *The Caspian Legal Status and Riparian States' Outlook on the Southern Corridor*, European Gas Hub. https://www.europeangashub.com/wp-content/uploads/2018/07/Liakopoulou_Caspian.pdf.

Mammadov, Elmir. 2016. 'Management of Caspian Biodiversity Protection and Conservation.' In *The Handbook of Environmental Chemistry*, by Damià Barceló and Andrey Kostianoy, 1–34. Berlin: Springer.

Ministry of Foreign Affairs Azerbaijan. 2018. 'Azerbaijan, Turkmenistan signed bilateral documents.' November 22. Accessed November 23, 2018. http://un.mfa.gov.az/news/4/3231.

Ministry of Foreign Affairs Azerbaijan. 2017. 'Xarici işlər nazirinin müavini Xələf Xələfovun Xəzər dənizinin hüquqi statusu haqqında Konvensiyanın hazırlanması üzrə Xəzəryanı dövlətlərin xarici işlər nazirlərinin müavinləri səviyyəsində Xüsusi İşçi Qrupunun 48-ci iclasında çıxışı.' The Special Working Group (SWG) for drafting a Convention on the legal status of the Caspian Sea at the level of deputy foreign ministers of the littoral states: 48th session. January 25. Accessed January 26, 2017. http://www.mfa.gov.az/az/news/881/4648.

Ministry of Foreign Affairs of Kazakhstan. 2018. 'Legal status of the Caspian Sea.' August 12. http://mfa.gov.kz/en/content-view/pravovoj-status-kaspijskogo-morya.

Monshipouri, Mahmood. 2016. 'Pipeline politics in Iran, Turkey and South Caucasus.' In *The Great Game in West Asia*, by Mehran Kamrava, 57–83. New York: Oxford Press.

Mustafayev, Nurlan. 2016. 'The Southern Gas Corridor: legal and regulatory developments in major gas transit pipeline projects.' *Journal of World Energy Law and Business* 9: 370–387.

Nadim, Farhad, Amvrossios Bagtzoglou, and Jamshid Iranmahboob. 2006. 'Management of Coastal Areas in the Caspian Sea Region: Environmental Issues and Political Challenges.' *Coastal Management* 34 (2): 153–165.

Nazarli, Amina. 2017. 'Azerbaijani FM: Final document on Caspian Sea status almost agreed.' July 17. Accessed July 20, 2017. https://www.azernews.az/nation/116349.html.

Newell, Joshua, and Laura Henry. 2016. 'The state of environmental protection in the Russian Federation: a review of the post-Soviet era.' *Eurasian Geography and Economics* 57 (6): 779–801.

News Central Asia. 2014. 'Caspian Summit at Astrakhan – The Outcome.' September 30. Accessed June 12, 2017. http://www.newscentralasia.net/2014/09/30/caspian-summit-at-astrakhan-the-outcome/.

Nuriyev, Elkhan. 2015. 'Russia, the EU and the Caspian Pipeline Gambit.' September 27. Accessed July 16, 2018. http://www.ensec.org/index.php?option=com_content&view=article&id=584:russia-the-eu-and-the-caspian-pipeline-gambit&catid=131:esupdates&Itemid=414.

Pawletta, Barbara Janusz. 2015. *The Legal Status of the Caspian Sea*. Berlin: Springer.

Petersen, Alexandros. 2016. *Integration in Energy and Transport*. London: Lexington Books.

President. 2018. 'Fourth Ministerial Meeting of Southern Gas Corridor Advisory Council held in Baku.' February 15. Accessed February 2018. https://en.president.az/articles/27051/print.

108 *Environmental issues*

President. 2014. 'Speech by Ilham Aliyev at the 4th summit of the heads of state of Caspian littoral states.' September 29. Accessed September 2018. https://en.president.az/articles/13039.

Pritchin, Stanislav. 2019. 'Russia's Caspian Policy.' *Russian Analytical Digest* 235: 2–6.

Radio Free Europe. 2002. 'Caspian: Ashgabat Summit Ends Without Agreement.' April 24. Accessed September 10, 2018. https://www.rferl.org/a/1099503.html.

Rakel, Eva. 2009. 'Environmental Security in Central Asia and Caspian Region: Aral and Caspian Sea.' In *Facing Global Environmental Change*, by Hans Günter Brauch, 725–729. Berlin: Springer.

Shadrina, Ekaterina. 2007. 'The Great Caspian Caviar Game.' *A Russian Journal on International Security* 13 (1): 55–78.

Tehran Convention Secretariat. 2018a. 'The Conference of the Parties Sixth Meeting.' September 24. Accessed September 29, 2018. http://www.tehranconvention.org/IMG/pdf/TC_COP6.16_CEIC_Fin.pdf.

Tehran Convention Secretariat. 2018b. 'Extraordinary meeting of the Conference of the Parties.' July 20. Accessed July 24, 2018. http://www.tehranconvention.org/IMG/pdf/Agenda_ECOP_Meeitng_July_2018_Moscow_EN.pdf.

Tehran Convention Secretariat. 2015. 'The Conference of the Parties Sixth Meeting (Prepatory).' November 15. Accessed September 2016. http://www.tehranconvention.org/spip.php?article112.

Tehran Convention Secretariat. 2014. 'The Conference of the Parties Fifth Meeting.' May 2014. Accessed September 2016. http://www.tehranconvention.org/spip.php?article76.

Tehran Convention Secretariat. 2012. 'The Conference of the Parties Fourth Meeting.' December 12. Accessed September 2016. http://www.tehranconvention.org/IMG/doc/LOP_last_f.doc.

Tehran Convention Secretariat. 2010. 'Caspian Sea: State of the Environment.' Analysis, Geneva: United Nations Environment Programme.

Tehran Convention Secretariat. 2008. 'Conference of Parties Second Meeting.' December 12. Accessed August 20, 2016. http://www.tehranconvention.org/cop2/TC%20COPII%20INF%205%20Final%20report%20%20eng%20_.pdf.

Tehran Convention Secretariat. 2007a. 'Caspian Strategic Action Programme Implementation: A Regional Review and Assessment.' Evaluation, Tehran Convention Secretariat.

Tehran Convention Secretariat. 2007b. 'Transboundary Diagnostic Analysis Revisit.' Evaluation, Tehran Convention Secretariat.

The World Bank. 2019. 'Data for Azerbaijan, Russian Federation, Turkmenistan, Kazakhstan, Iran, Islamic Rep.' August 10. Accessed August 10, 2019. https://data.worldbank.org/?locations=AZ-RU-TM-KZ-IR.

Torbakov, Igor. 2002. 'Russia to Flex Military Muscle in the Caspian Sea With an Eye on Future Energy Exports.' July 31. Accessed September 10, 2018. https://eurasianet.org/russia-to-flex-military-muscle-in-the-caspian-sea-with-an-eye-on-future-energy-exports.

TRAFFIC Report. 2018. 'Understanding the Global Caviar Market.' Assessment, Cambridge: TRAFFIC and WWF.

Trend. 2018. 'Caspian littoral states to assess impact of economic activity in Caspian basin on ecology.' July 20. Accessed July 20, 2018. https://en.trend.az/azerbaijan/society/2931800.html.

Uddin, Shams. 1997. 'The New Great Game in Central Asia.' *International Studies* 34 (3): 1–13.

United Nations Economic Commission for Europe. 2011. 'Environmental Performance Review Azerbaijan.' Performance Review, Geneva: United Nations Commission for Europe.

United Nations Economic Commission for Europe. 2004. 'Environmental Performance Review Azerbaijan.' United Nations, Geneva: United National Economic Commission for Europe.

United Nations Environment Programme. 2017. 'Caspeco Program.' March 12. Accessed April 20, 2017. http://projects.inweh.unu.edu/inweh/display.php?ID=4090.

Van Uhm, Daan, and Dina Siegel. 2016. 'The illegal trade in black caviar.' *Trends in Organized Crime* 19 (1): 67–87.

Villa, Matteo. 2014. 'Escaping the Tragedy of Commons: Environmental Cooperation in the Caspian Sea.' In *The Caspian Sea Chessboard*, by Carlo Frappi and Azad Garibov, 73–89. Italy: Egea.

Wong, Sarah. 2012. *Environmental Threats to the Caspian Sea.* Washington: University of Washington.

Yablokov, Alexei. 2010. 'The Environment and Politics in Russia.' *Russian Analytical Digest* 79 (10): 2–4.

Young, Oran. 2006. *Analyzing International Environmental Regimes.* Cambridge, MA: The MIT Press.

Yusin, Lee. 2005. 'Toward a New International Regime for the Caspian Sea.' *Problems of Post-Communism* 52 (3): 37–48.

Zimmintskaya, Hanna, and James Von Gelderen. 2010. 'Is the Caspian Sea a sea: why does it matter?' *Journal of Eurasian Studies* 2 (1): 1–14.

Zonn, Igor. 2001. 'The Caspian Sea: Threats to its Biological Resources and Environmental Security.' In *The Security of the Caspian Sea Region*, by Gennady Chufrin, 69–82. Oxford : Oxford University Press.

4 Cooperation around post-Soviet transnational infrastructure projects in the Caspian Sea

Introduction

This chapter will illustrate that cooperation among the Caspian littoral states is not limited to environmental issues. The development of cooperation habits, which was started in the CEP, continued and was reinforced through the BTC pipeline.[1]

To propose an alternative reading of the developments surrounding the natural resources in the area, this chapter analyzes the three phases of the BTC project: planning of the pipeline, construction of the pipeline, and the use of the pipeline, none of which has been adequately addressed yet. Although the relevant literature recognizes the pivotal importance of the BTC oil pipeline, it fails to analyze its entanglement with wider regional processes and the material networking of the Caspian Sea region. Therefore, scant scholarship has been devoted to the effects of transnational infrastructure projects on the strategies of regional cooperation and exchange in the Caspian Sea region. Taking this into account, the core argument of this chapter is that the BTC is much more than a piece of energy infrastructure because it is the main impulse for interaction between international and regional actors which has facilitated numerous connections in a highly contingent world. This chapter aims to situate the technical and material networks needed for cooperation in this broader political, economic, and social analysis of the Caspian Sea region. It aims to make visible a hidden material cooperation in the Caspian Sea region.

This chapter contains four parts. The first part provides background information about the BTC pipeline, the three phases of the BTC project, and its timeline. The second part outlines the New Great Game views on three phases of the BTC project. The third and main part of the chapter discusses the three identified phases of the BTC project in light of the insights derived from my revised functionalism. More specifically, this part of the chapter illustrates that, during the planning phase, there was great uncertainty about the amount of extractable natural resources and how this would impact the foreign policies of the states in the region, which led New Great Game scholars to make to one-sided assumptions and exaggerations.

DOI: 10.4324/9781003189626-5

Transnational infrastructure projects 111

However, financial, technical, and social issues, not geopolitical challenges, prevented the project from going forward and led to significant delays during the construction phase. The third part of this chapter argues that without the network of multiple actors, (companies, NGOs, and IGOs), for example, it would have been impossible to overcome these obstacles. In the fourth part, the role of the pipeline after its construction is revealed by answering the question of how the transnational pipeline infrastructure influences the interaction of different actors, state as well as non-state, and how it connects the landlocked countries of the Caspian Sea to global networks. More concretely, it shows that the BTC pipeline encouraged specific forms of cooperation rather than rivalry among the Caspian littoral states. Following the construction of the pipeline, the relevant literature has mainly explained the potential benefits and influence of the BTC pipeline in terms of the relationship between Azerbaijan, Georgia, and Turkey, but these are not the only states that benefit from the BTC pipeline. The Caspian littoral states, namely Kazakhstan, Turkmenistan, and even Russia also use this transnational infrastructure to transport their natural resources. This chapter shows the benefits of the BTC pipeline for these littoral states.

Background of the BTC pipeline

On 20 September 1994, after three and a half years of extensive negotiations, Azerbaijan and a consortium of foreign oil companies (mainly Western) signed a Production Sharing Contract (PSC) in order to develop Azerbaijan's Azeri-Chirag-Gunashli Deepwater (ACG) oil reserves. This would later come to be known as the 'contract of the century' (BP Azerbaijan 2018a). Following this, a number of pipeline routes were initially explored to transport the oil to international energy markets, including one going east from the Caspian Sea to China, another heading south to Iran, and a further one extending the existing pipeline connections of Baku-Novorossiysk (Sovacool and Cooper 2013).[2]

However, the economic sanctions imposed on Iran by the US, the poor state of the existing Baku-Novorossiysk pipeline, and the fact that other routes tended to terminate at the Black Sea, requiring oil to be transferred along the Bosporus (which was already congested with tanker traffic), together resulted in all parties preferring a route leading from Baku through Tbilisi to Ceyhan. This pipeline links the Sangachal Terminal, situated on the shores of the Caspian Sea, to the marine terminal in Ceyhan, on Turkey's Mediterranean coast. On 29 October 1998, the presidents of Azerbaijan, Turkey, Georgia, and Kazakhstan, signed the Ankara Declaration in support of the BTC pipeline (Baran 2005). In a similar show of support, the US Secretary of Energy Bill Richardson attended the signing ceremony. A year later, an intergovernmental agreement was signed by the presidents of Azerbaijan, Turkey, Georgia, Turkmenistan, and Kazakhstan in Istanbul on 18 November 1999 (Sovacool and Cooper 2013). US president Bill Clinton

112 Transnational infrastructure projects

attended this signing ceremony so as to reaffirm the West's political and economic support for the BTC project, as well as that of the Western companies involved in the pipeline's planning and construction (Baran 2005).

The Azerbaijani and Georgian sections of the pipeline were completed in 2005. The pipeline finally became operational in June 2006 and was operated by BP (BP Azerbaijan 2016b). The timeline for the project from 1994 to 2006 is presented in Figure 4.1.

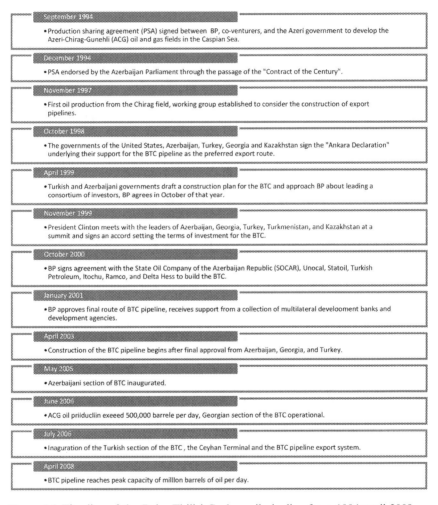

Figure 4.1 Timeline of the Baku-Tbilisi-Ceyhan oil pipeline from 1994 until 2008.
Note: The figure shows important decisions, achievements, and agreements.
Source: Author's own compilation.

The New Great Game views on the BTC pipeline

This section introduces the arguments of the New Great Game literature specific to the BTC pipeline in order to make the discussion more concrete. To do so, it shows whether and how the New Great Game literature mentions and explains the BTC project.

From the very first day of the BTC project's existence, the weak rivalry in the Caspian Sea has been described as a new geographical site of the New Great Game (Bahgat 2003; Karasac 2010; Kober 2000; Jaffe and Manning 1998). By using 19th-century geopolitical thinking, the literature describes Russia, Armenia, and Iran as the main rivals to the development of any pipeline in the Caspian Sea because it is viewed as a way to avoid Russian infrastructural imperialism and its monopoly on infrastructure. The US, Turkey, and the EU are described as saviours of local actors on the other hand, because they are taken to be the alternative to Russian and Iranian imperial plans.

During the planning phase of the BTC, the relevant literature was mainly pessimistic and sceptical about the potential for a successful construction of the pipeline because of conflicts in Chechnya, Abkhazia, Nagorno-Karabakh and the uncertain legal status of the Caspian Sea (Alam 2002; Cohen 2002; Karasac 2010; Kober 2000). According to Kober (2000, 2–4), Washington's support for the BTC increased the existing tensions in the Caspian Sea region as the pipeline would bypass Russia and Iran. Additionally, a number of warfare scenarios were predicted in the early 2000s. For instance, the relevant literature argued that by supporting Armenia, Iran could disrupt or sabotage the pipeline. According to Cohen:

> Iran also is carefully expanding defence ties with Armenia, a country technically at war with Azerbaijan. With Iranian instigation, Armenia would be capable of disrupting and threatening the Baku–Tbilisi–Supsa and future Baku–Tbilisi–Ceyhan pipelines, since a part of their route is located less than 30 miles from the Armenian–Azerbaijani ceasefire lines.
> (Cohen 2002, 5)

Due to the uncertain legal status of the sea and the presence of potentially vast oil fields, Haghayeghi (2003) argued that the legal dispute between the littoral states might eventually reach the point of military means being used. In the early 2000s, some scholars even claimed that there was a large chance that Azerbaijan would begin a war with Armenia following the construction of the BTC pipeline (Bayulgen 2009; Kim and Eom 2008). Kim and Eom claim that:

> ...at present Azerbaijan is exercising self-restraint in conflicts with Armenia for the stabilization of the BTC enterprise, but once Azerbaijani oil begins to be exported to world markets in a stable manner

114 *Transnational infrastructure projects*

> through the BTC there is a large chance that Azerbaijan will begin a war
> with Armenia through its augmented military.
>
> (Kim and Eom 2008, 102)

During the construction phase, Russia, Iran, and Armenia were again argued
to be among the main causes of almost every technical, economic, and political issue. For example, Ismailzade (2006, 22) argued that Russia actively
utilized and provoked various environmental NGOs to lobby against the
construction of the BTC pipeline. According to Ismailzade (2006) these
groups staged numerous demonstrations outside the Caspian Sea region and
tried to draw the attention of donor agencies to environmental concerns
reportedly associated with the construction of the pipeline. In the early years
of the new millennium, Russian energy company Lukoil became one of the
BTC pipeline's shareholders; it was thus claimed that Lukoil became part of
this project due to Russian political pressure. However, Lukoil quit the project in 2002 for economic reasons. Ironically, it was again argued that Lukoil
wanted to sabotage the project by selling its shares (Ismailzade 2006).

The pipeline became operational in 2006 and the relevant literature argued
that Russia and Iran lost the long-term battle for the BTC pipeline (Kubicek
2013). In doing so, the New Great Game scholarship moved on to discuss
the next transnational project, namely the Southern Gas Corridor. However,
there are still several unanswered questions such as: Has Azerbaijan started a
conflict with Armenia due to oil money? And how did Azerbaijan, Georgia,
and Turkey solve technical, economic, and social challenges? During the
planning phase the literature argued that Russia and Iran were against this
project but it is not clear whether they changed their position or not after its
construction. Although the pipeline has already been in use for more than a
decade, the literature has not answered these questions.

The planning, construction and post-construction phases in the functionalist framework

This section offers a different interpretation of the geopolitical uncertainties
in the Caspian Sea region. More specifically, it explains why the New Great
Game scholarship exaggerates the geopolitical uncertainties in the planning
phase, thereby overlooking economic, technical, and social challenges in the
construction phase. In doing so, it illustrates that these issues made
cooperation between multiple actors necessary and feasible.

Planning the BTC pipeline: geopolitical uncertainty

First, in the early 1990s as well as first years of the new century a number of
political events played a key role in creating the grounds for geopolitical
uncertainty. For example, because of the Nagorno-Karabakh conflict
between Azerbaijan and Armenia, the pipeline route was not sufficiently

Transnational infrastructure projects 115

secure. Furthermore, the legal status of the Caspian Sea was not clear, and the littoral states were struggling to come to an agreement on it. Due to this uncertain legal status of the sea, it was also difficult to determine the ownership of several oil fields at sea – namely, Araz, Alov, and Sharg. In this regard, there was ongoing disagreement between Azerbaijan, Iran and Turkmenistan as claimants (Lelyveld 2001). Nevertheless, the BTC pipeline was not the main reason for these political disagreements because it was a social process in which the newly independent states were trying to identify certain legal, economic and political borders. These countries lived under the Soviet Union and its political, economic, and legal rules for several decades. In the same vein, after the 1990s Iran had to deal with the four new Caspian Sea neighbours. Naturally, during this transition period it was more likely to have disagreements. However, these political events provided the academic literature with a suitable ground for using their realist line of perspectives, thus the BTC become a scapegoat for these events.

Second, when reviewing the academic literature, newspapers and official speeches published throughout the 1990s, one realizes that large amounts of scholarship were devoted to predicting the Caspian Sea's energy reserves and tended to cite reserve figures that ranged from the optimistic to unrealistic. This scholarship includes Alam 2002; Bahgat 2003; Kim and Blank 2016; Kleveman 2003; Jaffe and Manning 1998; Ruseckas 1998. The most commonly used estimate for the region's oil reserves was 200 billion barrels, with no distinction made between 'proven' and 'possible' reserves in the late 1990s. In this sense, both academics and politicians fell into this trap and exaggerated the amount of natural resources without checking facts and figures. For example, in July 1997 US Deputy Secretary of State Strobe Talbott described the Caspian Sea oil reserves as being 'as much as two hundred billion barrels of oil' (Kleveman 2003, 7). Later, US Secretary of State James Baker would go even further: 'Caspian oil may eventually be as important to the industrialized world as Middle East oil is today' (*New York Times* 1997). In the late 1990s, a number of academic works used these statements of politicians to strengthen their New Great Game assumptions (see e.g., Kleveman 2003). For example, Pipes argued that the Caspian region holds 'oil reserves estimated to be at least as large as those of Iraq and perhaps equal to those of Saudi Arabia' (Pipes 1997, 73). These exaggerations may seem unimportant. But in some cases, particularly when the overly optimistic figure of 200 billion barrels is wrongly compared to total global reserves of about one trillion, it can enhance international attention paid to the region in the short term and unwittingly cause subsequent conflicting understandings, deep suspicion about motives and information struggles (Conca 2001).

Considering Russia's oil production, Moscow should not have taken any notice of relatively marginal amounts of oil being produced by Azerbaijan. Russia's overall production of the commodity is significantly greater in volume generating some 11.16 million barrels per day (Henderson and

116 *Transnational infrastructure projects*

Grushevenko 2017). Current BTC production does not even amount to 5 percent of this output level. According to BP Azerbaijan (2018c), the BTC has the throughput capacity 1.2 million barrels of oil a day and the highest daily flow-rate of 1.06 million barrels to date was achieved on 21 July 2010. For example, from 2006 until 2018 the BTC pipeline carried just 3 billion barrels of oil to the Ceyhan marine terminal in Turkey (BP Azerbaijan 2018c). Because of this, one may argue that neither Russia nor the other great powers should worry about the amounts of oil produced in Azerbaijan.

Considering this, it can be concluded that the planning phase of the pipeline faced political and economic uncertainties in the early 1990s due to a number of weak and strong forms of geopolitical events and inaccurate statements of politicians. However, the relevant literature also had a tendency to present every development through the lens of geopolitics and great power manoeuvring in the early 1990s. More specifically, while the first phase of the pipeline project faced a number of natural political and economic events, the academic literature over-interpreted these challenges. In using inaccurate information, much of the analysis that has been conducted is of dubious standard with facts being accepted without question, and used without being subjected to any semblance of academic rigor. Therefore, a false and misleading image of the BTC pipeline has been created in the relevant literature. Such outdated 19th-century geopolitical thinking is likely inevitable because of natural resources, the uncertain legal status of the Caspian Sea, and the regional conflicts, but awareness about it needs to be raised as this awareness leads to new insights regarding the shortcomings of dominant academic and political practices. The geopolitical scholarship does not tell the full story about Caspian Sea pipeline politics because this scholarship is remarkably silent on challenges that energy projects face after the planning phase.

Construction of the BTC pipeline: challenges besides geopolitics

Throughout the construction phase, the pipeline faced a number of technical, environmental, and economic challenges, namely engineering failures, unstable oil prices, and social protests. These challenges should be considered as important elements of the pipeline politics since they have the capacity to affect security, geography and economy of any infrastructure. More specifically, these challenges are among the main issues that can halt the pipeline construction and affect its future. Considering their economic, social, and technical scopes, they are beyond the capacity of one single actor to solve and therefore they require and push multiple actors to cooperate and coordinate their functional capacities. Considering a number of technical challenges, the following sections illustrate that it was not Russia, Iran, or Armenia but the issues themselves that led to significant delays during the construction process and meanwhile increased the overall cost of the BTC project.

Technical challenges

The first technical challenge faced was unexpected engineering failures. In 2004 a number of consultant engineering companies reported problems with cracking in the pipeline caused by the SP 2888 coatings used in the Azerbaijani and Georgian sections of it (*The Guardian* 2004). More specifically, the Azerbaijani and Georgian sections of the pipeline had been found to be defective because the coating used on joints between sections of the BTC turned out to be insufficient. This defect could have led to an oil leak and thus to environmental pollution (*The Guardian* 2004). As a result, these sections had to be repaired, which meant the project took more time, attracted unnecessary international attention and cost more money. WorleyParsons, the lead independent consultant engineering firm involved in the project, criticized the inaction of the BTC project management team, which had allowed the problems to become greater than necessary. This issue increased the concerns of international investors backing the pipeline. Among them, the Banca Intesa (Italian Bank) had expressed apprehension about the technical problems and later dropped the BTC project completely for this very reason (*Financial Times* 2004).

Similarly, the dispute over the significance of SP 2888 coating[3] became particularly intense during the course of an enquiry by the United Kingdom Parliament's House of Commons on Trade and Industry into the activities of the UK government's Export Credit Guarantee Department (ECGD). It was found that SP 2888 is not a high-quality material, as was shown by the technical issue of its cracking. The UK Parliament devoted considerable time to the use of this material, and it also questioned the involvement of BP and the ECGD in this project (Barry 2013a, 143). In other words, the coating issue garnered transnational political significance and it was the primary issue that was discussed in the House of Commons regarding this. The underestimated technical issue led to unnecessary risk because the political discussion occurred before the decision of the ECGD to finance the BTC pipeline (Barry 2013a). This means that this technical issue put the involvement of the ECGD and the UK government at risk. Considering their international reputation, their EU membership, and their networking capabilities, it can be argued that if the ECGD and the UK withdrew their support for the BTC, it would increase the financial risk to investors because it would show that the UK government does not have any interest in the completion of the project.

Additionally, harsh weather conditions and unexpected archaeological findings created further technical challenges. The BTC pipeline corridor climbs gradients as high as 3,000 metres in some places, and is almost 2,000 kilometres long, with increased pressure being required to move oil up and down inclinations and slopes (Pipeline and Gas Journal 2006). It was argued that unexpected snowstorms and harsh weather conditions made some parts of the pipeline inaccessible for up to four months, which accounted for

118 *Transnational infrastructure projects*

delays at an extra cost of USD 270 million (Pipeline and Gas Journal 2006). Originally, it was estimated that the project would cost USD 2.1 billion but the technical issues changed this estimation (Sovacool and Cooper 2013). Finally, once construction began, contractors encountered more archaeological sites and unexplored places along the pipeline route than the planners had anticipated, which also led to delays and extra technical work and financial costs.

Economic challenges

The pipeline project additionally faced a multitude of economic hurdles. During the planning phase, project sponsors assured the governments of Azerbaijan, Georgia and Turkey that the BTC pipeline would cost approx. USD 2.1 billion; then it was increased to USD 3.6 billion, while in the end it came to cost approximately USD 4 billion to build (British Petroleum 2012). Sovacool and Cooper (2013) argue that much of the cost overruns resulted from underestimating the expense of environmental and social impact assessments. In the year 2000 three members of the consortium – Lukoil, ExxonMobil, and Penzoil – withdrew from the project for economic reasons. As mentioned earlier, Italian investor Banca Intesa also pulled out of the consortium in 2004, which led to construction delays and extra financial outlays. Following this event, the head of SOCAR said delays to construction work on the project could increase its costs by about USD 400 million. It is important to note that every day of delay cost BP potential oil revenues (see Pipeline and Gas Journal 2006). Additionally, in 2004 the price of oil was less than USD 40 per barrel, creating pressure to complete the project before the commodity's value bottomed out entirely (OECD Data 2018).

Another economic challenge was the land acquisition and compensation process for the BTC pipeline. To address this process and its impacts, the BTC project needed a comprehensive and well-structured programme. However, according to an International Finance Cooperation (IFC) report 'BTC contractors underestimated the scale and complexity of the land acquisition process and how much lead time and resources this would require in countries where land registration systems and land records were weak or nonexistent' (International Finance Cooperation 2006, 19). Hence in many cases the BTC project had to start from scratch, initiating land survey work and identifying thousands of rights holders which ultimately took considerably longer than originally anticipated and therefore induced additional spending requirements and construction delays. Because of these economic issues, the BTC pipeline ended up costing, as noted, USD 4 billion.

Considering Azerbaijan's and Georgia's weak economy at the start of the new century, it can be argued that these extra economic costs created significant financial losses for them. Initially, BP aimed to transport the first oil from Baku to Ceyhan in late 2004 but this plan was postponed multiple times due to the technical delays. The daily cost of the delays has been

Transnational infrastructure projects 119

estimated to be approximately USD 4 million, so every day the completion of the project was delayed was quite costly (Ismailova 2004). This was especially unwelcome since Azerbaijan's and Georgia's economic growth contracted by almost 60 percent between 1990 and 1995, because of economic troubles related to the collapse of the Soviet Union. According to the World Bank report (September, 2002), following the dissolution of the Soviet Union, the Azerbaijani economy declined more sharply than that of the average CIS country and this decline was accompanied by significant inflation. Both Azerbaijan and Georgia had a low GDP, which was less than USD 5 billion in the early 2000s (Luecke and Trofimenko 2008). In this regard, every day of delay hit extra hard as Azerbaijan and Georgia had come to depend on the potential oil revenues for their economic development. Other international partners questioned the profitability of the project due to these issues. Attracting new investors was not easy because Azerbaijan and Georgia were considered too risky to invest in due to their own regional conflicts and internal issues (Sovacool and Cooper 2013).

Social and environmental challenges

Throughout the construction phase of the BTC, active protests by a number of environmental NGOs and grassroots movements were another core challenge that the BTC project stakeholders had to confront. Organizations such as Friends of the Earth, the Kurdish Human Rights Project, and Bankwatch Network staunchly opposed the pipeline project. They sent letters to high-profile members of the World Bank and BP, and organized protests at the offices of the European Bank for Construction and Development (EBRD) (Carroll 2009). In August 2002, a coalition of NGOs released a series of fact-finding reports based on investigative missions to Turkey, Azerbaijan, and Georgia, excoriating the project for the threat that the pipeline's construction and operation posed to the environment (e.g., risks of oil spill and loss of biodiversity) (Carroll 2011; Molchanov 2011). In 2004, Tamar Libanidze, Georgian minister of the environment, halted the construction of the Borzhomi section in that country due to these environmental risks (Burton 2004). In contrast to the New Great Game literature, this example shows that it was not Russia, Armenia, or Iran but one of the BTC pipeline's key stakeholders, Georgia, who blocked the pipeline's construction because of environmental issues.

Another barrier was social protests. The BTC venture was hit by worker discontent in 2004. Laborers in both Azerbaijan and Georgia argued that the companies involved in the laying of the pipeline were engaging in unfair workplace practices (Ismailova 2004). On 28 February, 2004, about 400 workers employed by the Greek-based Consolidated Contractors International Co. went on strike in the Kurdamir Districts of Azerbaijan, due to perceived social injustice and discrimination both in terms of wages and ethnicity (Appelbaum 2004). Similarly, inhabitants of the Krtsanisi village in

120 *Transnational infrastructure projects*

Georgia went on strike because of the flawed the land acquisition and compensation process (Ismailova 2004). These protests did not stop the project but they played a significant role in slowing down the project, increasing international political attention and raising expenditure on it (Sovacool 2010).

Above all, these examples illustrate the central role of technical, economic, and environmental issues – which increased the costs of the project, led to delays, gave rise to investigations and, indeed, almost put an end to it entirely. These neglected material and non-material issues created obstacles for the BTC project, threatened the success of it and increased the overall cost from USD 2.1 billion to USD 4 billion. From a functionalist perspective, these examples also indicate that political agreement is not the only decisive condition for the realization of complex infrastructure. Rather, non-political requirements also need to be fulfilled.

Network of actors

Because of the scope and complexities of these technical, economic, and social challenges, it can be argued that they are beyond the capacity of any single state to solve. Therefore, these issues have produced an environment where Azerbaijan, Georgia, and Turkey must now rely on the involvement and coordination of multiple actors, namely IGOs, NGOs, financial institutions, and TNCs. The reason for this is that they offer the required resources that most states lack, such as professional personnel, technology, organizational capacity, access to the world market, support from their home countries, and financial power. As is explained in revised functionalism, the cooperation of two or more outside actors in a transnational infrastructure project can reduce serious financial, political, and security risks, which such projects often encounter (see chapter 2). This section illustrates, therefore, exactly how a network of actors with varying interests provided systematic and functional coordination for the BTC pipeline project.

Energy companies

One of the key actors in coordination are multinational oil companies, such as BP, Chevron, SOCAR, Inpex, and Statoil Hydro, who between them offered a number of the required resources to transport landlocked oil to international markets. The first important point that needs to be highlighted is the economic leverage that multinational energy companies have. The BTC is owned and operated by a consortium of eleven international oil companies, being managed overall by BP. Figure 4.2 illustrates BTC's shareholders.

Considering the high cost of the project (USD 3.6 billion) and low GDP of Azerbaijan (approximately USD 5 billion), it can be argued that their involvement decreased the cost of the pipeline in the early 2000s.. Due to their economic power, oil companies' investments are a strategic source of revenue

Transnational infrastructure projects 121

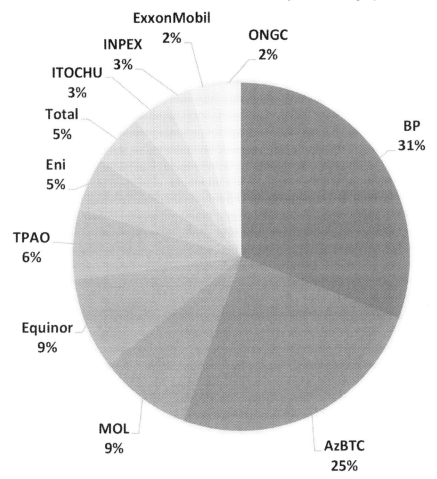

Figure 4.2 The BTC oil pipeline private shareholders in 2021.
Source: Author's own compilation.

and a key input to the budgets of the countries of the region. According to the World Bank (2002), the Azerbaijani economy started to recover after 1995 because the signing of Production Sharing Agreements (PSAs) with foreign oil companies brought USD 7.5 billion worth of investments to its economy. The PSAs also ensured hard currency revenues for the Azerbaijani economy in the long term (Petersen 2016). In the same vein, the EBRD report (2004, 131) highlights that in Georgia the BTC project contributed to growth in the construction and communications sectors, where output increased by almost 21 percent and 38 percent respectively in 2004. The Azeri and Georgian governments were therefore intrigued by the idea of constructing a pipeline and the potential of earning substantial transit

122   *Transnational infrastructure projects*

revenues, so they were willing to do their best to attract the participation of international oil companies (Kalyuzhnova 2008). For example, BP has invested more than USD 36 billion in development of the ACG oil field since the 1994 agreement (the Wall Street Journal, April 19, 2019). The BTC transports the oil extracted from this oil field. In light of this, it can be argued that the involvement of these companies contributed to economic growth in Azerbaijan, Georgia, and Turkey by providing a substantial new revenue stream.

Besides their economic leverage, the involvement of Western energy giants comes with political and security advantages too. According to one interviewee in Baku, 'in the 1990s, Azerbaijan was willing to accept a ceasefire with Armenia to create a safe investment environment for international oil companies. In light of this, Azerbaijan was able to attract crucial energy companies to the pipeline project' (Interview, May 11, 2018). Additionally, in the early 1990s, one of the key issues was whether, and if so how, to include Russian energy companies. Nevertheless, Western energy companies were aware that the financing, resources and political realities in the Caspian Sea region required working together. Therefore, they sought to accommodate Russia by giving Lukoil a 10 percent stake – as the success of their project depended on good relations with Russia (Edwards 2003). Moreover, the active involvement of TNCs put Azerbaijan and Georgia on the map in terms of attracting foreign direct investment and gaining Western support for their sovereignty, resolving territorial conflicts and for ensuring security. For example, according to a local expert in Baku, 'due to the involvement of international oil companies, some Western countries (for example, the UK and the US) have paid more attention to the region's conflicts' (Interview, May 11, 2018). This attention was very important for Azerbaijan and Georgia, as it could help them to keep up diplomatic negotiations and prevent further violent clashes. Additionally, one interviewee in Baku mentioned that the 'active involvement of TNCs offers extra security to the BTC because it is the property of both Azerbaijan and the West' (Interview, May 11, 2018).

In addition, BP has implemented significant security measures along the energy route, mainly in the form of patrolling and monitoring. An expert from the company said that 'although protection of the pipeline is ultimately the responsibility of the relevant governments, BP is involved in addressing this security matter with its own measures too, such as providing advanced technology, training guards, implementing social projects, and offering financial support' (Interview, October 26, 2017). In Azerbaijan, BP has implemented facility protection and security guard services through its private security provider, Titan D, while closely cooperating with the Export Pipeline Protection Department, the Azeri government agency appointed for infrastructure security. Besides these measures, BP has also launched several social programs (e.g., repairing roads, supporting agriculture, educational initiatives etc.) along the pipeline's route to support local villages and gain their support. According to a representative of the company, in this way BP

Transnational infrastructure projects 123

can cooperate with local people and inform government officials in advance about any terrorist or sabotage plans.

Finally, the exploitation and transportation of oil from the Caspian Sea would never have been possible without modern technology, which the regional states lack. The technical expertise that remained after the dissolution of the Soviet Union was not sufficient to address geological challenges and exploit offshore reserves. According to Bayulgen (2009, 165), Azerbaijan's oil output decreased by approximately 30 percent between 1990 and 1996 because of the limitations of outdated technology. To combat this, BP has brought in advanced equipment from its research and development centres in the UK and US (BP Azerbaijan 2018a). In doing so, BP, together with the other consortium companies, has built several of the ACG's oil production platforms, such as West Azeri, East Azeri, Deepwater Gunashli, and West Chirag (BP Azerbaijan 2018a). These platforms have significantly increased the oil production of Azerbaijan. For example, the ACG produced 584,000 barrels per day in 2018 (BP Azerbaijan 2018a). Additionally, the consortium companies revitalized the technical capacities of Azerbaijan, Georgia and Turkey by facilitating the construction of advanced oil and gas processing plants and fabrication facilities (Sovacool 2010).They contributed to the upgrading of local experts' knowledge by offering a number of educational and capacity building training programs (BP Azerbaijan 2018b). In line with the theoretical proposition of this research, BP's contribution to the BTC project illustrates, therefore, that it offers many of the things that regional states lack and were not otherwise able to attain. It is, however, important to note that by involving themselves in the project, these companies have also benefitted significantly from it – by adding new reserves to their resource bases, by exploiting vast natural resources for significant profit, and by diversifying their portfolios away from reliance on fields in Alaska, the North Sea and South America (Sovacool and Cooper 2013). According to the EIA (January 7, 2019). Azerbaijan's proven oil reserves were approximately 7 billion barrels at the end of 2017. In contrast, the UK North Sea's proven oil reserves were approximately 5.6 billion barrels at the end of 2017 (Offshore Energy Today, November 8, 2018). In light of this, it can be argued that the BTC is valuable for BP and the other energy companies because they make a profit on it and it increases their resource diversity.

Private and public lenders

Despite the heavy investment of BP and other energy companies, covering all of the costs for this massive project has still required funding by international banks and financial IGOs – such as the World Bank, the IFC, and the ECGD, as well as the EBRD. Ensuring sound coordination between them was decisive in securing sustainable funding and reducing attendant political risks. Nevertheless, in the years from the end of the Cold War into the new century the regional countries lacked crucial lobbying and networking

124 *Transnational infrastructure projects*

experience. Furthermore, countries like Azerbaijan and Georgia were – as noted earlier – considered too risky for international banks and financial institutions to invest in. As such, one interviewee noted that:

> By using their access to global donor networks, the consortium companies – particularly BP – facilitated relations between Azerbaijan and financial institutions: the World Bank, EBRD, ECGD, EXIM Bank and IFC. BP has played a key role in all phases of the BTC project since the 1990s. It is one of the strong and popular European energy companies, and its involvement attracts other Western financial institutions and gives them more security and reliability.

These global financial institutions invested in the BTC pipeline as a way of helping Azerbaijan, Georgia, and Turkey graduate to the global economy (Petersen 2016; Sovacool and Cooper 2013). For example, EXIM Bank was only one of seven countries' export credit agencies involved in financing the project. From 2003 to 2005, EXIM Bank had to approve financing of up to USD 160 million to help complete the project (Bashir 2017). The IFC provided an overall investment expenditure of USD 250 million for the development of the BTC pipeline. Additionally, in 2003 the EBRD approved a twelve-year loan of up to USD 125 million for the BTC project itself and syndicated a ten-year USD 125 million loan to commercial lenders (Pyrkalo 2016). In December 2003, the ECGD approved a line of credit for the project of USD 450 million. According to Barry (2013a), the involvement of the ECGD in the project was intended to reduce the financial risk to investors – but also helped to ensure that the UK government in particular would have a direct interest in the eventual completion of the project.

Additionally, governments that received loans from the World Bank and other financial institutions are obliged to implement a package of reforms (relating to environmental, technical, and economic standards). Considering the pressure coming from different NGOs, these organizations worked with

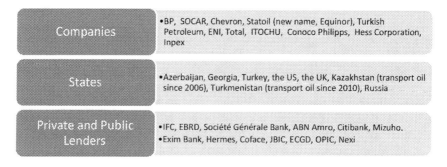

Figure 4.3 List of actors involved in the BTC oil pipeline.
Source: Author's own compilation.

Transnational infrastructure projects 125

the BTC consortium companies and three governments to help with land resettlements, fostering local businesses, and ensuring environmental compliance. To optimize Azerbaijan's management of its resource wealth, the World Bank Group advised the Azerbaijani government on the creation of the State Oil Fund of Azerbaijan (SOFAZ). To promote transparency, the Group facilitated the country's participation in the Extractive Industry Transparency Initiative (EITI); Azerbaijan would, however, leave this institution in 2017, due to its human rights problems. International oil companies and financial institutions together helped Azerbaijani and Georgian energy companies to transform from Soviet-era entities into more transparent, modern state-owned enterprises (Petersen 2016).

After becoming involved in the BTC, these actors offered their strong networks to help attract further financial support (in terms of private banks) and mitigate political risks. Nevertheless, as pointed out earlier, it has been argued that 'the private capital markets were not willing to loan to countries like Azerbaijan and Georgia because they are too risky' (Sovacool and Cooper 2013, 118). However, this situation changed thanks to the strong networks of the EBRD and IFC – who were able to guarantee the cheap lending of financial products to Azerbaijan and Georgia.

The two countries utilized these organizations' vast network of financial, social and environmental experts to ensure the minimization of costs and maximization of assets. They played the much-underappreciated role of risk mitigators in the process of opening up the Caspian Sea's riches and assisted in attracting the private leaders of the financial world – including Citibank, ABN Amro, and Société Générale – to help finance the remaining (minor) outstanding amounts (Carroll 2011). In line with the theoretical proposition of this book, this example illustrates that the power of actors rests in large part on their access to global donor and technical assistance networks that regional actors may not be able to otherwise reach (see chapter 2). The export credit agencies and bilateral financial institutions of the US, the UK, Japan, and others teamed up with the EBRD and IFC to lend more than just a hand. In total, the funding model proposed put up USD 1.7 billion of public money for the project in a 70/30 debt/equity structure (Carroll and Jarvis 2014). It has been claimed that 70 percent of the project costs were funded by a group of lenders that included the World Bank Group's IFC, EBRD and the export credit agencies of seven countries as well as a syndicate of fifteen commercial banks (IFC 2006).

These empirical findings reinforce the functional proposition that technical issues are beyond the political, economic and physical capacities of any individual actor to solve – thus requiring the involvement of multiple players. In line with this, it can be argued that the BTC project would not have been completed in a timely manner if a number of actors had not been part of the project. They pooled their resources to deal with specific issues. In many cases, they are highly appreciated because the legitimacy and supervision provided by IGOs like the World Bank Group and by private companies

126   *Transnational infrastructure projects*

were critical to securing public recognition and support from the US and EU governments for the project (Petersen 2016). Although the regional countries still have a weak rule of law, endemic corruption, and limited institutional capacities as well as transparency, these actors around them ensured that ultimately the BTC pipeline was successfully built according to certain Western standards.

Operating the BTC pipeline

The previous section illustrated the role of technical, economic, and social challenges in the planning and construction of the BTC. In doing so, it also explained in which ways different actors were involved in the BTC project during construction phase. The following section explains the BTC's entanglement with wider regional processes after its construction. When addressing the BTC project's socio-economic impact after its construction, the existing scholarship focusses mainly on the trilateral relationship between Azerbaijan, Georgia, and Turkey or, alternatively, competition between the littoral states (see e.g., Bayulgen 2009; Dikkaya and Ozyakisir 2008; Frappi and Valigi 2015;). However, from a functionalist perspective, the question is how the BTC as a material power has influenced the relationship between the Caspian littoral states since it become operational and whether the BTC has led to cooperation or enhanced the existing regional rivalry since its construction.

Pragmatic cooperation

Unlike the geopolitical assumptions, which predicted naval conflict and rivalry, the Caspian Sea countries actually started to show keen interest in the BTC route following the successful completion of the project. In line with the insights formulated in revised functionalism, the BTC has offered the Caspian littoral states an issue-specific opportunity to cooperate. More concretely, the BTC has offered the littoral states material integration opportunity as an alternative to naïve political integration path and regional conflict. While this material integration avoids nationalism, political differences, and sovereignty issues, it proposes profits and mutual dependency in the long term.

The first such example of cooperation is Kazakhstan. On June 16, 2006 Kazakhstan officially joined the BTC project – for which an agreement was signed in Almaty by the presidents of Kazakhstan and Azerbaijan (Radio Free Europe 2006). Due to the absence of an existing pipeline between the two countries, Kazakh crude oil is shipped to Baku across the Caspian Sea and then pumped through the 1,770-kilometre-long BTC on to Turkey's Mediterranean port of Ceyhan. After this, in November 2008 the national energy companies of Azerbaijan and Kazakhstan reached an agreement with respect to the development of a Trans-Caspian oil transport system to help

Transnational infrastructure projects 127

get Kazakhstani oil to international markets (The Moscow Times 2008). The network would be initially able to ship 500,000 barrels of oil daily (23 million tons a year), eventually increasing to 750,000–1.2 million barrels per day (35–56 million tons annually). The new Trans-Caspian oil transport system agreement and the commodity's shipment via the BTC pipeline indicate that despite some disagreements over transit tariffs and the use of Black Sea terminals, Azerbaijan and Kazakhstan are willing to cooperate on moving the latter's oil – and that, moreover, Kazakhstan is keen to improve its export capacities and is looking for options vis-à-vis diversifying export routes (Guliyev and Akhrarkhodjaeva 2009).

Kazakhstan has still managed to restore the pumping of hydrocarbon resources via the BTC pipeline, but not the KCTS project. Deliveries were resumed in November 2013 in accordance with the agreement between the Aktau Seaport and Tengizchevroil company that provides an annual exportation of four million tons of oil via Azerbaijan, of which 3 million are to be transported specifically via the BTC pipeline (Parkhomchik 2016, 143). According to the Azerbaijani State Statistics Committee, over 6.5 million tons of transit oil (from Turkmenistan and Kazakhstan) were pumped through the BTC pipeline in 2017, and 1.5 million transit oil were pumped in the first quarter of this year (Caspian Barrel 2018).

As a second example, in 2008 Azerbaijan and Turkmenistan signed a bilateral agreement suspending all previous exploration agreements concerning the disputed Kepez (Serdar) field until they solve all issues surrounding the field (Eurasianet 2012). In the same year, Azerbaijan paid off USD 44.8 million of debt owed to Turkmenistan (Valiyev 2009). From July 2010 onwards Turkmenistan started to transfer its oil through the BTC pipeline. Despite the Azeri-Chirag-Kepez oil fields – which the literature of the great powers argued would eventually lead to (naval) warfare between the two countries – the BTC pipeline has, in fact, provided these two countries with the opportunity to enhance their cooperation. According to BP Azerbaijan, the pipeline is capable of handling some 800,000 barrels per day and Turkmen oil accounts for 4–5 percent of this flow volume (Radio Free Europe 2010). For example, 371,206 tons of Turkmen oil was transported via the BTC pipeline in June 2016 alone (Ismailova 2016). This number increased to 4.2 million tons in 2018 (Trend 2019). Since there is no pipeline connection between Turkmenistan and Azerbaijan, oil is brought to Baku aboard tankers. The BTC pipeline is functional for Turkmenistan because by joining the pipeline, Turkmenistan has diversified its oil export options to include one that does not pass through Russia and has also secured access to international energy markets through an alternative route. These days, Azerbaijan and Turkmenistan are furthermore in the process of discussing the transportation also of Turkmen gas to Europe through the 'Southern Gas Corridor.'[4]

Additionally, the bilateral relations between Azerbaijan and Turkmenistan intensified in 2018. For example, Azerbaijan and Turkmenistan's presidents

128 *Transnational infrastructure projects*

met in Ashgabat and Baku in 2018 (Trend 2018). In 2018, the leaders signed a number of agreements to facilitate further cooperation such as increasing shipping between trade ports, visa facilitation, avoiding double income and property taxation, and establishing a joint committee for transport as well as logistics (Ministry of Foreign Affairs Azerbaijan 2018). These examples illustrate that the cooperative practices, which were started during the CEP, continued and facilitated collaboration in other areas. However, it is important to note that Azerbaijan and Turkmenistan have done little to develop their non-oil sectors, which represent only a limited share of their total exports, less than approximately 5 percent in terms of gross gains (ADB 2019). This means that cooperation between Azerbaijan and Turkmenistan is mainly dominated by hydrocarbon sectors. In other words, since there is a lack of production and development in non-oil sectors, there is limited room for expanding cooperation into different sectors.

Furthermore, a week before Kazakhstan officially committed to the pipeline an Iranian official said Tehran wanted to explore the BTC export option too. According to Mahmoud Khagani, the chief of the Caspian Sea Department of the Iranian Oil Ministry 'we are currently exploring for oil in the southern Caspian Sea. Our relations with Azerbaijan have been developing so successfully that, if we get positive results in the southern Caspian, we could discuss possible cooperation' (Eurasianet 2006). Although this aim was not fulfilled due to reasons of it being commercially unprofitable and of limited natural resources in the southern section of the Caspian Sea, this political statement illustrates that Iran was also keen to seek new options regarding reaching Western energy markets. In 2018 Tehran and Baku discussed the possibility of establishing a joint oil company for the exploration of natural resources in the Caspian Sea (Trend 2018a).

Finally, in 2009 Russia's largest oil producer, Rosneft, became interested in options to export oil through the BTC pipeline. Rosneft's president, Sergei Bogdanchikov, told the press: 'if the project meets the economic interests of both sides, naturally we will be able to export our oil through the BTC' (Azernews 2009). In response to this, Rovnag Abdullayev, president of SOCAR, said: 'if an appeal is received, it may be considered, and even its realization in the future is possible' (Azernews 2009). However, this idea has, to date, ultimately not moved beyond abstract statements, because it is argued that the BTC pipeline is economically less appealing for Russia (Azernews 2009). Despite this, negotiations have continued between SOCAR and Rosneft from time to time. Moreover, in 2014 Lukoil showed interest in transporting its oil via the BTC pipeline (Daly 2014). Then that company announced, on 16 May 2014, that its oil would soon be delivered to Europe via the BTC pipeline (Daly 2014). In the same month, Lukoil delivered a trial batch of 30,000 tons of oil via the pipeline. According to BP Sustainability Report (2018b, 10), the BTC pipeline carried volumes of crude oil and condensate from Russia in 2018. Since it constitutes a commercial secret, uncovering the exact amount of transported Russian oil is not possible. During

Transnational infrastructure projects 129

my fieldwork interviews, a local expert from Azerbaijan posited that Lukoil intends to transport approximately 500,000 tons of oil this way (Interview, October 27, 2017). In light of this, it can be argued that the BTC is even functional for Russia because it provides its energy companies an alternative route to transport their natural resources.

The amount of cooperation among the littoral states could still increase in the future for three main reasons. First, as mentioned above, the BTC pipeline transports oil from the ACG field, but that field's oil production has modestly decreased since 2012 (EIA 2019). If this decline continues, there will be more capacity for the other littoral states to transport their natural resources through BTC pipeline. Coincidentally, oil production at the Kazakhstan's oil fields might increase in the future, which would entail an increased demand for export routes (Reuters 2019). The BTC can offer the additional functional route needed to transport Kazakh oil. Second, the Legal Status Convention was signed in August 2018, which ensures the application of binding legal norms to shipping across the Caspian Sea and provides for a clearer picture of the movement of oil tankers and construction of submarine pipelines. More concretely, the Legal Status Convention (see Article 14) provides clarity about the necessary requirements for constructing submarine cables and pipelines between the littoral states (Kremlin 2019). Considering the increase in Kazakh oil production, Azerbaijan, and Kazakhstan might decide to extend the BTC pipeline and construct additional submarine pipeline to transport Kazakh oil. Finally, although the Legal Status Convention does not explicitly mention oil fields the ownership of which is disputed between Iran and Azerbaijan (e.g., the Alov-Sharg-Araz oil field) or between Azerbaijan and Turkmenistan (e.g., the Azeri-Chirag-Kepez oil field), the agreement and its articles can be used as a starting point for finding common ground in these disputes. For example, Azerbaijan and Iran signed a memorandum of understanding on joint development of offshore hydrocarbon fields in the Caspian Sea in 2018 (President 2018).

As explained in chapter 3, the littoral states came together in the CEP in the 1990s. The empirical findings in the case study of the BTC illustrate that despite geopolitical challenges, cooperation among the littoral states has spread from cooperation on environmental concerns to cooperation on transnational infrastructure projects. Of course, this does not mean that the CEP has explicitly encouraged the littoral states to join the BTC project. However, the CEP is the first place where the littoral states started to experience and establish the practice of cooperation, interaction, negotiation and trust. Therefore, the CEP can be construed as the icebreaker among the littoral states in the 1990s. In this regard, the above-mentioned examples illustrate that the stage for cooperative habits, which was set by the CEP, continued and became even more compelling throughout the BTC project.

Additionally, these empirical findings reinforce the theoretical proposition that post-construction the transnational BTC infrastructure has changed the dynamics of the New Great Game in the region, by offering a functional

130 *Transnational infrastructure projects*

system for pragmatic cooperation. More specifically, once a technological artifact (e.g., pipeline) is constructed, it can practically facilitate or restrict interaction, communication and transportation of people, social life, or other goods and services (Bijker 2001). In contrast to the New Great Game literature, these empirical findings also illustrate that the social relations among and the interests of the Caspian littoral states are not fixed or given. The BTC pipeline should be viewed as a way of bringing different actors together and increasing their interaction capacities. It is indeed true that infrastructure becomes 'strategic' because of the number of connections that it makes possible in a highly contingent world (Latour 2005). In this regard, transnational infrastructures (like the BTC) should be considered as an important transformative element of the Caspian Sea.

The BTC is a material power as it affects security, economy, politics, geography, diplomacy, and state-society relations in the region. The completion of the BTC pipeline has changed the positions of the littoral states, enhanced regional interaction capacities, and connected landlocked countries to both global and regional networks. Existing uncertainty and hostility have decreased to some extent, which has furthermore enhanced the interest of the littoral states in the project. Cooperation between them is occurring because they stand to benefit greatly from it, as each possesses a resource that the other two lack. Both energy and transport are valuable enterprises that promise to bring financial reward. It is a pragmatic, flexible, and technocratic cooperation unfolding, as the littoral states can be part of these activities with respect to their interests and resources while there is no requirement either to contribute to the project or to stay out of it. Therefore, it is necessary to determine those activities which are common, where they are common and to what extent they are common.

Conclusion

The transnational infrastructure of the BTC pipeline should not be viewed in isolation, rather its complexity and sophistication must be taken into full consideration. This is because, first and foremost, the BTC project is not just made up of metal pipes and black gold, but also of the extensive legislation, logistics, and state and non-state authorities that also all help support it. The chapter has revisited the three phases of the BTC pipeline project: planning of the pipeline; construction of the pipeline; and use of the pipeline. This chapter first, illustrated that the planning phase was dominated by geopolitical assumptions due to the exaggeration of the amount of natural resource reserves as well as to political, economic, and technical uncertainties. More specifically, both academics and politicians overestimated the extent of the Caspian Sea oil and gas reserves. This enhanced the international attention paid to the region in the short term, and also unwittingly caused subsequent conflicting understandings of it, deep suspicion about motives, and information struggles. Thus, a false image of the region has been created.

Transnational infrastructure projects 131

Second, it has been illustrated in this chapter that the New Great Game literature presents an incorrect picture when it comes the BTC, as the relevant scholarship overlooks and underestimates the actual technical, economic, and social challenges of cross-national infrastructure projects. This chapter has shown there were other conditions for and challenges to the realization of the complex BTC project besides purely political ones that were more influential to the type and extent of cooperation between the littoral states. What this chapter has highlighted, which the hitherto dominant state-centric narrative neglected, are the technical, social, environmental, and economic issues that created unanticipated obstacles for the BTC project and led to lengthy delays (which increased the project's cost), the launching of investigations, and almost, indeed, halting the project entirely. During the construction phase, one of the BTC pipeline's key stakeholders, Georgia, temporarily blocked the project because of environmental issues, for example. The UK Parliament investigated and questioned the involvement of BP and ECGD in the project vis-à-vis technical and material failures. Finally, the project was delayed due to massive protests by workers, NGO pressures, and land acquisition disputes. Contrary to the state-centric New Great Game assumptions, this chapter has illustrated that these were the issues which made cooperation of multiple actors necessary and feasible during the construction phase. More specifically, these challenges were only resolved due to the systematic support and networking of multiple players namely, transnational energy companies, intergovernmental organizations, and international banks. In line with revised functionalism's insights, this chapter illustrated that without the strong financial, political, technical, and lobbying support these actors gave the BTC, it would never have been completed.

Finally, this chapter has shown that the New Great Game literature has neglected the role of the BTC pipeline after its construction. More specifically, it has illustrated that cooperation among the Caspian littoral states was not limited to the CEP. The formation of cooperation habits, which was begun in the CEP, continued and grew stronger through the BTC project. The successful construction of the pipeline has done more than just enable the Caspian Sea to gain international prominence and power. It has transformed the region and the states in it. While the pipeline was already operational in 2006, this aspect has so far been ignored by the relevant literature. Since its construction the pipeline has changed the dynamics of the Great Game in the region by offering a functional system for pragmatic cooperation despite a number of geopolitical disputes and uncertainties. The BTC pipeline came to be regarded as 'strategic' because of the number of connections it makes possible in a highly contingent world. Previously existing uncertainty and hostility between the littoral states have decreased somewhat, which has increased their stake in this project. In this regard, the BTC pipeline has been successful in creating pragmatic, flexible, and technocratic cooperation as any littoral state can be part of these activities with respect to their preferences and resources while there is no requirement to either to join

132 *Transnational infrastructure projects*

the project or be excluded from it. There are long-standing issues between the littoral states, such as the uncertain legal status of the sea and the contested nature of its resources, but the BTC pipeline has created room to circumvent these restrictions while still addressing issue-specific needs. Considering this, it can be argued that, when analyzing the region, it is necessary to determine which activities are communal, where they are communal, and the extent to which they are communal.

All in all, the BTC pipeline is functional for multiple actors as it addresses shared and different interests. It is functional for social interests because it provides people with jobs and because of the pipeline, companies have launched several social projects. The BTC is functional for the ruling elite of several states because it enhances their power position, economic income, legitimization, connects them to the international arena, and provides them an alternative route for transporting their natural resources. It serves the ruling elite because the BTC provides the international market with energy resources and the elite might use this for their own benefit during diplomatic discussion. The BTC is also functional for TNC because BP and other energy companies make profit, increase their resource diversity, and it is a functional way for them to enter the Caspian Sea. The BTC is also functional because it has brought new constrains. More specifically, it increased the cost of regional conflicts or aggressiveness, which serves the interests of international organizations. Of course, the BTC has several negative functional effects as well. Because of this infrastructure, human rights are neglected or ignored by the international community.

Notes

1 This chapter was published in *East European Politics Journal* in 2019. The link for the article: https://doi.org/10.1080/21599165.2019.1612372.
2 The Baku–Novorossiysk pipeline is a 1,330-kilometre long oil pipeline, running from Sangachal Terminal in Azerbaijan to Novorossiysk Terminal on the Black Sea coast, in Russia. The pipeline first became operational in 1997.
3 Used for coating of girth welds, as well as valves, fittings, pipe, ballast tanks, ships, and marine structures. Ideally suited for coating of pipe to be used for slip bore/ directional drilling due to its superior abrasion, impact, and gouge resistance properties. Also used for exterior coatings of pipelines in buried or immersed services. Advantage: excellent adhesion to grit blasted steel surfaces, Fusion Bond Epoxy and Fiber Reinforced Plastic.
4 The Southern Gas Corridor (SGC) is a term used to describe planned infrastructure projects aimed at improving the security and diversity of the EU's energy supply by bringing natural gas from the Caspian region to Europe.

Bibliography

Akiner, Shirin. 2004. *The Caspian: Politics, Energy and Security.* London: Routledge.
Alam, Shah. 2002. 'Pipeline politics in the Caspian Sea Basin.' *Strategic Analysis* 26 (1): 5–26.

Transnational infrastructure projects 133

Appelbaum, Alec. 2004. 'Protests Over Working Conditions Unlikely to Slow Caspian Pipeline.' March 1. Accessed December 12, 2017. https://eurasianet.org/p rotests-over-working-conditions-unlikely-to-slow-caspian-pipeline.

Allison, Roy. 2008. 'Russia Resurgent? Moscow's Campaign to "Coerce Georgia to Peace".' *International Affairs* 84 (6): 1145–1171.

Ashworth, Lucian, and David Long. 1999. *New Perspectives on International Functionalism.* London: Macmillan Press.

Asian Development Bank. 2019. 'ADB Economic Diversification Support for Azerbaijan Proves Challenging: Independent Evaluation.' January 28. Accessed January 29, 2019. https://www.adb.org/news/adb-economic-diversification-support-azerbaija n-proves-challenging-independent-evaluation.

Azernews. 2009. 'Russia's Rosneft seeks to export oil via BTC.' September 23. Accessed September 12, 2017. https://www.azernews.az/oil_and_gas/14615.html.

Bahgat, Gawdat. 2003. 'Pipeline Diplomacy: The Geopolitics of the Caspian Sea Region.' *International Studies Perspective* 3 (3): 310–327.

Baran, Zeyno. 2005. 'The Baku-Tbilisi-Ceyhan Pipeline: Implications for Turkey.' In *The Baku-Tbilisi-Ceyhan Pipeline: Oil Window to the West*, by Starr Frederick and Svante Cornell, 103–119. Uppsala: Central Asia-Caucasus Institute and Silk Road Studies.

Barry, Andrew. 2013a. *Material Politics.* Sussex: Wiley Blackwell.

Barry, Andrew. 2013b. 'The Translation Zone: Between Actor-Network Theory and International Relations.' *Journal of International Studies* 41 (3): 413–429.

Bashir, Omar S. 2017. 'The Great Games Never Played: Explaining Variation in International Competition Over Energy.' *Journal of Global Security Studies* 2 (4): 288–306.

Bayramov, Agha. 2018. 'Dubious nexus between natural resources and conflict.' *Journal of Eurasian Studies* 9: 71–82.

Bayramov, Agha. 2016. 'Silencing the Nagorno-Karabakh Conflict and Challenges of the Four-Day War.' *Security and Human Rights* 27 (1–2):116–127.

Bayulgen, Oksan. 2009. 'Caspian energy wealth: social impacts and implications for regional stability.' In *The Politics of Transition in Central Asia and the Caucasus*, by Amanda Wooden and Christoph Stefes, 163–189. New York: Routledge.

BBC. 2008. 'Q&A: Conflict in Georgia.' November 11. Accessed September 20, 2018. http://news.bbc.co.uk/2/hi/europe/7549736.stm.

Bijker, Wiebe E. 2001. 'Technology, Social Construction of.' In *International Encyclopedia of the Social and Behavioral Sciences*, 15522–15527. Oxford: Blackwell Publishing.

British Petroleum. 2016a. 'Baku-Tbilisi-Ceyhan.' Accessed October 25, 2017. http://www.bp.com/en_az/caspian/operationsprojects/pipelines/BTC.html.

British Petroleum. 2016b. 'First Quarter 2018 Results.' May 17. Accessed May 25, 2018. https://www.bp.com/en_az/caspian/press/businessupdates/first-quarter-2018-results.html.

British Petroleum. 2016c. 'Shah Deniz Stage 2: Operations and Projects.' Accessed August 3, 2016. http://www.bp.com/en_az/caspian/operationsprojects/Shahdeniz/SDstage2.html.

British Petroleum. 2012. 'BTC Project Environmental and Social Annual Report.' https://www.bp.com/content/dam/bp-country/en_az/pdf/lenders-reports/2012-BTC-Annual-lenders-report.pdf, Baku: British Petroleum.

BP Azerbaijan. 2018a. 'Azeri-Chirag-Deepwater Gunashli.' September 20. Accessed September 21, 2018. http://www.shah-deniz.com/azeri-chirag-deepwater-gunashli/.

134 *Transnational infrastructure projects*

BP Azerbaijan. 2018b. 'First Quarter 2018 Results.' May 17. Accessed May 23, 2016. https://www.bp.com/en_az/caspian/press/businessupdates/first-quarter-2018-results. html.

BP Azerbaijan. 2018c. 'BTC celebrates 3 billion barrels of oil export.' July 16. Accessed July 16, 2018. https://www.bp.com/en_az/caspian/press/features/btc_3M_billion_barrels_of_oil_export1.html.

Bryman, Alan. 2016. *Social Research Methods.* Oxford: Oxford University Press.

Burton, Adrian. 2004. 'The BTC Oil Pipeline Mystery.' *Frontiers in Ecology and the Environment* 2 (7): 344–345.

Carroll, Toby. 2011. 'The Cutting Edge of Accumulation: Neoliberal Risk Mitigation, the Baku-Tbilisi-Ceyhan Pipeline and its Impact.' *Antipode* 44 (2): 281–302. doi:10.1111/j.1467-8330.2011.00891.x.

Carroll, Toby. 2009. *Pipelines, Participatory Development and the Reshaping of the Caucasus.* Singapore: Center on Asia and Globalisation, Lee Kuan Yew Public School, National University of Singapore.

Carroll, Toby, and Darryl Jarvis. 2014. *The Politics of Marketing Asia.* New York: Palgrave.

Caspian Barrel. 2018. 'Baku-Tbilisi-Ceyhan oil pipeline will increase shipment of Turkmen oil to world markets.' April 27. Accessed May 10, 2018. http://caspianba rrel.org/en/2018/04/baku-tbilisi-ceyhan-oil-pipeline-will-increase-shipment-of-turkm en-oil-to-world-markets/.

Caspian Barrel. 2016. 'Transportation of transit oil via BTC significantly increased.' July 15. Accessed October 25, 2017. http://caspianbarrel.org/?p=17031.

Ceccorulli, Michela, Carlo Frappi, and Sonia Lucar. 2017. 'On regional security governance once again: how analysis of the Southern Caucasus can advance the concept.' *European Security* 26 (1): 59–78.

Cohen, Ariel. 2002. *Iran's claims over Caspian Sea resources.* Washington: The Heritage Foundation.

Coole, Diana. 2013. 'Agentic Capacities and Capacious Historical Materialism: Thinking with New Materialisms in the Political Sciences.' *Millennium: Journal of International Studies* 41 (3): 451–469.

Conca, Ken. 2001. 'Environmental Cooperation and International Peace.' In *Environmental Conflict*, by Paul F Diehl and Petter Gleditsch, 225–250. Colorado: Westview Publisher.

Daly, John C. 2014. 'Russian Oil to Feature in Baku-Tbilisi-Ceyhan Pipeline—Circumventing Possible Sanctions?' May 30. Accessed September 12, 2018. https://jam estown.org/program/russian-oil-to-feature-in-baku-tbilisi-ceyhan-pipeline-circumve nting-possible-sanctions/.

Dikkaya, Mehmet, and Deniz Ozyakisir. 2008. 'Developing regional cooperation among Turkey, Georgia and Azerbaijan: Importance of Regional Projects.' *Perceptions* 13 (1–2):93–118.

Dodds, Klaus. 2005. *Global Geopolitics: A Critical Introduction.* Essex: Pearson Education.

EBRD. 2004. 'Transition Report.' London: EBRD. https://www.ebrd.com/downloads/ research/transition/TR04.pdf.

Edwards, Matthew. 2003. 'The New Great Game and the new great gamers: Disciples of Kipling and Mackinder.' *Central Asian Survey* 22 (1): 83–102.

Energy Information Administration. 2019. 'Country Analysis Executive Summary: Azerbaijan.' January 7. Accessed January 8, 2019. https://www.eia.gov/beta/interna tional/analysis_includes/countries_long/Azerbaijan/azerbaijan_exe.pdf.

Transnational infrastructure projects 135

Eurasianet. 2012. 'Azerbaijan & Turkmenistan: Renewing Caspian Sea Energy Dispute.' July 11. Accessed September 12, 2018. https://eurasianet.org/azerbaijan-turkmenistan-renewing-caspian-sea-energy-dispute.

Eurasianet. 2006. 'BTC: Kazakhstan Finally Commits to the Pipeline.' June 19. Accessed September 12, 2018. https://eurasianet.org/btc-kazakhstan-finally-commits-to-the-pipeline.

EXIM. 2004. 'Project and Structured Finance: BTC Pipeline.' Accessed December 12, 2018. https://www.exim.gov/what-we-do/project-structured-finance/transactions.

Export-Important Bank of the United States. 2003. 'Ex-im Bank $160 million Loan Guarantee to support 1,100 oil pipeline in Central Asia.' *Export-import Bank News.* December 9. https://www.exim.gov/news/ex-im-bank-160-million-loan-guarantee-support-1100-mile-oil-pipeline-central-asia.

Financial Times. 2004. 'Intesa in talks over exit from pipeline project.' December 1. Accessed September 1, 2016. https://www.ft.com/content/0759c694-43d5-11d9-af06-00000e2511c8.

Forsgren, Mats. 2008. *Theories of the Multinational Firm.* Cheltenham: Edward Elgar.

Frappi, Carlo, and Marco Valigi. 2015. 'Patterns of Cooperation in the South Caucasus Area.' Working Paper, ISIPI.

German, Tracey. 2012. 'The Nagorno-Karabakh Conflict between Azerbaijan and Armenia: Security Issues in the Caucasus.' *Journal of Muslim Minority Affairs* 32 (2): 216–229.

Guliyev, Farid, and Nozima Akhrarkhodjaeva. 2009. 'The Trans-Caspian Energy Route: Cronyism, Competition and Cooperation in Kazakh Oil Export.' *Energy Policy* 37 (8): 3171–3182.

Haghayeghi, Mehrdad. 2003. 'The Coming of Conflict to the Caspian Sea.' *Problems of Post-Communism* 50 (3): 32–41.

Henderson, James, and Ekaterina Grushevenko. 2017. 'Russian Oil Production Outlook to 2020.' *The Oxford Institute for Energy Studies.* February. Accessed March 2, 2017. https://www.oxfordenergy.org/wpcms/wp-content/uploads/2017/02/Russian-Oil-Production-Outlook-to-2020-OIES-Energy-Insight.pdf.

Hendrix, Cullen. 2015. 'Oil Prices and Interstate Conflict.' *Conflict Management* 17 (3): 87–103.

Hennink, Monique, Inge Hutter, and Ajay Bailey. 2011. *Qualitative Research Methods.* London: SAGE Publications.

Henrich-Franke, Christopher. 2014. 'Functionalistic Spill-over and Infrastructure Integration: The Telecommunication Sectors.' In *Linking Networks: The Formation of Common Standards and Visions for Infrastructure Development*, by Martin Schiefelbusch and Hans-Liudger Dienel, 95–115. London: Routledge.

Imber, Mark. 2002. 'Functionalism.' In *Governing Globalization*, by David Held and Anthony McGrew, 290–305. Cambridge: Polity Press.

International Finance Corporation. 2006. 'The Baku-Tbilisi-Ceyhan Pipeline Project.' World Bank. September. Accessed May 10, 2018. http://documents.worldbank.org/curated/en/174011468016223078/pdf/382160ECA0BTC1LOE0201PUBLIC1.pdf.

Iseri, Emre. 2009. 'The US grant Strategy and the Eurasian Heartlandin the twenty-first Century.' *Geopolitics* 14 (1): 26–46.

Ismailova, Leman. 2016. 'SOCAR reveals volume of oil pumping through BTC.' 13 July. Accessed May 10, 2018. https://www.azernews.az/oil_and_gas/99274.html.

Ismailova, Gulnara. 2004. 'Opponents of Baku-Tbilisi-Ceyhan Project Reactivated.' Accessed September 29, 2018. https://www.cacianalyst.org/publications/field-reports/item/9133-field-reports-caci-analyst-2004-6-30-art-9133.html.

136 *Transnational infrastructure projects*

Ismailzade, Fariz. 2006. *Russia's Energy Interests in Azerbaijan*. London: GMB Publishing Ltd.

Jaffe, Amy Myers, and Robert A. Manning. 1998. 'The myth of the Caspian Great Game: the Real Geopolitics of Energy.' *Global Politics and Strategy* 40 (4): 112–129.

Karasac, Hasene. 2010. 'Actors of the new 'Great Game', Caspian oil politics.' *Journal of Southern Europe and the Balkans* 4 (1): 15–27.

Kalyuzhnova, Yelina. 2008. *Economics of the Caspian Oil and Gas Wealth*. London: Palgrave Macmillan.

Keck, Margaret E, and Kathryn Sikkink. 1998. *Activists Beyond Borders. Advocacy Networks in International Politics*. Ithaca: Cornell University Press.

Kim, Younkyoo, and Stephen Blank. 2016. 'The New Great Game of Caspian energy in 2013–14: 'Turk Stream', Russia and Turkey.' *Journal of Balkan and Near Eastern Studies* 18 (1): 37–55.

Kim, Younkyoo, and Gu-Ho Eom. 2008. 'The Geopolitics of Caspian Oil: Rivalries of the US, Russia, and Turkey in the South Caucasus.' *Global Economic Review* 37 (1): 85–106.

Klare, Michael. 2001. *Resource Wars*. New York: Metropolitan Books.

Kleveman, Lutz. 2003. *The New Great Game: blood and oil in Central Asia*. New York: Grove Press.

Kober, Stanley. 2000. 'The Great Game Round 2.' *Foreign Policy Briefing* 63: 1–11.

Kubicek, Paul. 2013. 'Energy politics and geopolitical competition in the Caspian Basin.' *Journal of Eurasian Studies* 4: 171–180.

Latour, Bruno. 2005. *Reassembling the Social*. Oxford: Oxford University Press.

Lelyveld, Michael. 2001. 'Caspian: Tempers Flare In Iran-Azerbaijan Border Incident.' July 25. Accessed September 21, 2018. https://www.rferl.org/a/1097012.html.

Li-Chen, Sim. 1999. 'In search of security: Azerbaijan and the role of oil.' *the Journal of Communist Studies and Transition Politics* 15 (3): 24–53.

Luecke, Matthias, and Natalia Trofimenko. 2008. 'Redistribution of oil revenue in Azerbaijan.' In *The Economics and Politics of Oil in the Caspian Basin*, by Boris Najman, Richard Pomfret and Gaël Raballand, 132–157. New York: Routledge.

Mammadyarov, Elmar. 2007. 'A new way for the Caspian Region: Cooperation and Integration.' *Turkish Policy Quarterly* 6 (3): 39–46.

Menon, Rajan. 1998. *Treacherous Terrain: The Political and Security Dimensions of Energy Development in the Caspian Sea Zone*. Washington: The National Bureau of Asian Research.

Ministry of Foreign Affairs Azerbaijan. 2018. 'Azerbaijan, Turkmenistan signed bilateral documents.' November 22. Accessed November 23, 2018. http://un.mfa.gov.az/news/4/3231.

Mitrany, David. 1966. *A Working Peace System*. Chicago: Quadrangle Books.

Molchanov, Mikhail. 2011. 'Extractive Technologies and Civic Networks' Fight for Sustainable Development.' *Bulletin of Science, Technology & Society* 31 (1): 55–67.

Morningstar, Richard. 2003. *From Pipe Dream to Pipeline: The Realization of the Baku-Tbilisi-Ceyhan Pipeline*. Harvard: Council on Library Resources.

New York Times. 1997. 'America's Vital Interest in the "New Silk Road".' Accessed September 1, 2017. https://www.nytimes.com/1997/07/21/opinion/america-s-vital-inter est-in-the-new-silk-road.html.

OECD Data. 2018. 'OECD iLibrary Energy.' *Crude Oil Import Prices 2000–2016*. May 26. Accessed May 10, 2018. https://www.oecd-ilibrary.org/energy/crude-oi l-import-prices/indicator/english_9ee0e3ab-en.

O'Neal, John, Frances Oneal, and Zeev Maoz. 1996. 'The Liberal Peace: Interdependence, Democracy, and International Conflict.' *Journal of Peace Research* 33 (1): 11–28.

Offshore Energy Today. 2018. 'OGA: UK oil and gas reserves enough for 20+ years of production.' November 8. Accessed December 10, 2018. https://www.offshoreenergytoday.com/oga-uk-oil-and-gas-reserves-enough-for-20-years-of-production/.

Papava, Vladimer. 2005. 'The Baku-Tbilisi-Ceyhan Pipeline: Implications for Georgia.' In *The Baku-Tbilisi-Ceyhan Pipeline: Oil Window to the West*, by Frederick S Starr and Svante Cornell, 85–103. Uppsala: Central Asia-Caucasus Institute and Silk Road Studies.

Parkhomchik, Lidiya. 2016. 'Kazakhstan Pipeline Policy in the Caspian Sea Region.' In *Oil and Gas Pipelines in Black-Caspian Seas Region*, by Sergey S Zhiltsov, Igor S Zonn and Andrey G Kostianoy, 139–151. Berlin: Springer.

Petersen, Alexandros. 2016. *Integration in Energy and Transport: Azerbaijan, Georgia, and Turkey* (Contemporary Central Asia: Societies, Politics, and Cultures). London: Lexington Books.

Pipeline and Gas Journal. 2006. 'Mountainous Terrain And Weather Challenge Pipeline Pre-Commissioning.' August 26. Accessed January 20, 2017. https://www.ogj.com/articles/2005/10/georgian-section-of-btc-pipeline-opens.html.

Pipes, Richard. 1997. 'Is Russia Still an Enemy?' *Foreign Affairs* 76 (5).

Poussenkova, Nina. 2012. 'They went East, they went West…: the global expansion of Russian oil companies.' In *Russia's Energy Policies*, by Pami Aalto, 185–206. Northampton: Edward Elgar.

Pyrkalo, Svitlana. 2016. *BTC pipeline and cross-border energy projects: working for energy security.* April 28. Accessed May 10, 2018. https://www.ebrd.com/news/2016/btc-pipeline-and-crossborder-energy-projects-working-for-energy-security.html.

Radio Free Europe. 2010. 'Turkmen Oil Starts Flowing Through BTC Pipeline.' August 12. Accessed May 10, 2018. https://www.rferl.org/a/Turkmen_Oil_Starts_Flowing_Through_BTC_Pipeline/2126224.html.

Radio Free Europe. 2006. 'Kazakhstan Joins BTC Pipeline Project.' June 16. Accessed May 10, 2018. https://www.rferl.org/a/1069221.html.

Reuters. 2019. 'Oil output at Kazakhstan's Kashagan hits record of 400,000 bpd – sources.' June 5. Accessed June 6, 2019. https://www.reuters.com/article/kazakhstan-oil-kashagan-output/update-1-oil-output-at-kazakhstans-kashagan-hits-record-of-400000-bpd-sources-idUSL8N23C4WA.

Reuters. 2015. 'Energy & Oil.' Accessed October 25 2016. http://af.reuters.com/article/energyOilNews/idAFL5N0XX30F20150506.

Rosamond, Ben. 2005. 'The Uniting Of Europe And The Foundation Of EU Studies: Revisiting The Neofunctionalism Of Ernst B. Haas.' *Journal of European Public Policy* 12 (2): 237–254.

Rosenau, James. 2002. 'Governance in a New Global Orders.' In *Governing Globalization: Power, Authority and Global Governance*, by David Held and Anthony McGrew. Cambridge: Polity Press.

Ruseckas, Laurent. 1998. *Energy and Politics in Central Asia and the Caucasus*. Seattle: The National Bureau of Asian Research.

Sewell, James Patrick. 1966. *Functionalism and World Politics*. Princeton: Princeton University Press.

Siddi, Marco. 2017. 'The EU's Botched Geopolitical Approach to External Energy Policy: The Case of the Southern Gas Corridor.' *Geopolitics* 24 (1): 124–144.

138 *Transnational infrastructure projects*

Sovacool, Benjamin K. 2010. 'Exploring the Conditions for Cooperative Energy Governance: A Comparative Study of Two Asian Pipelines.' *Asian Studies Review* 34 (4): 489–511.

Sovacool, Benjamin K, and Christopher JCooper. 2013. 'The Baku-Tbilisi-Ceyhan Oil Pipeline.' In *The Governance of Energy Megaprojects*, by Benjamin K Sovacool, 111–136. Chelthenham: Edward Elgar.

Spiegel Online. 2008. 'Fears over Stability of Georgian Pipeline.' August 13. Accessed September 20, 2018. https://www.spiegel.de/international/world/fears-over-stabili ty-of-georgian-pipeline-russia-should-not-have-a-stranglehold-on-resources-a-5718 55.html.

Talbott, Strobe. 1997. 'A Farewell to Flashman: American Policy in the Caucasus and Central Asia.' June 21. Accessed September 12, 2016. https://1997-2001.state.gov/ regions/nis/970721talbott.html.

The Guardian. 2004. 'Cracked joints found in BP's Georgia pipeline.' November 17. Accessed September 1, 2016. https://www.theguardian.com/money/businessnews/ story/0,1265,-1352859,00.html.

The Wall Street Journal. 2019. 'BP, Partners to Invest $6 Billion in Offshore Azerbaijan Project.' April 19. Accessed May 20, 2019. https://www.wsj.com/articles/bp -partners-to-invest-6-billion-in-offshore-azerbaijan-project-11555700733.

Trend News Agency. 2019. 'Azerbaijan reveals projected volumes of Turkmen oil transit via BTC pipeline.' March 23. Accessed March 23, 2019. https://en.trend.az/ business/energy/3036065.html.

Trend News Agency. 2018. 'Iran in talks with int'l oil companies to start co-op with SOCAR (Exclusive).' May 15. Accessed May 18, 2018. https://en.trend.az/iran/ business/2903013.html.

The Moscow Times. 2008. 'Astana, Baku Set Up Oil Shipping Links.' November 17. Accessed June 10, 2018. http://old.themoscowtimes.com/sitemap/free/2008/11/arti cle/astana-baku-set-up-oil-shipping-links/372420.html.

Tsereteli, Mamuka. 2009. *The impact of the Russian-Georgian War on the South Caucasus Transportation Corridor.* Washington: Jamestown.

Valiyev, Anar. 2009. 'Azerbaijan and Turkmenistan's Dispute over the Caspian Sea.' *PONARS Eurasia Policy Memo* 87: 1–4.

World Bank Report. 2002. 'Azerbaijan Country Brief.' Baku Office: *The World Bank Group.* http://web.worldbank.org/archive/website00998/WEB/PDF/AZERBAIJ.PDF.

5 A new round in the Caspian pipeline game
The Southern Gas Corridor

Introduction

This chapter aims to show whether and in what way cooperation on the BTC pipeline has spilled over into the SGC project. With the help of revised functionalism, this chapter unpacks the effects of the SGC on cooperation and exchange in the Caspian Sea. Chapter 3 illustrated that environmental cooperation created conditions for signing the Legal Status Convention.

This chapter is made up of four parts. The first part provides background information about the SGC project, the three phases of the SGC project, and its timeline. The second part outlines the New Great Game views on the SGC project. It shows that the relevant literature portrays the SGC project as the second round of the New Great Game in the Caspian Sea. In doing so, it again only presents Russia, Gazprom, Iran, and the regional conflicts as the main geopolitical and security challenges for the SGC project. The third and main part of the chapter discusses the three identified phases of the SGC project. This part of the chapter illustrates that during the planning phase, the SGC project faced challenges beyond and besides those posed by Russia, Gazprom, and Iran. It shows that there was great uncertainty about the direction of gas pipelines and how this would impact the financial support Western energy companies were willing to provide. More specifically, it shows that there was significant internal competition among the European energy companies and the SGC had to compete with other European pipeline projects rather than Russia or Gazprom's natural gas pipeline. Furthermore, this part of the chapter shows that the relationship between Azerbaijan, the US, and Turkey grew cold during the planning phase of the SGC because of Turkish-Armenian rapprochement. This cold relationship put the direction of the SGC project under question during the planning phase.

Additionally, the third part of this chapter illustrates how an Italian city halted the SGC project rather than Russia, Iran or other geopolitical powers during the construction phase. Chapter 4 explained that transnational infrastructure does not only connect point A to B point but it also engages with social, technical, and environmental challenges. This chapter develops this

DOI: 10.4324/9781003189626-6

140 *A new round in the Caspian pipeline game*

argument by showing why, where, and when social, technical, and environmental challenges led to remarkable political and economic consequences in the SGC project. In doing so, it argues that without the network of multiple actors, companies, NGOs, and IGOs for example, it would have been impossible to overcome these obstacles during the construction phase. Finally, this chapter illustrates that cooperation among the Caspian littoral states is not limited to the CEP and the BTC pipeline. The formation of cooperation habits, which was begun in the CEP and the BTC, continued and grew stronger through the SGC project.

Background of the SCG project

The SCG pipeline also has the more poetic name 'Nabucco'. It was named after the opera that a group of energy executives saw one night while discussing the idea for the pipeline. More specifically"

> …one evening in 2002 in Vienna, a small group of Austrian energy executives took their colleagues from Turkish, Hungarian, Bulgarian, and Romanian firms to see a rarely performed Verdi opera. It recounted the plight of Jews expelled from Mesopotamia by King Nebuchadnezzar. Before the event, the officials spent the day sketching out a plan for a pipeline that could transport natural gas every year across their countries and into European markets. The sources of this gas would not be Russia, but Azerbaijan, maybe Iran one day, and with a US-led war against Saddam Hussein looking increasingly likely, possibly the gas fields of northern Iraq. Following this fascinating music concert, the energy executives continued their discussion at dinner. The opera they attended that night was called Nabucco, and that is the name they gave their new pipeline project during the dinner.
>
> (as cited in Freifeld 2009)

The Nabucco project was designed as a 3,900 km pipeline from Turkey to Austria via Bulgaria and Hungary that would carry up to 31bcm of gas to Europe, with an estimated construction cost of over USD 8 billion (Skalamera 2016).

The main suppliers were expected to be Azerbaijan, Turkmenistan, Iraq, and Iran. The original project was also backed by several EU member states and the US. While the Nabucco project had already been in planning since 2002, it gained strong political momentum in 2009–2010, when – against the background of a March 2009 surge in oil prices and the second Russo–Ukrainian 'gas war' – the EU allocated USD 200 million from its own budget to Nabucco (De Micco 2015). The European Commission also appointed a European Coordinator, Jozias Van Aarsten, to facilitate the project's realization and to promote dialogue among member states and energy companies. However, despite the strong support of the EU, the Nabucco project was abandoned in

A new round in the Caspian pipeline game 141

2013. A number of factors led to the project's failure: a lack of support from main EU companies, EU clients' limited demands for gas, the high price of construction, and competition from rival projects (De Micco 2015). These points will be discussed in detail later in this chapter.

Following the official cancelation of the Nabucco project, the South Caucasus Pipeline (SCP), the Trans-Anatolian-Gas Pipeline (TANAP), and the Trans-Adriatic-Pipeline (TAP) became the new pipelines of the SGC project, which will bridge a distance of 3,500 kilometres from the Caspian Sea into Europe, cover elevation differences of over 2,500 metres, and run over 800 metres below sea level. It will deliver 16bcm gas from Azerbaijan's Shah Deniz 2 field to Europe. The SGC project is a complex challenge involving many different stakeholders – including six governments, eleven energy companies, and more than five private as well as public lenders. In the same vein, during the construction phase 24,000 people work on the project in Azerbaijan and Georgia, more than 6,000 in Turkey and over 2,000 already work on the territory of Greece, Italy and Albania (see British Petroleum 2018).

The SCP (the first leg of the SGC) runs through Azerbaijan to Georgia, which has been in operation since late 2006. It is also known as the Baku-Tbilisi-Erzurum (BTE) pipeline, which runs parallel to the BTC oil pipeline for 429 miles through Azerbaijan and Georgia before ending in Erzurum, Turkey. The TANAP (the second leg of the SGC) runs through Turkey and was completed in 2018 (Report 2018). The TAP (the third leg of the SGC) runs through Greece, Albania, and Italy but is still under construction and expected to be completed in 2020. According to British Petroleum (2016), the project is intended to deliver 16bcm of Shah Deniz natural gas, of which 6bcm will be delivered to Turkey and 10 bcm will be transported to the European energy market. Besides this, several scholars argue that the SGC pipeline capacity could be scaled up to more than 50bcm if Turkmenistan joins the project (Grigas 2017; Rzayeva 2015).

Because the SCP and the TANAP have been constructed and the TAP has been 85 percent completed (Trend 2018b), the EU seeks to attract Kazakhstan and Turkmenistan to the SGC project. Therefore, future plans include a potential fourth leg to the project – a Trans-Caspian Pipeline (TCP) to bring additional gas from Turkmenistan and Kazakhstan to Azerbaijan and satiate the SGC project with additional resources. For example, after the Fourth Ministerial Meeting of the SGC Advisory Council, in Baku in February 2018, it was suggested that Turkmenistan was ready to actively engage with the project and Maros Sefcovic, the European Commission vice president of energy, confirmed that discussions were continuing with the Turkmen government (Pirani 2018, 2).

The New Great Game: the second round

This section introduces the claims of the New Great Game literature specific to the SGC project in order to make the discussion more concrete. To do so,

142 *A new round in the Caspian pipeline game*

it shows whether and how the New Great Game literature mentions and explains the SGC project.

During the planning phase of the SGC, the relevant literature argued that the New Great Game has entered a second round in the Caspian Sea, which is again a competition between two blocks: Russia, China and Iran contra the EU, Turkey, the US and Azerbaijan (Kamrava 2016; Kim and Blank 2016; Kusznir 2013; Siddi 2017; Stegen and Kusznir 2015). A notable development in this second round is that besides Russia and Iran, China has become one of the key players in the Caspian Sea region with the opening of an oil pipeline from Kazakhstan and a gas pipeline from Turkmenistan (Kiernan 2012). In light of this, the relevant scholarship argues that the main aim of the second round of the New Great Game is controlling the transnational natural gas pipelines of the Caspian Sea region (Kamrava 2016; Kusznir 2013).

During the planning phase of the SGC project, the relevant literature argued that two gas pipelines, namely the South Stream from Russia and the SGC from the Caspian Sea, would compete with each other for the European energy market (Kiernan 2012; Kim and Blank 2016). Kim and Blank (2016) argue that the South Stream aims to isolate Ukraine from Europe and increase Central and Southeast European gas dependency. This would help strengthen Russia's political position in the Balkans. In this regard, the SGC project is construed as the rival to Russian gas as it provides an alternative to the South Stream pipeline (Kim and Blank 2016, 40; Kusznir 2013). In the same vein, Kiernan (2012, 35) argues that the South Stream pipeline's main purpose is to decrease the SGC's economic and political impact on Europe. According to Kusznir, the EU's (energy) interests conflict with those of Russia and China. In this regard, 'the future of the SGC project will depend on the EU's ability to deal with Russia and China in the region' (Kusznir 2013, 5). Similar to the EU, China seeks to diversify its sources of imported natural gas supplies. In doing so, China seeks to persuade Azerbaijan, Kazakhstan and Turkmenistan to export their gas resources to the Chinese market (Kubicek 2013; Stegen and Kusznir 2015). Yenikeyeff (2011, 61) argues that 'Russia prefers the active involvement of China, rather than that of the EU and the US, because Russia views China as a partner against EU-US bloc.'

However, the South Stream did not receive enough support from the EU because it did not meet the EU diversification of supply strategy. In response to this, Russia decided to change the pipeline direction to Turkey, and called it the Turkish Stream. It is argued that Russia did this in order to increase Turkey's natural gas dependency and minimize the SGC's influence (Kim and Blank 2016; Siddi 2017). According to Kim and Blank 'Moscow could exploit that reliance to place enormous pressure on Turkey to downgrade the TANAP-TAP line and to block the SGC's intentions to connect Caspian-area gas producers directly to European markets' (Kim and Blank 2016, 37–38). In the same vein, Kusznir (2013, 5) claims that 'when the transport of

A new round in the Caspian pipeline game 143

Shah-Deniz gas via TANAP will start, Moscow will end its support to Turkey in tackling the country's growing gas demand, potentially leading to gas shortage.' During the planning phase of the SGC, the relevant literature argued that the failure to realize the SGC would marginalize Azerbaijan, restrict its access to key European customers, frustrate its ability to move toward Europe and entail the decrease of its sovereignty, which would also be a serious defeat for the EU.

Similar to the BTC pipeline, the SGC project has faced a number of economic, environmental and technical challenges during the construction phase. For example, the inhabitants of the Puglia region in Italy protested against the last phase of the SGC because the SGC might damage the region's environment and tourism (La Republicca 2013). A number of environmental NGOs sent an open letter to the EIB to halt the financing for the SGC project (Bankwatch Network 2017). Considering this, the relevant literature again depicted Russia as the main cause of the environmental protests because of Russia's strong presence in Italian energy market. Gurbanov (2017a) argued that Russia is behind these environmental protests, as it wants to stop the SGC. According to Gurbanov (2017a), 'the gambit was part of a long-running coordinated campaign, involving various NGOs and European political parties, to put pressure on the EU to slow down the implementation of the SGC and undermine its ability to attract funding from international financial institutions.' As a result, the relevant literature claimed that Russia finances and encourages the local government and population against the SGC pipeline during the construction phase.

Like the BTC pipeline, the New Great Game literature describes the Nagorno-Karabakh and the South Ossetia conflicts as one of the main security threats to the SGC project in the region (Kucera 2012; Siddi 2017). More specifically, it is argued that it is an insecure gas transport route as Russia can support its military ally Armenia in the South Caucasus to sabotage the SGC project. According to Siddi:

> Russia has considerable influence in the Nagorno-Karabakh conflict as Armenia's military ally and arms supplier to both Armenia and Azerbaijan. Russia's sales of modern military equipment to both sides contribute to volatility in the region. Thus, the security situation in the area casts serious doubts on the appropriateness and reliability of projects such as the SGC.
>
> (Siddi 2017, 7)

As mentioned above, the SGC project is almost ready because the SCP and the TANAP pipelines have been constructed and the TAP is 85 percent complete. The EU seeks to expand the SGC project and the TCP pipeline, which would stretch between Turkmenbashi (Turkmenistan) and Baku (Azerbaijan) and may also include a connection between the Tengiz field in Kazakhstan and Turkmenbashi, might therefore become the fourth leg of

144 *A new round in the Caspian pipeline game*

the SGC project. Since the SGC project has almost been completed, the New Great Game literature argues that Iran and Russia will not allow the expansion of the SGC project through the construction of the TCP. The TCP project is still at the planning stage and like other pipeline projects, there are still a number of financial, political and technical uncertainties that have to be dealt with. By using the familiar lines of argumentation, the New Great Game literature, first, argued that Russia and Iran intentionally postponed the Legal Status Convention to prevent the TCP project (Kusznir 2013; Siddi 2017; Stegen and Kusznir 2015; Verda 2016). For example, Nuriyev (2015) argues that Iran and Russia used the existing environmental concerns to block or hinder crude oil shipping and the construction of pipelines between Azerbaijan, Kazakhstan and Turkmenistan. In the same vein, Siddi argued that for 'the import of Turkmen gas, an offshore pipeline crossing the Caspian Sea would have to be built, an endeavour that is complicated by the uncertain legal status of the sea and the opposition of Russia and Iran (both are riparian states and can veto the legal process)' (Siddi 2017, 132).

As mentioned in chapter 3, the Legal Status Convention was signed in August 2018. Ironically, following the signing of this legal agreement, the relevant literature claimed that the Legal Status Convention includes environmental articles (e.g., 1, 11, 14, 15) which Russia and Iran could use to block the TCP project (Anceschi 2019; Garibov 2018; Gurbanov 2018; Ismayilov 2019). According to the Anceschi (2019), the Legal Status Convention provides Russia and Iran with extensive environmental monitoring powers, which they use to influence the construction of any transport infrastructure side lining Russia or Iran.

As it did in the discussion about the BTC pipeline, the scholarship comes from a fixed mindset revolving around power, rivalry, and insecurity to explain all developments in the planning, construction, and post-construction phases of the SGC project. In doing so, it fails to view the political and economic changes since the BTC pipeline, and it assumes that everything in the Caspian Sea region is also fixed. It can be seen that the relevant literature does not recognize the difference between different infrastructure projects, namely the BTC pipeline, the SGC project, and the TCP. It also does not see the difference between uncertain legal status of the Caspian Sea and the signing of the Legal Status Convention since Russia and Iran are portrayed as the only ones to benefit from both situations. This is because the literature does not take note of the CEP and the Tehran Convention (see chapter 3). It therefore does not discuss the four ecological protocols of the Tehran Convention, of which three protocols had been discussed and signed by the littoral states by 2018. The fourth ecological protocol, called the EIA, was signed in July 2018. Since the relevant literature is not aware of the Tehran Convention and its four protocols, it assumes that the EIA was included by Russia and Iran to block the future pipeline projects in the Caspian Sea. Due to this ignorance, the New Great Game literature fails to explain or even see the complex interconnection between the ecological articles, the Legal Status Convention, and the infrastructural projects, and it therefore offers an incorrect explanation.

Discussion: the planning, construction and post-construction phases

If one reads only the New Great Game literature, one will assume that the SGC project competes only with the Russian gas pipeline projects, namely the South Stream, for the European gas market. To dismantle the narrow explanation of the New Great Game literature, this section analyses the three phases of the SGC project through revised functionalism. More specifically, this section illustrates that the SGC project has faced challenges beyond and besides Russia, Iran, and China during the three phases.

Planning the SGC project

The following sections illustrate that during the planning phase the SGC project faced three main uncertainties which negatively influenced the feasibility of the project. First, unlike the BTC pipeline, the SGC project lacked the support of the US because the US increased its political and economic interests in other energy projects, such as the pipeline from Turkmenistan to Afghanistan. The second issue is that there was a cold relationship between Azerbaijan and Turkey during the planning phase due to the Turkish-Armenian rapprochement, which pushed Azerbaijan towards Russia. The third issue is that the SGC faced strong competition from other European pipeline projects, and because of this it was lacking in European support during the planning phase as well. These points are important because as explained in other chapters, any infrastructure project needs to have resourceful external actors in order to strengthen its feasibility in the planning phase. The main argument of this section is, as was the case with the BTC pipeline, the New Great Game literature exaggerates the role of Russia and Gazprom and misses the actual nature of the challenges faces in the planning phase. The following sections show that the SGC project was challenged by states that were supporters of the BTC, such as the US and Turkey, energy companies, and internal European pipelines rather than just by Russia during the planning phase. The following sections also show that the New Great Game literature does not only miss new changes and developments, but it also fails to see changes that are important for geopolitics.

Decline of US interests in the Caspian Sea

Similar to the BTC pipeline, the SGC struggled with a number of uncertainties. One of them was the US government's and energy companies' support for other regional energy projects. As explained in chapter 3, both the US government and its energy companies played a key role in development of

146 *A new round in the Caspian pipeline game*

the BTC oil pipeline, but its energy companies (e.g., Chevron and Exxon) are not actively engaged with the SGC. While reviewing the SGC shareholders, it can be seen that the US companies are not part of this project (see SGC Partners below). Instead Russian and Iranian energy companies (NIOC and Lukoil) are major stakeholders in the project at 10 percent each. It is a remarkable difference, because these companies were not part of the BTC pipeline. Unlike the New Great Game literature, this also means that Russia and Iran are (in)directly part of the SGC project. However, during the planning phase, the involvement of NIOC and Lukoil created uncertainty because of the economic sanctions imposed on Iran and Russia by the US (Gutterman and Grojec 2018; Paraskova 2018). The other project shareholders feared that the SGC could also be target of the US economic sanctions.

Additionally, during the planning phase, it was argued that the administration of President Barack Obama was not as forthright in promoting a direct gas link to Europe as the previous Democratic administration of Bill Clinton, which promoted the BTC oil pipeline in the 1990s (Kiernan 2012; Shiriyev and Davies 2013). Instead, the Obama administration showed active support for the Turkmenistan-Afghanistan-Pakistan-Indian (TAPI) pipeline. In January 2013, for example, the US assistant secretary for South and Central Asian affairs stated that 'the TAPI project is one of the most important regional integration projects, because it will provide Turkmen gas for the growing Indian market, but it will also provide very substantial transit revenue for Afghanistan and Pakistan' (Kiernan 2012, 37). The US promotion of the TAPI pipeline is not intended to exclude American support for the SGC, but ensuring Afghanistan's stability following the withdrawal of NATO troops in 2014 was the highest priority for the Obama administration.

Finally, the Turkish-Armenian rapprochement between 2009 and 2011 had caused a cold relationship between Azerbaijan and the US. In light of this, Washington did not appoint a US ambassador to Azerbaijan until late 2010 (Shiriyev and Davies 2013). Washington's behaviour during this period irritated some Azerbaijani officials (Eurasianet 2010). The rapprochement is discussed in detail in the following section. Later, the Obama administration nominated Matthew Bryza as the next US ambassador to Azerbaijan. However, the US Senate did not support Bryza's appointment because the Armenian-American lobby had successfully opposed his appointment and several senators accused Bryza of having a pro-Azerbaijani bias (Radio Free Europe 2011). In response to this, the Obama administration bypassed the usual Senate confirmation processes and sent Bryza to Azerbaijan on an interim basis (Radio Free Europe 2010). However, Bryza did not receive sufficient support from the Senate, and he was replaced by Richard Morningstar, who served as the State Department's special envoy for Eurasian energy. Only after that did the SGC project start to receive strong support from the US, as Morningstar frequently iterated the US's support for the

A new round in the Caspian pipeline game 147

regional energy projects. Considering this, it can be argued that unlike the BTC pipeline, the SGC project did not received strong support from the US until late in its planning phase.

Turkish-Azerbaijani energy ties

Similar to the BTC pipeline, TANAP is an important part of the SGC project as it connects Azerbaijan to Europe through Turkey. The New Great Game literature takes Turkey's support for granted. However, this section shows that Azerbaijan and Turkey had a cold relationship between 2009 and 2010 because of Turkish foreign policy towards Armenia. Due to the cold relationship between Ankara and Baku, the SGC transit negotiations between the two countries took two years and Azerbaijan even considered a route through Russia as an alternative transit route.

The relationship between Turkey and Azerbaijan grew cold due to the possibility of normalized relationships between Turkey and Armenia becoming ever more likely in 2009. According to Shiriyev and Davies (2013), the US was pressing Turkey to normalize relations with Armenia without emphasizing the Nagorno-Karabakh dispute. This approach alarmed Baku in 2008. There were reports in the Azerbaijani press that Azeri President Ilham Aliyev had considered suspending gas deliveries to Turkey in response to the normalization process (Azernews, 2009). Also, President Aliyev boycotted the summit meeting of the Unsponsored Alliance of Civilisations Initiative which assembled in Istanbul in April 2009. Shortly after the summit, Aliyev publicly condemned the rapprochement initiative, calling it 'a mistake' (Shiriyev and Davies 2013, 191).

Baku started to use its energy card in order to discourage Turkish-Armenian rapprochement. For example, at official meetings and conferences across the EU, Azerbaijani officials suggested that Azerbaijan might consider shifting the direction of its energy cooperation towards Russia, which would decrease Turkey's energy hub policy (Whitmore 2009). In the same vein, on October 14, 2009, the SOCAR signed an agreement to sell 500 million cubic meters of gas to Russia's Gazprom starting in 2010, at a price of USD 350 per 1000 cm (Gazprom 2009). In the same vein, Russia proposed to increase the amount of gas purchases in the future. This meant Azerbaijan sent the message that Turkey should include Azerbaijan's demands in its negotiations with Armenia, because otherwise Azerbaijan would consider transiting its natural resources through Russia, which would decrease Turkey's transit role in European energy security. The deal also led to uncertainty over Azerbaijan's desire to transit its natural gas through the SGC project. During the crisis in Turkish-Azerbaijani relations, Ankara feared that by signing energy contracts with Russia's Gazprom, Baku was distancing itself from Turkey, which could damage Turkey's ambitions to become a regional energy hub. This also means that the cold relations created an opportunity for Russia to influence Azerbaijan's gas transition. There has been speculation that the problems in

148   *A new round in the Caspian pipeline game*

relations between Ankara and Baku could result in Azerbaijan accepting Russia's offer to purchase all the gas that will be produced in the second phase of the Shah Deniz project (Eurasianet 2010).

However, the rapprochement between Armenia and Turkey was halted and following this, strategic relations between Turkey and Azerbaijan have intensified, particularly in the energy sector. This was followed by the starting the cooperation on the TANAP gas pipeline in 2012. Considering this, one may argue that the cold relationship between Baku and Ankara could have blocked the SGC project, which would have forced Baku to choose the alternative Russian route to export its oil. Unlike the New Great Game arguments, it was not Russia but the US who pushed the rapprochement process and created the cold relationship between Baku and Ankara. Seen through the lens of revised functionalism, these developments illustrate that the regional dynamics are not fixed or constant, but tend to change. The changing dynamics and complex interconnection between different developments should be explained in order to understand the full picture in the Caspian Sea region. This section has also illustrated that the New Great Game picture is again wrong because the relevant literature misses crucial developments that are important for its geopolitical arguments.

Internal competition: Nabucco/Nabucco West versus TAP

This section outlines the constructive competition between different European pipelines and energy companies. More specifically, it shows that the SGC project had to compete with different energy pipelines and energy companies besides the Russian South Stream and Gazprom during the planning phase. In contrast to the New Great Game literature, this section argues that the main barrier for the SGC project was its competition with other European projects rather than the South Stream pipeline. This section illustrates that the meaning, value, and importance of the SGC project had to change during the planning phase. It is necessary to view and explain these changes, because they influenced how actors like Russia and Gazprom perceive the SGC, which accordingly influenced how they behaved in the construction phase.

As explained above, the SGC consists of three pipeline networks. The third pipeline is called the TAP, which connects Turkey to Greece and Italy. While discussing the TAP, the New Great Game literature describes the EU as the main supporter of the project. In other words, it takes the EU support of this pipeline for granted. In doing so, the literature illustrates the Russian South Stream project as the TAP's only competitor. However, the relevant literature neglects that the TAP project faced resistance within the EU because it had its own pipeline preferences, such as the Nabucco, Nabucco West, and Interconnector Turkey-Greece-Italy (ITGI) projects. Therefore, the EU was not always supporting the TAP project and to gain its support the TAP and the consortia behind it had to compete with other internal projects and energy companies (European Commission, March 4, 2010). Figure 5.1 illustrates the three rounds of internal competition between the projects.

Initially the Nabucco and ITGI projects were officially recognized as a project of European interest by the EU and represented the EC's tactical option to deliver Caspian supplies to Europe through Greece and Italy (European Commission 2010). By contrast, the TAP project was supported neither by an institutional ceremony, nor by a special endorsement of President Barroso (Meister and Vietor 2011). Despite the general support for all projects, the European Commission attached political priority to the Nabucco pipeline (Grewlich 2011). The reason is that the Nabucco project was intended to bring 31 bcm of gas from the Caspian Sea to Europe. It was expected that the TAP project, which was not yet supported by Italy and Greece, would be very difficult to realize as it could not compete with that amount (Reuters 2012b).

The first round of competition was between the TAP and the ITIGI shareholders. The ITIGI shareholders were Edison (Italy) and DEPA/DESFA (Greece). The initial shareholders of the TAP were Statoil (Norway), EGL (Switzerland), and E.ON (Germany). According to Prontera (2017), the ITIGI project was quite feeble compared to the TAP because both pipelines would follow similar routes, but Greece was struggling with economic crisis. Due to this economic crisis, Greece decided to privatize its energy company DEPA, but it failed to find investors because of company's financial position. This put Greece and DEPA's economic power under question, which increased TAP's feasibility as it has more shareholders with strong economic power. As a result, in 2012, the Shah-Deniz consortium dropped the ITGI project (Azernews 2012). While the reason for this decision remains unknown, Greece's economic vulnerability is consistently proposed as one of the reasons for choosing the TAP project.

After the ITGI project had been dropped, the TAP company lobbied intensively to gain support from Italy and Greece because they had been supporting the ITGI (Prontera 2017, 2015). After their initial hesitation,

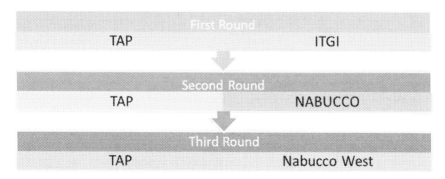

Figure 5.1 Three rounds of internal competition between different natural gas projects.
Source: Author's own compilation

150 *A new round in the Caspian pipeline game*

both Rome and Athens demonstrated their political and diplomatic support for the TAP because of its similarity to the ITGI project (*Hurriyet Daily News* 2012). Additionally, the TAP would create significant economic benefits Greece and Italian energy and construction companies. Considering the economic situation in these countries, it can be argued that it increased the attractiveness of the TAP's position. Because of this, both Rome and Athens took action to facilitate its realization in different ways. Italy and Greece (and Albania) signed agreements to support the project and granted the TAP a 25-year exemption from Third Party Access for its complete initial capacity of 10 bcm (a decision confirmed by the European Commission), for example. They also (especially Italy) worked to create a wider inter-state coalition to increase EU support for this pipeline (De Micco 2015). Both governments strengthened their bilateral diplomatic engagement with Azerbaijan to facilitate its completion (Prontera 2017). Following this, two competitor projects remained in the game, namely Nabucco and the TAP.

The second round of competition was between the TAP and the Nabucco project. However, in this round the TAP's position was more difficult as the European Commission, besides supporting it politically and diplomatically, funded the Nabucco consortium with a grant covering 50 percent of the cost of its feasibility study and decided to grant the project a 25-year-long 50 percent exemption from Third Party Access requirements (Baev and Øverland 2010). However, in 2012 the original Nabucco project (31 bcm) downscaled to Nabucco West (16bcm) (European Commission 2012). There were multiple reasons for this, the first being that Azerbaijan and Turkey announced the construction of the TANAP which overlapped with the Nabucco's eastern section in Turkey. The TANAP was intended to serve fewer countries than the original Nabucco project, as its capacity was only16 bcm, but it was expected to be less expensive than the EU project (Reuters 2012a). Second, the Nabucco pipeline could not find sufficient gas to feed the pipeline other than Azerbaijani gas (Skalamera 2016). Due to this, the major European companies (e.g., EDF, GDF-Suez, Eni, E.ON, and RWE) would not commit to the project (Wiesmann 2012). As a result, it had to be revamped as Nabucco West.

However, the EC supported Nabucco West project diplomatically and politically as well (European Commission 2012). Nabucco West was intended to compete for the Azerbaijani Shah-Deniz 2 gas field; it would run from the Greek-Turkish border to Austria through Bulgaria, Romania, and Hungary. However, in 2012 one of the shareholders (Germany's RWE company) of the Nabucco West project dropped its support, which negatively influenced the project (Wiesmann 2012). Following this, the Nabucco West project also broke down due to its commercial disadvantages, technical infeasibility, and complex and untimely decision–making procedures. It was argued that Nabucco West was more expensive than the TAP (Skalamera 2016). Finally, on June 28, 2013 the TAP project was selected over the Nabucco West by the Shah-Deniz consortium (European Commission 2013).

A new round in the Caspian pipeline game   151

It can be argued that the planning phase of the SGC project has been more complex and more difficult than the purely geopolitical description makes it out have been. More specifically, if one zooms out, one can only see Russia as the main obstacle for cooperation. But if one zooms in, one sees that the SGC project has faced three rounds of competition between different energy pipelines, states, and energy companies besides and beyond Russia and Gazprom. In contrast to the New Great Game arguments, the value, meaning, and importance of the SGC was not fixed but changed at each round of competition. Accordingly, this change influence how the EU, Russia, and the assorted energy companies perceived the SGC project. In this regard, it is necessary to consider state, corporate, and material competitions while discussing the planning stage of the SGC.

Constructing the SGC project

The following section analyzes the construction phase of the SGC project, particularly the TAP, its third leg. The reason for choosing the TAP pipeline is that the SCP, the first leg of the SGC, is already operational and the TANAP, the second leg of the SGC, did not face severe protests within Turkey because of the authoritarianism of the Turkish regime. However, among the SGC pipelines, the TAP has faced a wealth of resistance from Albanian, Greek, and Italian cities. More specifically, throughout the construction phase, the TAP faced several intertwined technical, environmental, social, and economic challenges. By not discussing these challenges, the New Great Game literature falls into the common trap of geopolitical studies and assumes that Russia, Gazprom, have to be behind them. However, this section illustrates that the relevant literature paints a reductive picture again because it does not explain why, where, and when social, technical, and environmental challenges acquire unexpected political and economic consequences. The relevant literature does not see how and why these challenges lead functional cooperation between multiple actors (state, non-state and semi-state). This section explores these challenges, their causes, and their actual influence on the development of the TAP project during the construction phase.

Technical challenges

The first technical challenge was the incomplete geographical facilities the project had to work with. In order to construct and transport the pipelines and technical equipment, the TAP companies needed to repair or even build roads, facilities and bridges. For example, in Albania an access bridge was refurbished, in service of the TAP project, using a structural strengthening method that allowed keeping the bridge open for road traffic (TAP 2017a). The bridge, 92m long and 7m wide, is located in Mbrostar, at the entrance to the town of Fier, and serves as the main access point along the route from Durrës to the south of Albania. The location and the volume of daily traffic did not allow the bridge to

152 *A new round in the Caspian pipeline game*

be closed for a complete replacement of the deck, so another non-intrusive technique was needed. At the end of 2016, TAP completed the upgrade of approximately 58km of access roads, the construction of two new bridges, and refurbishment of 40 bridges in Albania (TAP 2017b).

The second technical challenge was the unexpected discovery of historical settlements. While clearing the pipeline route for the Albanian section, construction workers brought to light an ancient settlement, which had been inhabited for an extensive period of time from the early Iron Age to the 10th century, in Korça, south-eastern Albania (Tirana Times 2017). Due to this discovery, construction was suspended for over a month (Azernews 2017).

The third challenge was the transportation of olive trees in Italy. The TAP's route passes through ancient olive groves and over pristine beaches in the Italian region of Puglia, which relies on these idyllic landscapes for its major industry, tourism. That caused a standoff between global energy interests and local business interests. The most contentious issue was that of a grove of 1,900 olive trees (Kucera and Shiriyev 2017). However, transplanting the trees – some of which are more than 1,000 years old – was a delicate operation as they had to be transported during certain months, and the construction had to wait until the right time. However, this process cost extra effort, money, and time because both local authority and the inhabitants of the Puglia region objected to the process. In addition to moving the olive trees, the project had to meet a checklist of more than 30 other conditions, which led to fresh delays (Natural Gas World 2017). These included measures to preserve the natural environment and wildlife habitats – on land and at sea. The TAP developers began moving the first of roughly 10,000 trees in 2018, but local opposition to moving them slowed the process, as a result it cost an extra few months, shortening the construction timetable and jeopardizing the TAP developer's goal to deliver gas into Italy in 2020 (Reuters 2017b). Although the TAP developers secured government clearance for the pipeline, Renzi's government attached 66 demands – some of which could only be fulfilled with the cooperation of local authorities (Reuters 2016). Due to these circumstances, the EIB has announced that its financial support depends on environmental and social conditions. More specifically, if any TAP company wants to receive financial support, it needs to help settle the local issues in Italy first (European Investment Bank 2018).

Social and environmental challenges

The SGC project has faced several social and environmental obstacles since the first day of the construction phase, just like the BTC pipeline, such as active protests by a number of NGOs and environmental grassroots movements. Environmental and human rights NGOs, as well as representatives of local population, have sent letters to the World Bank, the European Parliament, the EBRD, the IFC, and BP to stop the SGC (Counter-Balance 2016). While the three pipelines have faced several challenges the TAP, the final leg of the pipeline running into Europe, represents the biggest chance protesters have of disrupting the project as the TAP has faced opposition movements in Greece, Albania, and Italy.

The TAP project has previously been contested in the Puglia region in Italy. The Puglia Regional Committee on the Environmental Impact Assessment rejected the TAP proposal in 2012, questioning the environmental compatibility of the project in relation to its intended landing place on the Puglia mainland (Prontera 2017). After the selection of the TAP route by the Shah-Deniz 2 consortium, a new proposal from TAP identified a point of arrival on the mainland near San Foca, in the municipality of Melendugno (near Lecce), but local protests, as well as opposition from the Puglia region, increased (La Republicca 2013). Following this, the Puglia Regional Committee on the Environmental Impact Assessment rejected the TAP proposal again in January 2014 (Colluto 2014). This second negative judgement from the regional committee, along with the opposition of local communities, severely complicated the TAP's attempts to realize the plans. The TAP company started a campaign at the local level to 'win friends' by offering sponsorship to local events in the communities affected by the pipeline's route. However, this promotional campaign did not appease local protests (Papadimitriou 2014). On the contrary, it prompted stronger debate at the local and the national levels. This debate did not lessen, although the Italian Ministry of the Environment voiced positive opinions regarding the realization of the TAP at the end of August 2014 (Prontera 2017).

TAP's website has pointed out the so-called benefits that 'the pipeline is environmentally friendly and compatible with the area and will have no impact on tourism' (TAP 2017a). Some believe the investment will breathe new life into the area, others fear it will threaten the region's tourism in Melendugno. Local concern is that the pipeline will make landfall at the popular Puglia beach of San Foca famous for its sparkling blue waters (Squires 2017). This is an area where young people especially are highly dependent on tourism for their daily sustenance. Therefore, if any kind of accident were to happen the region might lose its touristic attraction.

Throughout these protests, the Five Star Movement, Bankwatch Network, local Italian environmental groups, and even local Italian governors have been constantly opposing the TAP. For example, one of the opposition leaders, Beppo Grillo, said 'if they come to build a pipeline in any part of Puglia, even if they bring their army, we will line up our army' (Reuters 2014). These groups constantly organized protests in order to stop the construction of the TAP project. During one of the business events, a dozen mayors, who feared that the pipeline would destroy the environment and the safety of their communities, staged a protest against the government's support for the project. They were demanding that, instead of supporting it, the Italian government and the EU should drop the project (Counter-Balance 2015). In the same vein, Puglia governor Michele Emiliano had been lobbying Rome to shift the pipeline's landing point. He publicly denounced the

154 *A new round in the Caspian pipeline game*

removal of the first 211 olive trees (out of the 1,900 to be moved in total) in a post on Facebook and called moving the trees illegal, and this statement rapidly spread in the news (Bankwatch Network 2017). Eventually, the Lazio Regional Administrative Court (TAR) suspended a permit from the Ministry for the Environment for the removal of the olive trees on the TAP gas pipeline site in Melendugno, Puglia, because of these systematic protests (The Italian Insider 2017).

Because of these protests, the TAP shareholders and the EU were concerned about the prospect of delays. According to EU official Elena Gerebizza; 'time is running out and the landing point in Italy is still an issue. The project is not moving ahead, the resistance is well-grounded in expert analysis, technical issues have not been solved, and political consensus is lacking' (as cited in Kucera and Shiriyev 2017). In the same vein, SOCAR's vice president, Vitaly Baylarbayov, voiced his concern that local Italian opposition:

> creates a risk for the realization of the project (Bankwatch Network, April 13, 2017). Another Azerbaijani official mentioned 'it is all about (local) politics. One would hardly believe that a few hundred olive trees could outweigh the huge benefits the country could get'.
>
> (as cited in Kucera and Shiriyev 2017)

Several officials and academics are arguing, without proof, as they did in the case of the BTC pipeline, that Russia is behind these environmental protests, because it wants to stop the TAP from being realized (Gurbanov 2017b). The protests even attracted the attention of Anders Fogh Rasmussen, secretary-general of the North Atlantic Treaty Organisation (NATO), and former prime minister of Denmark, who argued that:

> Russia, as part of their sophisticated information and disinformation operations, engaged actively with so-called non-governmental organisations – environmental organisations working against shale gas – to maintain European dependence on imported Russian gas.
>
> (*The Guardian* 2014)

However, Rasmussen acknowledged that he had no proof and mentioned that 'it is my interpretation' (*The Guardian* 2014). Using unfounded statements such as this, the existing literature proposed Russia as the main cause. It was suggested that Russia finances and encourages the local government and population against the TAP.

However, to depict Russia as the sole reason behind the controversy over the pipeline's construction in Italy is too reductive as it is not a single dispute, but rather a collection of local and global disputes that led to unanticipated consequences. These disputes include internal political struggle in Italy, difference in economic development between Italian regions, international opposition to the activities of transnational energy companies, and global protests for preserving the environment (Barry and Gambino 2019). These global and local systematically intertwined issues have blocked the short route the TAP could have taken in Italy. For example, an expert from BP said:

> I am sceptical about the involvement of Russia in this issue because in Italy local and main government bodies do not like each other, therefore it is an internal issue. This makes it difficult to get a permit for construction.
>
> (Interview, October 26, 2017)

During an informal meeting an expert from TANAP pipeline shared his very similar view that:

> ...it is a local politics that caused the delay, because political parties want to play every card they can to get support from local people. Additionally, the government structure of Italy is very different that of Turkey, Georgia and Azerbaijan because municipalities or provinces have more decision-making power.
>
> (Interview, June 18, 2019)

Although the Five Star Movement party won the election and came to power in 2018, it did not halt the TAP. More specifically, Luigi Di Maio, the Italian Deputy Prime Minister and member of the Five Star Movement, mentioned that he gave the green light for the TAP in 2018 (Euractiv 2018).

Additionally, it can be seen that Russian energy companies promoted and supported the SGC project. For example, Lukoil is part of the SGC, which owns a 10 percent stake of the Shah-Deniz field, and received USD 1 billon credit from international finance institutions for this project (Lukoil Press Release 2015). This also means that the Russian company, and indirectly Russia, owns 10 percent of a gas project that was devised by Europe as an alternative to Russian gas. Moreover, Gazprom has publicly announced its interest in transporting its gas through the future expansion of the TAP (Reuters 2017a). Additionally, despite close relations between Rome and Moscow, Rome had already condemned Russia's annexation of Crimea and agreed to several rounds of EU sanctions targeting Moscow (Bloomberg 2014). These examples illustrate that to depict Russia as the sole reason for these local protests in Italy is too reductive as there are issues beyond and beside those clearly caused by Russia in Italy.

Economic challenges

Similar to that of the BTC pipeline, the estimated cost of the SGC project has changed over time due to the technical, social, and environmental

156 *A new round in the Caspian pipeline game*

challenges that had to be overcome. Initially, it was estimated that the project would cost approximately USD 35 billion and this estimate was later increased to USD 45 billion (Farchy 2015). However, the cost estimation was decreased again to USD 41.5 billion (Azernews 2017b). Azerbaijan's share in the USD 40 billion SGC project is around USD 11.5 billion, half of which will have been borrowed from international financial institutions and commercial banks (Azernews 2017b). However, due to low oil prices, the Azerbaijan economy has faced severe economic devaluations which have diminished the financial support for the country's part in the realization of the SGC (Deloitte 2018). Amidst volatile oil prices, securing financing was of primary importance for the timely implementation of this strategic energy transit corridor. Speaking in autumn of 2016, the deputy vice president of Azerbaijan's State Oil Company (SOCAR), Vitaly Baylarbayov, argued that the changing market situation, marked by volatile oil prices, had made strategic planning more difficult and impacted negatively on SOCAR's investment portfolio (Euractiv 2016).

While Azerbaijan managed to raise USD1.05 billion in eurobonds on the international financial markets to fund the SGC's segments, additional external financing was still needed to cover the remaining funding (*Financial Times* 2016). Azerbaijan's former minister of energy Natig Aliyev confirmed that 'the timely realization of the project depends on financial support' (Gurbanov 2016). According to Afgan Isayev, the director general of the SGC Closed Joint Stock Company (SGC-CJSC), the total cost of the SGC's realization for Azerbaijan amounted to some USD11.5 billion. The company had already fulfilled half of its financial commitments by raising around USD 6 billion of the required sum for its shares (Azernews, 2016).

Overall, the social, technical, and environmental challenges have led to significant delays, political attention, and extra financial costs as they did in the realization of the BTC project. Initially, the TAP was expected to be finished in January 2019, but the project was finally completed in December 2020. One may argue that every project involved extra costs and delays, and the cost inflation and delays in this project should therefore not be exaggerated. With this in mind, there are three distinguishing points that need to be highlighted. First, one of the supporters of the SGC project, Italy, halted the last leg of the SGC project, which is not an expected or calculated delay. This is an important point because this issue could put the feasibility of the project in question (Barry and Gambino 2019).

Second and related to this, the power, resistance, and the role of the Italian city councils should be considered. The above-mentioned examples show that despite the strong support of the Italian government, the local municipality can stop, postpone, or delay the USD 40 billion project because of olive trees. This means that the relevant literature needs to consider actors beside states and different government structures while discussing transnational projects. If the project is agreed upon at state level, it does not mean that the deliberations are over, because there are likely to be further requirements that need to be fulfilled,

A new round in the Caspian pipeline game 157

as outlined above. Third, these delays and extra economic costs happened while the oil price was below USD 40 per barrel and Azerbaijan was struggling with internal economic and political turmoil. This means the technical issues came to be combined with unexpected issues that led to extra costs, risks, and frustration. As a result, this delay has increased the economic challenges to the project because Azerbaijan needs to pay its debts and every day of delay cost Azerbaijan potential energy revenue. Additionally, these issues made it difficult to get extra loans as the project was becoming too risky to finance. While these findings do not deny that geopolitics play a role in the project, geopolitics nevertheless do not represent the whole picture.

Considering the technical, political, and economic scope of these issues, it can be argued that these problems can only be solved on both a national and regional level at very high costs, and they thus require the involvement of actors above and beyond just states to be financed and solved. More specifically, the SGC project created functional challenges, which led multiple actors (state, non-state, and semi-state) to cooperate because their connections and interaction helped to deal with the functional challenges in this project.

Network of actors

According to Skalamera (2016), political agreement is only one instrumental, but not the decisive condition, for the realization of complex infrastructure projects. Thus, it is too simple to assume that just because the strategic rationale for a certain energy infrastructure project is strong, gas will flow. For the SGC, the first hurdle is addressing the above-mentioned challenges. Second, the investors must ascertain that the SGC is economically viable and superior to alternative transport routes. Because of this, there has to be a transnational energy company or consortium of transnational energy companies willing to commit to leading the SGC project. More specifically, facing these challenges also demands the functional services of multiple actors, namely energy companies and public, as well as private, lenders. These actors are likely to offer the required services, however, because they are looking to make a profit, diversify their energy sources, and address human needs. These motives induce international technical and political cooperation because multiple actors have to pool their resources for the common goal, namely transporting gas through the SGC. The following section explains who the key actors, besides states, involved in shaping and constructing the SGC project are and how their preferences (political and economic) and networks affect the capacity, opportunity, and will of governments (e.g., ministries, parliaments, presidents etc.) to cooperate.

Energy companies

The key actors in the SGC project are multinational energy companies, such as BP, SNAM, Enagas, Lukoil, and Petronas who offered a number of the

158 A new round in the Caspian pipeline game

required resources to transport landlocked natural gas to the European markets, as was the case with the BTC pipeline project. These resources include financial investment, political influence, security personnel and material, and advanced technology. The first important point that needs to be highlighted is the economic leverage that multinational energy companies have. Although the SGC involves six states (Azerbaijan, Turkey, Georgia, Albania, Greece, and Italy), its economic cost is beyond their financial capacity. Because oil prices have dropped, these countries (particularly Azerbaijan) desperately need international economic support. As mentioned above, Azerbaijan's investment share in the SGC project is approximately USD 11 billion, which means the rest of the project needs to be financed by different actors. In light of this, the Shah-Deniz (the main supplier field of the SGC) is shared by seven co-ventures among which BP owns the biggest percentage at 28.8 percent and is leading the Shah Deniz II project. The second largest stakeholder in this project is Turkish Petroleum (TP) with 19 percent, then comes Petronas with 15.5 percent, SOCAR with 10 percent, Lukoil with 10 percent, NIOC 10 percent, and SCC 6.7 percent (British Petroleum 2016). In the same vein, ownership of the three pipelines (SCP, TANAP, and TAP) is also divided among several multinational energy companies. Figure 5.2 shows the actors involved in the SGC project.

This means the USD 40 billion economic cost of the SGC project has been divided among these companies. The strong financial contribution of the consortium companies increased the feasibility of the SGC project because these companies divided the economic risks. To do so, they have also applied for loans from private and public lenders in order to finance the project. For

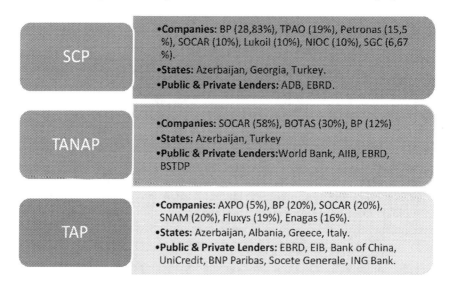

Figure 5.2 List of actors involved in the Southern Gas Project.
Source: Author's own compilation.

A new round in the Caspian pipeline game 159

example, according to the Enagas's report of 2016, the company invested 84.8 million euros in the TAP project in the first half of 2017 (Enagas 2016). In the same vein, Lukoil received USD 1 billion of credit from the EBRD for the SGC project (Antidze 2014). This example illustrates, in contrast to what the New Great Game literature concludes, that Lukoil is not one of the geopolitical tools Russia uses to implement its foreign policy goals. It is, however, important to note that these companies benefit significantly from involving themselves in the SGC project, because the SGC adds new reserves to their resource bases and diversifies their energy portfolios. These benefits induce energy companies to offer functional services and facilitate international technical cooperation.

The second important point that needs to be mentioned is the internal and external political power of BP, SNAM, Enagas, and SOCAR. The international energy companies have good relationships with their home governments, who provide them with the ability to strongly influence the decisions of local governments (see chapter 3). In this sense, having BP, SNAM, Fluxys, and Enagas on board with the SGC project has secured the support of several European capitals. For example, one of the shareholders of SNAM is the Italian government, and the involvement of SNAM in the SGC makes the Italian government part of that project. Additionally, although BP only has a small share in the TAP project, it played an important role in solving the Italian olive tree problem. An expert from BP mentioned that during this time, BP helped coordinate the discussion between local and central government to work towards a solution and continue construction. Another example that has mostly been kept from the relevant discussion is that of the US's sanctions against Russia. As mentioned above, the Russian and Iranian energy companies Lukoil and NIOC own 10 percent of the Shah-Deniz field. This meant that the US sanctions against Russia and Iran could also influence the Shah-Deniz II project. In order to alleviate the impending US sanctions, BP, together with Azerbaijani government, used its strong lobbying network in the US senate to get exceptions for Lukoil and NIOC in the sanctions (Paraskova 2018). If they had not got this exception the SGC project would have faced difficulties. In terms of networking, BP, being a European company, helps SOCAR implement systematic coordination and cooperation with other European companies. BP has great expertise and a strong network in the European market, but SOCAR is new at this and therefore BP shares its expertise to facilitate coordination among the TAP companies.

The third important point is security. The companies involved play a key role for the security of the SGC project, as the companies involved in the BTC pipeline did for that project. Remarkably, this aspect has been neglected by both geopolitical and geo-economic literature. According to an expert from TANAP, several security measures are needed to ensure the safe operation of the pipeline, such as physical, procedural, and electronic measures. Physical security includes building fences, lighting the perimeter, and

160 *A new round in the Caspian pipeline game*

creating clear zones, gates, doors, and locks. Procedural security includes drawing up and implementing risk management plans as well as emergency response procedures by defining and assigning the roles and actions and coordinating with the public security providers involved. Electronic security measures include CCTV systems, access control systems, intrusion detection systems, and warning systems. These security measures are provided by the relevant energy companies. For example, BP sets out certain security standards for the pipeline countries to implement and follow. If BP realizes that the suggested security measures are not enough, it gets involved and asks the relevant governments to expand the security requirements. When doing so, BP offers financial and technological support, such as drones. BP and SOCAR have implemented social support programmes in six countries to gain the public's support, as they did in the BTC pipeline project. According to an expert from BP, 'these social programs are important for the security of pipeline because the project gains the support of local people through them, which means local people grow willing to inform the government of threats that arise.'

Finally, the exploitation and transportation of natural gas from the Caspian Sea would never have been possible without advanced technology, which the states in this region lack. This has led the consortium companies to revitalize the technical capacities of the states in this region by offering modern gas processing plants and fabrication facilities. They supported local experts by offering several educational and capacity-building training programmes. These examples show that these companies do many of the things traditionally, sometimes exclusively, associated with the state. However, it is also worth reiterating that these companies exploit the natural resources of the Caspian Sea to gain extra revenue from it. In doing so, only a few cities, mainly those on the pipeline's route, benefit from these companies' financial contributions, while others are neglected. Additionally, these companies prefer to side line human rights issues within certain countries (e.g., Azerbaijan and Turkey) and focus mainly on economic benefits.

Private and public lenders

Although quite a number of TNCs and states are already involved, the realization of the SGC project requires the involvement of more actors, as those currently involved cannot cover all the cost of the project. To construct the 3,500 km SGC pipeline, which crosses seven countries and represents a total investment of approximately USD 40 billion, systematic financial support from a number of financial institutions, such as the EBRD, ADB, BSTDB, ING Bank, and the World Bank has proven necessary. Because of this, companies and states have used their strong lobbying and networking power to gain support from these financial institutions. For example, an expert from BP said:

A new round in the Caspian pipeline game 161

...by using its strong reputation, BP has played an important role in attracting international financial organizations and banks to the SGC project. BP is a European company; it has strong risk management and environmental and technical standards. Therefore, banks and financial institutions trust BP and its opinion.

(Interview, October 26, 2017)

Another example of companies using their stature to gain private and public lenders' support is Lukoil. In 2015, Lukoil signed a twelve-year credit facility agreement with a consortium of banks to borrow USD 1 billion, of which the EBRD, the ADB, and the BSTDB would provide USD 560 million. The remaining amount, USD 440 million, is provided for a period of ten years by a commercial banking syndicate comprising of the ING Bank, Bank of China, UniCredit AG, and Société Générale via the B Loan programs of the EBRD and ADB (Lukoil Press Release 2015).

Figure 5.3 shows international loans from different public banks.

The total cost of the TANAP project is USD 8.6 billion. On December 20, 2016 the World Bank approved two USD 400 million loans to Turkey and Azerbaijan for the TANAP project (World Bank 2016). A day later, on December 21, 2016 the Asian Infrastructure Investment Bank (AIIB) allocated USD 600 million to a loan for the TANAP project (AIIB 2016). In the same year, the EBRD declared its intention to grant a loan of up to USD 1.59 billion for the TAP project and another large loan for the TANAP project (Trend 2016). The total TAP project cost is more than USD 4.5 billion of which the EBRD supplied approximately USD 1.5 billion in loans. Finally, in 2016 additional modest financial support (just over USD 14 million) came from the European Commission (EC) under the European Union's special Connecting Europe Facility (CEF) funding instrument. The money will be directed toward archaeological investigations and excavation studies for the TAP project, within the framework of the EU's priority energy projects (European Commission 2016). After becoming involved in the SGC

USD2.8 Billion	• European Investment Bank (EIB)
USD 1.8 Billion	• World Bank Group
USD 1.7 Billion	• European Bank for Reconstruction and Development (EBRD)
USD 1.3 Billion	• Asian Development Bank (ADB)
USD 0.6 Billion	• Asian Infrastructure Investment Bank (AIIB)

Figure 5.3 International loans from different public banks.
Source: Author's own compilation.

162 *A new round in the Caspian pipeline game*

project, these institutions have used their networks and lobbying power to attract funding from several private and governmental banks. However, when investing in this project, these institutions require certain environmental and social standards and measurements from the energy companies and countries. By using their economic leverage, these institutions push energy companies and countries to follow these requirements in order to secure the funding. For example, EBRD has yet to decide to confirm one of the loans for the project due to environmental protests and complaints. However, it is also important to mention that these institutions have closed their eyes to the human rights abuses in Azerbaijan. They have not really used their economic leverage to put pressure on the Azerbaijani government.

These examples highlight two important factors that have been overlooked to some extent. First, the SGC is indeed a mediating interface as it manages to bind multiple actors together, which creates mutual interdependency and alliances. More concretely, the infrastructure project has brought several actors and their network together on economic, social, and technical issues on the pipeline's route. Contrary to conclusions drawn from state-centric assumptions, these actors not only include states but also companies, financial institutions, NGOs, and IGOs. Second, and related, each actor offers specific and functional contribution (e.g., economic, political, social, technical, and security) to deal with certain challenges. After recognizing their mutual dependency, these actors pooled their resources to complete this infrastructure project. The multiple networking ties between these actors generated continuous interaction by invoking the image of connectedness between individuals and organizations on the one hand and private and public actors on the other. The guidance and governance of the projects would have been unreliable without their involvement.

Operating the SGC: expectations versus reality

The case of the BTC pipeline has illustrated that it is possible to find room for more pragmatic cooperation among the littoral states after the successful completion of an oil infrastructure project. As discussed in chapter 4, the Caspian littoral states have started to use the BTC oil pipeline as an alternative to their old oil transport routes. Additionally, chapter 3 explained that the Legal Status Convention, which was signed in August 2018, created suitable conditions for building undersea pipelines in the Caspian Sea. This section shows whether and how cooperation on the CEP and the BTC pipeline has spilled over to the SGC project. The following section explains the ways in which the SGC became entangled with wider regional processes after its construction. More specifically, this section explains how the recently signed Legal Status Convention can affect the SGC project and whether and how the SGC project affects the possibility, likelihood, and severity of regional conflicts.

A new round in the Caspian pipeline game 163

Pragmatic cooperation: the TCP

Similar to the BTC project, the SGC project has offered the Caspian littoral states and external powers an issue-specific opportunity to cooperate. The relevant literature focuses on the states in the region and on external states, namely Russia, Iran, and China while discussing the SGC project. This means that the scholarship neglects other actors, such as Iranian and Russian energy companies (Lukoil and NIOC) and China's financial institution (the AIIB), even though Lukoil and NIOC are already part of the Shah-Deniz Consortium and hold a 10 percent share each. As explained above, Lukoil received a loan of USD 1 billion from the EBRD for the SGC project (Antidze 2014). Additionally, the NIOC got an exception from Western sanctions due to its involvement in the SGC project. In the same vein, Mahmoud Vaezi, Chief of Staff to the President of Iran, mentioned that Iran was considering transporting its gas to Europe by means of the TANAP gas pipeline (SNAM 2014). Finally, China is part of the SGC indirectly through the AIIB, which was initiated and launched by China and granted a USD 600 million loan to support the SGC project in 2016 (AIIB 2018). Considering this, one may ask why Iran and Russia's national energy companies are part of the SGC project if the states themselves are against this project? Are they trying to sabotage the SGC project? If so, then why did Lukoil borrow USD 1 billion? Of course, the New Great Game scholars would find answer to these questions in line with their Great Game explanation, but in reality, their involvement means that China, Iran, and Russia are part of this project indirectly and will benefit from it. These examples also show that even if there is a 'Great Game', it is about constructive cooperation rather than destructive rivalry.

Additionally, Turkmenistan and Kazakhstan have expressed their interest to join the SGC project, like they did with the BTC pipeline, as it would offer them an alternative route to reach the European energy market. For example, gas accounts for nearly two-thirds of Turkmen exports and it is almost exclusively sold to Russia, Iran and China (Natural Gas World 2015). Ever since the completion of the Central Asia-China Pipeline, Turkmenistan has supplied a substantial portion of China's gas demand through the infrastructure in Uzbekistan and Kazakhstan (Socor 2012). The SGC project would offer Turkmenistan an opportunity to diversify its pipeline routes and establish relations with the West, allowing it to drive up the price of its oil by making China and the West outbid each other. In this sense, this is the significance of the opportunity to diversify the export routes. One of the ways to connect Central Asia to the SGC project is to build the fourth leg of the project, the so-called TCP. This new underwater pipeline is expected to transport 30 bcm of Turkmen gas from Turkmenbashy to the Sangachal Gas Terminal in Azerbaijan, from where it would be transported to Europe (Cason 2015). When this pipeline idea was initially presented, both Kazakhstan and Turkmenistan supported the TCP option (European Commission

164 *A new round in the Caspian pipeline game*

2011). For example, the Turkmen President expressed his support for the project when he met with the top EU officials in 2011. Following this, on May 1, 2015, Azerbaijan, Turkmenistan, and the EU signed the Ashgabat Declaration to develop energy cooperation between the parties (European Commission 2015a). Turkmenistan even considered the possibility of shipping compressed natural gas (CNG) to Azerbaijan by tankers, decompressing it there, and transporting it onward through the SCG to Europe. This development is remarkable because it shows that the practice of cooperation between the littoral countries has not been limited to the CEP and the BTC, but has moved into other areas.

To show its interest in the project, Turkmenistan sent a delegation to the Fourth Ministerial Meeting of the SGC, which was held in Baku in 2018. During his opening speech, President Aliyev of Azerbaijan explicitly stated:

> I am glad that representatives of friendly countries, Romania and Turkmenistan, are also attending this meeting for the first time. Their participation in this meeting also demonstrates that they attach great importance to our project.
>
> (as cited in President 2018)

In the same vein, Parviz Shahbazov, Azerbaijan's Energy Minister, noted that:

> ...the volume of Azerbaijani gas transported along the SGC may be increased at the expense of gas from Turkmenistan. The participation and statements of representatives of Turkmenistan and Romania at the fourth Ministerial Meeting of the SGC Advisory Council also confirm that interest in the project is gradually increasing.
>
> (Trend 2018b)

Additionally, as explained in chapter 3, the Legal Status Convention provides clarity about the requirements for constructing the TCP and was agreed on by Azerbaijan, Turkmenistan, and Kazakhstan. More specifically, Article 14 of the Legal Status Convention states that the littoral states may construct submarine pipelines on the bed of the Caspian Sea if they are compliant with environmental standards and requirements of the Tehran Convention. In doing so, 'submarine cable and pipeline routes shall be determined by agreement with all the parties the seabed sector of which is to be crossed by the cable or pipeline' (Kremlin 2018). This means that one of the points of uncertainty between Azerbaijan, Turkmenistan, and Kazakhstan has been resolved. This also illustrates the interconnection between environmental, legal, and infrastructural cooperation in the Caspian Sea region. More concretely, the Legal Status Convention, the Tehran Convention, and the environmental documents of the CEP offer common base for the governments of the littoral states, and they can refer to these documents while discussing the

A new round in the Caspian pipeline game   165

TCP project. In light of revised functionalism, it can be argued that these examples illustrate that the cooperative practices, which were started during the CEP and the BTC pipeline project, continued and facilitated collaboration between the littoral states in other areas.

It is worth noting that there are other issues that still need to be resolved in order to construct the fourth leg of the SGC project. First, Turkmenistan's policy of gas transport requires the buyer to assume all risks from the Turkmen border onward (Cason 2015). This means those who want Turkmen gas must build the pipeline to Turkmenistan to receive it. Azerbaijan does not have enough money to build this pipeline and it is still engaged in covering the SGC's costs (Azernews 2017a). Second, as mentioned above, any transnational infrastructure project requires the strong financial support of actors besides states. Because of this, it is still not officially confirmed whether the TCP project can secure sufficient financing from European companies and public as well as private lenders to match its political endorsement. Considering the current low oil prices, many European companies are hesitant when it comes to the risks of financing complex pipeline projects. Third, Azerbaijan wants to deliver its own natural gas to Europe first because Azerbaijan has enough natural gas capacity to supply the promised 16 bcm. Therefore, Baku will only greenlight the TCP pipeline if it turns out its natural gas capacity is not enough to fulfil the promise of supplying 16 bcm of natural gas. In 2019, BP announced that there might be another giant gas field in the Caspian Sea, which would increase the capacity of the SGC project (Bloomberg 2019). As mentioned above, Baku also got a Third Party Access Exception from the EU, which means Azerbaijan can have a monopoly over the transport of natural gas through the SGC and can reject the transportation of natural gas from third parties.

However, there are cooperation initiatives besides the TCP project in other areas, such as the development of seaports. The littoral states have started modernizing their ports in the Caspian Sea to facilitate more transportation options and to improve regional and global connectivity by establishing free trade zones. Meanwhile, the boards of the littoral states' seaports have organized regular meetings to exchange ideas and sign cooperation memorandums (Port of Baku 2018). An expert from an Azerbaijani port said:

> ...although each Caspian state has its own port, the main aim of these ports is to cooperate rather than compete. The reason for this is that there is strong interdependency and networking between the five ports. They aid each other in terms of capacity, transportation, bureaucracy, customs service, and regional and global connectivity.
>
> (Interview, June 1, 2018)

To strengthen the regional and global economic connectivity, Turkmenistan organized the First Caspian Economic Forum in 2019 (Trend 2019a). During

166 *A new round in the Caspian pipeline game*

the forum, the littoral states signed a number of documents related to transport, industry, agriculture, infrastructure, and diplomacy (Trend 2019a).

Overall, it can be argued that the habit of coming together that took shape in the CEP and the BTC pipeline project continued to flourish in the Caspian Sea region, and the SGC project created a new interest and pride in continuing cooperation among the littoral states. Of course, this does not mean that the CEP and the BTC pipeline have explicitly encouraged the littoral states to join the SGC project. However, as is illustrated in chapters 3 and 4, the CEP and the BTC project are the initial places where the littoral states started to experience and establish the practice of environmental and infrastructure cooperation, interaction, negotiation, and trust. However, it is worth noting that the littoral states mainly produce and export natural resources, meaning that non-energy-related industry sectors represent only a limited share of their total exports (ADB 2019). This in turn means that, since there is a lack of production and development in non-energy-related industry sectors, there is limited room and thus need for expanding cooperation beyond transportation of oil and gas. As mentioned in revised functionalism, spill-over between different sectors or issue areas only occurs if there is a need or necessity. In this sense, if the littoral states do not establish a competitive industry sector outside the energy industry, economic and political agreements, documents or treaties will only play an important role on paper.

Conclusion

This chapter has analysed the planning, construction, and post-construction phases of the SGC project. First, the chapter illustrated that Western support and interests are not granted or fixed but that they change according to the size, value, and meaning of the project taken on. In contrast to the way it acted in the BTC pipeline project, the US government increased the amount of attention it paid to Afghanistan and to alternative energy projects in the region. In the same vein, its energy companies did not involve themselves in the SGC. This absence was counteracted by the Russia and Iran's energy companies, Lukoil and NIOC. Additionally, Azerbaijan had cold relations with one of the key transit countries, Turkey, because it sought to normalize relations with Armenia, Azerbaijan's enemy. This situation called Turkey's role as a transit country into question and created room for Russia as an alternative transit country. During the planning phase of the project, the SGC also had to compete with the EU's internal energy pipelines in order to gain financial and political support from European energy companies as well as private and public lenders. These uncertainties influenced the feasibility, value, and importance of the SGC project during the planning phase.

Second, the chapter highlighted that political agreement was only one of the instruments, not the decisive condition, needed to complete the SGC project. This chapter has shown that the SGC faced technical, environmental, and economic challenges during its construction phase, which necessitated the cooperation of multiple actors (state, non-state and semi-state) because their connection and interaction were needed to help deal with these challenges. As shown, a local Italian municipality stopped construction on a USD 40 billion project because of olive trees and environmental pollution, despite the Italian government's strong support of the project. A local municipality's actions led to frustration, delays, extra costs, and political difficulties during the construction phase of the project. These construction challenges were resolved due to the systematic support and networking of multiple players, namely transnational energy companies (BP) and private and public lenders (the World Bank Group), as was the case with the BTC pipeline. In line with revised functionalism's insights, this chapter illustrated that the interaction and cooperation of these actors increased the political and economic feasibility of the SGC project because they pooled their political, technical, and economic resources to deal with the shared construction challenges.

Finally, this chapter illustrated that cooperation among the Caspian littoral states was not limited to the BTC project and the CEP. The practice of cooperation, which was established by the CEP and strengthened by the BTC, has continued and spilled over to the SGC project. Turkmenistan and Kazakhstan have expressed their interest in joining the SGC project, as they did with the BTC project, and constructing the fourth pipeline, the TCP. Because the BTC pipeline has already been constructed, the littoral states have experienced options for transporting natural resources from Kazakhstan and Turkmenistan to Azerbaijan. In light of this, Azerbaijan, Kazakhstan, and Turkmenistan have increased the frequency of their official meetings in order to thoroughly discuss the possibility of the latter two joining the SGC project. Although Russia and Iran are not transporting their natural resources through the SGC, their respective energy companies are among the shareholders of the project and are working together with other actors to complete the SGC in 2020. As explain in revised functionalism, the littoral states are part of the SGC project with respect to their interests, capacities, and resources.

To prevent Euro-centric expectations, this chapter has argued that the habit of cooperation among the littoral states is mainly focused on the Caspian Sea's natural resources because the littoral states have done little to develop the non-energy-related sectors of their industry, which represent only a limited share of their total exports. Although the littoral states have signed a number of documents, agreements, and treaties with regard to agriculture, tourism, technology, and customs, one can observe a very limited cooperation in these fields, because these sectors are not nearly as developed and advanced as the energy sector in the Caspian Sea region. This means that the current cooperation can spill over into different areas only if they diversify their non-energy industry. Otherwise, the above-mentioned non-energy-related agreements are unlikely to move beyond words on paper.

Bibliography

Ahrari, Ehsan M. 1994. 'The dynamics of the new great game in Muslim Central Asia.' *Central Asian Survey* 13 (4): 525–539.

Akiner, Shirin. 2004. *The Caspian: Politics, Energy and Security.* London: Routledge.

Alam, Shah. 2002. 'Pipeline politics in the Caspian Sea Basin.' *Strategic Analysis* 26 (1): 5–26.

Amirova-Mammadova, Sevinj. 2017. *Pipeline Politics and Natural Gas Supply from Azerbaijan to Europe.* Wiesbaden: Springer.

Anceschi, Luca. 2019. 'Caspian Energy in the Aftermath of the 2018 Convention: The View from Kazakhstan and Turkmenistan.' *Russian Analytical Digest* 235: 6–9.

Antidze, Margarita. 2014. 'Rosneft eyes Azeri gas, oil pipeline use-SOCAR.' June 4. Accessed October 25, 2016. http://af.reuters.com/article/commoditiesNews/idAFL6 N0OL2W820140604?pageNumber=1&virtualBrandChannel=0.

Asian Infrastructure Investment Bank. 2016. 'AIIB approves $600 million to support energy project of Azerbaijan.' December 21. Accessed September 2, 2017. https://www.aiib.org/en/news-events/news/2016/20161222_001.html.

Azernews. 2017a. 'Europe still interested in the Trans-Caspian gas pipeline.' May 19. Accessed October 12, 2017. https://www.azernews.az/oil_and_gas/113422.html.

Azernews. 2017b. 'Cost of Southern Gas Corridor project revised.' October 13. Accessed October 14, 2017. https://www.azernews.az/oil_and_gas/120498.html.

Azernews. 2016. 'Azerbaijan's commitment on SGC fulfilled by half.' December 23. Accessed December 24, 2016. https://www.azernews.az/oil_and_gas/106901.html.

Azernews. 2012. 'ITGI Project not considered for Shah Deniz project on exporting Azerbaijani gas to EU.' February 2. Accessed September 12, 2016. https://azertag.az/en/xeber/ITGI_Project_not_considered_for_Shah_deniz_project_on_exporting_Azerbaijani_gas_to_EU-220753.

Baev, Pavel, and Indra Øverland. 2010. 'The South Stream versus Nabucco pipeline race: geopolitical and economic (ir)rationales and political stakes in mega-projects.' *International Affairs* 86 (5): 1075–1090.

Bankwatch Network. 2018. 'Southern Gas Corridor Loans from Public Banks.' July. Accessed August 1, 2018. https://bankwatch.org/project/southern-gas-corridor-eur o-caspian-mega-pipeline.

Bankwatch Network. 2017. 'Why no Trans-Adriatic Pipeline (NO TAP), here or elsewhere.' April 17. Accessed October 25, 2017. https://bankwatch.org/blog/why-no-trans-adriatic-pipeline-no-tap-here-or-elsewhere.

Bankwatch Network. 2016. 'Risky business – Who benefits from the Southern Gas Corridor.' Accessed June 2016. https://bankwatch.org/risky-business.

Bankwatch Network. 2015. 'Pipe Dreams: Why the Southern Gas Corridor will not reduce EU dependency on Russia.' January 21. Accessed October 12, 2017. https://bankwatch.org/press_release/pipe-dreams-why-the-southern-gas-corridor-will-not-r educe-eu-dependency-on-russia.

Barry, Andrew, and Evelina Gambino. 2019. 'Pipeline Geopolitics: Subaquatic Materials and the Tactical Point.' *Geopolitics* 25 (1): 1–35.

Bashir, Omar S. 2017. 'The Great Games Never Played: Explaining Variation in International Competition Over Energy.' *Journal of Global Security Studies* 2 (4): 288–306.

Bayulgen, Oksan. 2009. 'Caspian energy wealth: social impacts and implications for regional stability.' In *The Politics of Transition in Central Asia and the Caucasus*, by Amanda E Wooden and Christoph H Stefes, 163–189. New York: Routledge.

Bittner, Jochen. 2018. 'Who Will Win the New Great Game?' April 26. Accessed July 10, 2018. https://www.nytimes.com/2018/04/26/opinion/russia-china-west-power.html.

Bloomberg. 2019. 'BP Thinks It's Sitting on Another Giant Gas Field in the Caspian.' January 10. Accessed January 2019. https://www.bloomberg.com/news/articles/2019-01-10/bp-thinks-it-s-sitting-on-another-giant-gas-field-in-the-caspian.

Bloomberg. 2014. 'Putin's Stance on Ukraine Supported by Minority of Nations.' March 14. Accessed September 2018. https://www.bloomberg.com/graphics/infographics/countries-react-to-russian-intervention-in-crimea.html.

Blum, Douglas. 2002. 'Beyond Reciprocity: Governance and Cooperation around the Caspian Sea.' In *Environmental Peacemaking*, by Ken Conca and Geoffrey Dabelko, 161–190. Baltimore: The John Hopkins University Press.

British Petroleum. 2018. 'First Quarter 2018 Results.' May 17. Accessed May 23, 2016. https://www.bp.com/en_az/caspian/press/businessupdates/first-quarter-2018-results.html.

British Petroleum. 2016. 'Shah Deniz Stage 2: Operations and Projects.' Accessed December 18, 2017. http://www.bp.com/en_az/caspian/operationsprojects/Shahdeniz/SDstage2.html.

Cason, Bryce. 2015. 'The Trans-Caspian pipeline: implications for the five littoral states.' *Journal of World Energy Law and Business* 8 (3): 1–11.

Colluto, Tiziana. 2014. 'Tap, Regione Puglia boccia l'approdo a San Foca. E rimette in gioco Brindisi.' January 14. Accessed September 12, 2016. https://www.ilfattoquotidiano.it/2014/01/14/tap-regione-puglia-boccia-lapprodo-a-san-foca-e-rimette-in-gioco-brindisi/843653/.

Coote, Bud. 2017. *The Caspian Sea and Southern Gas Corridor A View from Russia*. Washington: Atlantic Council.

Counter-Balance. 2016. 'Open Letter: The EIB should not finance the Southern Gas Corridor.' January 28. Accessed March 12, 2017. http://www.counter-balance.org/wp-content/uploads/2016/01/NGO-Open-Letter_EIB-President_Southern-Gas-Corridor_28-01-2016.pdf.

Counter-Balance. 2015. 'Italian mayors protest again the Trans Adriatic Pipeline.' September 22. Accessed October 10, 2018. http://www.counter-balance.org/italian-mayors-protest-again-the-trans-adriatic-pipeline/.

Deloitte. 2018. 'Business Outlook in Azerbaijan. Evaluation.' Baku: Deloitte Baku Office.

De Micco, Pasquale. 2015. 'Changing pipelines, shifting strategies: Gas in south-eastern Europe and the implications for Ukraine. Belgium: European Parliament Policy Department.' July. Accessed June 10, 2016. http://www.europarl.europa.eu/RegData/etudes/IDAN/2015/549053/EXPO_IDA(2015)549053_EN.pdf.

De Wilde, Jaap. 1991. *Saved From Oblivion*. Aldershot: Dartmouth.

Dodds, Klaus. 2005. 'Screening Geopolitics: James Bond and the Early Cold War films (1962–1967).' *Geopolitics* 10 (2): 266–289.

Dodds, Klaus. 2003. 'Licensed to Stereotype: Geopolitics, James Bond and the Spectre of Balkanism.' *Geopolitics* 8 (2): 125–156.

Dunlap, Ben. 2004. 'Divide and conquer? The Russian plan for ownership for the Caspian Sea.' *Boston College International Comparative Law Review* 27 (1): 115–130.

Euractiv. 2018. 'Italy's Di Maio warns against party divisions after TAP pipeline U-turn.' October 30. Accessed October 30, 2018. https://www.euractiv.com/section/elections/news/italys-di-maio-warns-against-party-divisions-after-tap-pipeline-u-turn/.

Eurasianet. 2012. 'Azerbaijan & Turkmenistan: Renewing Caspian Sea Energy Dispute.' July 11. Accessed September 12, 2018. https://eurasianet.org/azerbaijan-turkmenistan-renewing-caspian-sea-energy-dispute.

170 *A new round in the Caspian pipeline game*

Eurasianet. 2010a. 'Matthew Bryza Named New US Ambassador to Azerbaijan.' May 21. Accessed September 2018. https://eurasianet.org/matthew-bryza-nam ed-new-us-ambassador-to-azerbaijan.

Eurasianet. 2010b. 'Medvedev Visit to Baku Produces Gas Export Agreement.' September 3. Accessed September 2018. https://eurasianet.org/medvedev-visit-to-ba ku-produces-gas-export-agreement.

Eurasianet. 2006. 'BTC: Kazakhstan Finally Commits to the Pipeline.' June 19. Accessed September 12, 2018. https://eurasianet.org/btc-kazakhstan-finally-comm its-to-the-pipeline.

European Commission. 2018. 'Diversification of gas supply sources and routes.' June 20. Accessed June 20, 2018. https://ec.europa.eu/energy/en/topics/energy-security/ diversification-of-gas-supply-sources-and-routes.

European Commission. 2016. 'List of actions selected for receiving financial assistance under the second CEF Energy 2016 call for proposals.' February 17. Accessed March 12, 2018. https://ec.europa.eu/energy/sites/ener/files/documents/list_of_a ll_projects_receiving_eu_su.

European Commission. 2015a. 'Ashgabat Declaration.' May 1. Accessed May 2018, https://ec.europa.eu/commission/commissioners/2014-2019/sefcovic/announcements /ashgabat-declaration_en.

European Commission. 2015b. 'Commission Decision.' March 17. Accessed September 2018. https://ec.europa.eu/energy/sites/ener/files/documents/2015_tap_prolonga tion_decision_en.pdf.

European Commission. 2013. 'EU Commission welcomes decision on gas pipeline: Door opener for direct link to Caspian Sea. 'June 28. Accessed September 12, 2016. http://europa.eu/rapid/press-release_IP-13-623_en.htm.

European Commission. 2012. 'Commissioner Oettinger welcomes decision on "Nabucco West" pipeline.' June 28. Accessed September 12, 2016. http://europa.eu/ rapid/press-release_IP-12-720_en.htm.

European Commission. 2011. 'EU starts negotiations on Caspian pipeline to bring gas to Europe.' September 12. Accessed September 2017. http://europa.eu/rapid/p ress-release_IP-11-1023_en.htm.

European Commission. 2010. 'Economic Recovery: Second batch of 4-billion-euro package goes to 43 pipeline and electricity projects.' March 4. Accessed September 12, 2016. http://europa.eu/rapid/press-release_IP-10-231_en.htm.

European Investment Bank. 2018. 'The Southern Gas Corridor and the Trans Adriatic Pipeline (TAP).' February 6. Accessed March 12, 2018. http://www.eib.org/en/infocen tre/press/news/topical_briefs/2018-february-01/southern-gas-corridor-trans-adriatic-pipel.

Enegas. 2016. 'Annual Report. Annual Report.' http://www.enagas.es/WEBCORP-sta tic/InformeAnual2016/sites/default/files/annual_report_2016_0.pdf.

Farchy, Jack. 2015. 'Baku seeks alternatives as Azerbaijan oil production declines.' March 12. Accessed September 12, 2016. https://www.ft.com/content/b86cb5b4-be 99-11e4-8036-00144feab7de.

Freifeld, Daniel. 2009. 'The Great Pipeline Opera.' *Foreign Policy*, 1–7. August 22. Accessed September 2016. https://foreignpolicy.com/2009/08/22/the-great-pipeline-opera/.

Garibov, Azad. 2018. 'Legal Status of the Caspian Sea is Finally Defined What is Next?' *Caucasus International* 8 (2): 179–195.

Gazprom. 2009. 'Gazprom and SOCAR sign Agreement on Azerbaijani gas purchase and sale terms.' June 29. Accessed April 2, 2015. http://www.gazprom.com/press/ news/2009/june/article66713/.

A new round in the Caspian pipeline game 171

Grigas, Agnia. 2017. *The New Geopolitics of Natural Gas.* London: Harvard University Press.

Guliyev, Farid. 2012. 'Political Elites in Azerbaijan.' In *Challenges of the Caspian Resource Boom: Domestic Elites and Policy Making* by Andreas Heinrich, and Heiko Pleines, 117–131. New York: Palgrave.

Guliyev, Farid, and Nozima Akhrarkhodjaeva. 2009. 'The Trans-Caspian Energy Route: Cronyism, Competition and Cooperation in Kazakh Oil Export.' *Energy Policy* 37 (8): 3171–3182.

Gurbanov, Ilgar. 2018. 'Caspian Convention and Perspective of Turkmenistan's Gas Export to Europe' *Caucasus International*, 8 (2): 159–179.

Gurbanov, Ilgar. 2017a. 'Propaganda Against Trans-Adriatic Pipeline Continues Under "Environmental Concerns".' April 26. Accessed May 20, 2017. https://jam estown.org/program/propaganda-trans-adriatic-pipeline-continues-environmental-c oncerns/.

Gurbanov, Ilgar. 2017b. 'Southern Gas Corridor Seeks Financial Backing Amidst Volatile Oil Prices.' March 9. Accessed March 10, 2017. https://jamestown.org/p rogram/southern-gas-corridor-seeks-financial-backup-amidst-volatile-oil-prices/.

Gurbanov, Ilgar. 2016. 'Falling Oil Prices and Its Implications for Azerbaijan's Gas Policy.' March 4. Accessed August 5, 2016. https://jamestown.org/program/fallin g-oil-prices-and-its-implications-for-azerbaijans-gas-policy/#.VzNZzoSLTIX.

Gutterman, Ivan, and Wojtek Grojec. 2018. 'A Timeline Of All Russia-Related Sanctions.' September 19. Accessed October 1, 2018. https://www.rferl.org/a/russia-sa nctions-timeline/29477179.html.

Grewlich, Klaus. 2011. 'International Regulatory Governance of the Caspian Pipeline Policy Game.' *Journal of Energy and Natural Resources Law* 29 (1): 87–116.

Hasanov, Huseyn. 2015. 'Trans-Caspian gas pipeline – promising project, says Turkmen president.' October 12. Accessed November 10, 2015. https://en.trend.az/busi ness/energy/2442726.html.

Hurriyet Daily News. 2012. 'Greece, Italy back Adriatic gas pipeline.' August 9. Accessed September 12, 2016. http://www.hurriyetdailynews.com/greece-italy-ba ck-adriatic-gas-pipeline-27381.

Iseri, Emre. 2009. 'The US Grand Strategy and the Eurasian Heartland in the Twenty-First Century.' *Geopolitics* 14 (1): 26–46.

Ismayilov, Murad. 2019. 'Azerbaijan and Russia: Towards a Renewed Alliance, for a New Era.' *Russian Analytical Digest* 232: 5–10.

ISPI. 2015. 'Italian Gas (Over)Supply: How the Crisis Reshaped Imports.' June 17. Accessed August 1, 2018. https://www.ispionline.it/en/energy-watch/italian-gas-over supply-how-crisis-reshaped-imports-13515.

Kamrava, Mehran. 2016. *The Great Game in West Asia.* New York: Oxford University Press.

Kiernan, Peter. 2012. *The Great Game for Gas in the Caspian.* London: The Economist.

Kim, Younkyoo, and Stephen Blank. 2016. 'The New Great Game of Caspian energy in 2013–14: "Turk Stream", Russia and Turkey.' *Journal of Balkan and Near Eastern Studies* 18 (1): 37–55.

Kleveman, Lutz. 2003. *The New Great Game: Blood and Oil in the Central Asia.* New York: Grove Press.

Koranyi, David. 2014. *The Southern Gas Corridor: Europe's Lifeline?* Rome: Istituto Affari Internazionali.

172 *A new round in the Caspian pipeline game*

Kubicek, Paul. 2013. 'Energy politics and geopolitical competition in the Caspian Basin.' *Journal of Eurasian Studies* 4: 171–180.

Kucera, Joshua. 2012. 'Armenian Military Simulates Attack On Azerbaijan's Oil.' October 17. Accessed January 20, 2019. https://eurasianet.org/armenian-milita ry-simulates-attack-on-azerbaijans-oil.

Kucera, Joshua, and Zaur Shiriyev. 2017. 'Azerbaijan: Energy Hopes vs. Italian Olive Groves.' January 20. Accessed January 21, 2017. https://eurasianet.org/azerbaija n-energy-hopes-vs-italian-olive-groves.

Kusznir, Julia. 2013. 'TAP, Nabucco West, and South Stream: The Pipeline Dilemma in the Caspian Sea Basin and Its Consequences for the Development of the Southern Gas Corridor.' *Caucasus Analytical Digest* 47: 1–7.

La Repubblica. 2013. 'Cos'è la Tap, il mega gasdotto che tanto piaceva all'amico di D'Alema.' November 29. Accessed September 12, 2016. http://espresso.repubblica.it/a ttualita/2013/11/29/news/il-salento-contro-il-gasdotto-arrivano-i-no-tap-1.143696.

Liakopoulou, Mariana. 2018. 'The Caspian Legal Status and Riparian States' Outlook on the Southern Corridor.' European Gas Hub. https://www.europeangashub. com/wp-content/uploads/2018/07/Liakopoulou_Caspian.pdf.

Lukoil. 2015. 'Lukoil obtains long term financing for second stage of Shah Deniz project in Azerbaijan.' August 7. Accessed September 10, 2017. http://www.lukoil. com/PressCenter/Pressreleases/Pressrelease?rid=50714.

Meister, Stefan, and Marcel Vietor. 2011. 'The Southern Gas Corridor and the South Caucasus.' November 1. Accessed September 20, 2016. https://dgap.org/en/ think-tank/publications/further-publications/southern-gas-corridor-and-south-cauc asus.

Mustafayev, Nurlan. 2016. 'The Southern Gas Corridor: legal and regulatory developments in major gas transit pipeline projects.' *Journal of World Energy Law and Business* 9: 370–387.

Natural Gas World. 2017. 'TAP cleared to resume work.' April 21. Accessed April 22, 2017. https://www.naturalgasworld.com/tap-cleared-to-resume-italy-work-37154.

Natural Gas World. 2015. 'Turkmenistan: The Diversification of Gas Export Market.' December 16. Accessed December 17, 2015. https://www.naturalgasworld. com/turkmenistan-the-diversification-of-gas-export-market-27160.

Norton-Taylor, Richard. 2001. 'The New Great Game.' March 5. Accessed July 10, 2018. https://www.theguardian.com/comment/story/0,3604,446490,00.html.

Nuriyev, Elkhan. 2015. 'Russia, the EU and the Caspian Pipeline Gambit.' September 27. Accessed September 28, 2015. http://www.ensec.org/index.php?option=com_ content&view=article&id=584:russia-the-eu-and-the-caspian-pipeline-gambit&cati d=131:esupdates&Itemid=414.

Offshore Energy Today. 2018. 'OGA: UK oil and gas reserves enough for 20+ years of production.' November 8. Accessed December 10, 2018. https://www.off shoreenergytoday.com/oga-uk-oil-and-gas-reserves-enough-for-20-years-of-producti on/.

Offshore Energy Today. 2010. 'E.ON Ruhrgas Gets 15% Combined Stake in Trans Adriatic Pipeline Project From Statoil and EGL.' May 20. Accessed September 2016. https://www.offshoreenergytoday.com/e-on-ruhrgas-gets-15-combined-stake-in-trans-ad riatic-pipeline-project-from-statoil-and-egl-2/.

Pannier, Bruce. 2009. 'China, EU Wait In The Wings For Access To Central Asia.' August 2. Accessed July 10, 2018. https://www.rferl.org/a/China_EU_Wait_In_ The_Wings_For_Access_To_Central_Asia/1790745.html.

A new round in the Caspian pipeline game   173

Papadimitriou, Jannis. 2014. 'TAP pipeline offers Europe new gas supply.' October 5. Accessed September 20, 2015. https://www.dw.com/en/tap-pipeline-offers-europe-new-gas-supply/a-17974204.

Paraskova, Tsvetana. 2018. 'U.S. Grants Iran Sanctions Waiver To Southern Gas Corridor.' August 8. Accessed August 10, 2018. https://oilprice.com/Latest-Energy-News/World-News/US-Grants-Iran-Sanctions-Waiver-To-Southern-Gas-Corridor.html.

Petersen, Alexandros. 2016. *Integration in Energy and Transport*. London: Lexington Books.

Pirani, Simon. 2018. 'Let's not exaggerate: Southern Gas Corridor prospects to 2030.' *The Oxford Institute for Energy Studies* 135: 1–30. https://www.oxfordenergy.org/wpcms/wp-content/uploads/2018/07/Lets-not-exaggerate-Southern-Gas-Corridor-prospects-to-2030-NG-135.pdf.

Port of Baku. 2018. 'Azerbaijan-Turkmenistan documents were signed.' November 23. Accessed November 24, 2018. http://portofbaku.com/en/news/192-A-ceremony-of-signing-Azerbaijan-Turkmenistan-docu/.

President. 2018. 'Fourth Ministerial Meeting of Southern Gas Corridor Advisory Council held in Baku.' February 15. Accessed February 2018. https://en.president.az/articles/27051/print.

President. 2014. 'Speech by Ilham Aliyev at the 4th summit of the heads of state of Caspian littoral states.' September 29. Accessed September 2018. https://en.president.az/articles/13039.

Prontera, Andrea. 2017. 'Forms of state and European energy security: diplomacy and pipelines in Southeastern Europe.' *European Security* 26 (2): 273–298.

Prontera, Andrea. 2015. 'Italian energy security, the Southern Gas Corridor and the new pipeline politics in Western Europe: from the partner state to the catalytic state.' *Journal of International Relations and Development* 21: 1–31.

Report. 2018. 'TANAP Opening Ceremony was held in Turkey.' June 12. Accessed June 22, 2018. https://report.az/en/energy/tanap-opening-ceremony-was-held-in-turkey/.

Reuters. 2019. 'Oil output at Kazakhstan's Kashagan hits record of 400,000 bpd – sources.' June 5. Accessed June 6, 2019. https://www.reuters.com/article/kazakhstan-oil-kashagan-output/update-1-oil-output-at-kazakhstans-kashagan-hits-record-of-400000-bpd-sources-idUSL8N23C4WA.

Reuters. 2017a. 'EU gets wake-up call as Gazprom eyes rival TAP pipeline.' February 14. Accessed February 15, 2017. https://www.reuters.com/article/us-gazprom-eu-tap-idUSKBN15T1LC.

Reuters. 2017b. 'TAP pipeline group close to breakthrough on Italian olive tree move.' March 7. Accessed March 8, 2017. https://www.reuters.com/article/italy-tap-idUSL3N1GK32R.

Reuters. 2016. 'Italian olive grove stands in way of European energy security.' October 4. Accessed October 5, 2016. https://www.reuters.com/article/us-italy-energy-trees-insight-idUSKCN1240GD?il=0.

Reuters. 2014. 'Iran says may sue BP for an Azeri oil spill.' January 23. Accessed August 20, 2015. https://uk.reuters.com/article/uk-iran-azeri-bp/iran-says-may-sue-bp-for-an-azeri-oil-spill-idUKBRE90S0I520130129.

Reuters. 2012a. 'Turkey, Azerbaijan sign accord on $7 bln gas pipeline.' June 26. Accessed September 12, 2016. https://www.reuters.com/article/turkey-azerbaijan-gas/update-1-turkey-azerbaijan-sign-accord-on-7-bln-gas-pipeline-idUSL6E8HQAVA20120626.

Reuters. 2012b. 'UPDATE 3-Shah Deniz consortium selects TAP for Italy pipeline option.' February 22. Accessed September 2018. https://www.reuters.com/article/

174 *A new round in the Caspian pipeline game*

shah-deniz/update-3-shah-deniz-consortium-selects-tap-for-italy-pipeline-option-id USL5E8DK31320120220.

Rzayeva, Gulmira. 2015. *The Outlook for Azerbaijani Gas Supplies to Europe Challenges and Perspectives.* Oxford: The Oxford Institute for Energy Studies.

Rzayeva, Gulmira, and Theodoros Tsakiris. 2012. *Strategic Imperative: Azerbaijani Gas Strategy and the EU's Southern Corridor. Baku: SAM Center for Strategic Studies.* Baku: Center for Strategic Studies.

Saivetz, Carol. 2003. 'Perspectives on the Caspian Sea Dilemma: Russian Policies Since the Soviet Demise.' *Eurasian Geography and Economics* 44 (8): 588–606.

Shiriyev, Zaur, and Celia Davies. 2013. 'The Turkey-Armenia-Azerbaijan Triangle: The Unexpected Outcomes of the Zurich Protocols.' *Perceptions* 23: 185–206.

Shlapentokh, Dmitry. 2013. 'Turkmenistan and military build up in the Caspian region: A small state in the post-unipolar era.' *Journal of Eurasian Studies* 4: 154–159.

Siddi, Marco. 2017. 'The EU's Botched Geopolitical Approach to External Energy Policy: The Case of the Southern Gas Corridor.' *Geopolitics* 24 (1): 124–144.

Skalamera, Morena. 2016. 'Revisiting the Nabucco Debacle.' *Problems of Post-Communism* 65 (1): 1–19.

Smith, Dianne L. 1996. 'Central Asia: A New Great Game?' *Asian Affairs* 23 (3): 147–175.

SNAM. 2014. 'Iran wants to join the Southern Corridor.' August 8. Accessed September 20, 2015. http://www.snam.it/en/Media/energy-morning/20140808_3.html.

Socor, Vladimir. 2012. 'Projects in Synergy: Trans-Caspian, Trans-Anatolian Gas Pipelines.' March 2. Accessed September 20, 2015. https://jamestown.org/p rogram/projects-in-synergy-trans-caspian-trans-anatolian-gas-pipelines/.

Socor, Vladimir. 2011. 'Turkmen President Supports Trans-Caspian Pipeline in Meeting With Top EU Officials.' January 20. Accessed September 20, 2015. https:// jamestown.org/program/turkmen-president-supports-trans-caspian-pipeline-in-mee ting-with-top-eu-officials/.

Squires, Nick. 2017. 'Olive groves in Italy become battleground over controversial gas pipeline.' March 29. Accessed September 12, 2018. https://www.telegraph.co.uk/ news/2017/03/29/olive-groves-italy-become-battleground-controversial-gas-pipeline/.

Startori, Nicolo. 2013. *Energy and Politics:Behind the Scenes of the Nabucco-TAP Competition.* Rome: Istituto Affari Internazionali.

Stegen, Karen Smith, and Julia Kusznir. 2015. 'Outcomes and strategies in the 'New Great Game': China and the Caspian states emerge as winners.' *Journal of Eurasian Studies* 6: 91–106.

TAP. 2017a. 'Pipeline construction in Albania.' April 1. Accessed August 20, 2017. https://www.tap-ag.com/the-pipeline/building-the-pipeline/in-albania.

TAP. 2017b. 'TAP Rehabilitated Road Empowers Albanian Villagers.' April 20. Accessed August 20, 2017. https://www.tap-ag.com/news-and-events/tap-stories/ 2017/04/20/tap-rehabilitated-road-empowers-albanian-villagers.

TAP. 2016. 'TAP Discovers Column Capital Part of 6th Century AD Religious Monument.' July 28. Accessed August 20, 2017. https://www.tap-ag.com/news-a nd-events/tap-stories/2016/07/28/tap-discovers-column-capital-part-of-6th-cen tury-ad-religious-monument.

The Economist Intelligence. 2015. 'Iran expresses interest in Southern Gas Corridor.' August 25. Accessed August 26, 2015. http://www.eiu.com/industry/article/1753453 959/iran-expresses-interest-in-southern-gas-corridor/2015-08-25.

The Economist Intelligence. 2007. 'The Great Game revisited.' March 22. Accessed February 19, 2018. https://www.economist.com/node/8896853.

The Italian Insider. 2017. 'Lazio court suspends TAP gas pipeline works.' April 7. Accessed April 8, 2017. http://www.italianinsider.it/?q=node/5218.

Tirana Times. 2017. 'Ancient Albanian settlement discovered in TAP works.' May 10. Accessed August 20, 2017. http://www.tiranatimes.com/?p=132346.

Trend. 2019a. 'Several agreements signed within Caspian Economic Forum in Turkmenistan.' August 19. Accessed August 19, 2019. https://en.trend.az/casia/turkmenistan/3103729.html.

Trend. 2019b. 'Azerbaijan reveals projected volumes of Turkmen oil transit via BTC pipeline.' March 23. Accessed March 23, 2019. https://en.trend.az/business/energy/3036065.html.

Trend. 2018a. 'Iran in talks with int'l oil companies to start co-op with SOCAR (Exclusive).' May 15. Accessed September 12, 2018. https://en.trend.az/iran/business/2903013.html.

Trend. 2018b. 'Energy minister: Southern Gas Corridor has prospects for expansion in Eastern, Central Europe, including Balkans (Interview).' May 8. Accessed May 8, 2018. https://en.trend.az/business/energy/2899703.html.

Trend. 2018c. 'Azerbaijani, Turkmen presidents hold one-on-one meeting.' November 22. Accessed November 22, 2018. https://en.trend.az/azerbaijan/politics/2983496.html.

Trend. 2018d. 'Caspian littoral states to assess impact of economic activity in Caspian basin on ecology.' July 20. Accessed July 20, 2018. https://en.trend.az/azerbaijan/society/2931800.html.

Trend. 2017. 'Iran: EU oversupplied, short-term gas export unprofitable.' May 25. Accessed May 26, 2017. https://en.trend.az/iran/business/2759013.html.

Trend. 2016. 'EBRD eyes support for TAP pipeline project.' July 27. Accessed July 28, 2016. https://en.trend.az/business/energy/2563188.html.

Trenin, Dmitri. 2003. 'A Farewell to the Great Game? Prospects for Russian-American Security Cooperation in Central Asia.' *European Security* 12 (3–4):21–35.

Tsurkov, Maksim. 2016. 'EBRD eyes support for TAP pipeline project.' July 27. Accessed July 28, 2016. http://en.trend.az/business/energy/2563188.html.

Verda, Matteo. 2016. 'The Foreign Dimension of EU Energy Policy: The Case of the Southern Gas Corridor.' In *EU Leadership in Energy and Environmental Governance*, edited by Jakub Godzimirski, 69–86. New York: Palgrave Macmillan.

Whitmore, Brian. 2009. 'Azerbaijan Could Scuttle Nabucco Over Turkey-Armenia Deal.' October 19. Accessed April 2, 2014. https://www.rferl.org/a/Azerbaijan_Could_Scuttle_Nabucco_Over_TurkeyArmenia_Deal/1855784.html.

Wiesmann, Gerrit. 2012. 'RWE set to quit Nabucco gas pipeline.' December 2. Accessed February 10, 2016. https://www.ft.com/content/278a8582-3c94-11e2-a6b2-00144feabdc0.

Yenikeyeff, Shamil Midkhatovich. 2011. 'Energy Interests of the 'Great Powers' in Central Asia: Cooperation or Conflict?' *The International Spectator* 46 (3): 61–78.

Conclusion

The starting point of this book was the notion that the New Great Game literature reflects the extended version of the James Bond movie *The World is Not Enough* because the misconceptions and stereotypes that fuelled the plot of the movie are also fuelling the relevant academic and media discussions. In the final scene of the movie, Bond defeats the Russian villains with help of an American nuclear expert named Jones. In doing so they help Electra achieve her family's dream of constructing an 800-mile pipeline from Azerbaijan to the Mediterranean. For this narrative, the movie draws upon longstanding Western stereotypes about the Caspian Sea region's reputation for rivalry, instability, and richness in natural resources. The movie's core ideological message about the Caspian Sea region is predominantly negative and hopeless, as is the relevant literature's core message. Because the Western agent saved the Caspian Sea region from the Russian villains in a 'winner takes all' fashion, we may conclude the movie even promotes the notion that geopolitics is a zero-sum game. One can observe this type of ending in many movies, but in the real world it works differently.

This book argued that the assumptions that the New Great Game literature is based on promote shallower and less systematic discussion because these assumptions ignore and misunderstand historical, material, political, economic, and normative differences in the Caspian Sea region. This book argued that because of this, the New Great Game literature does not only overlook developments, changes, and actors that are not identified in traditional geopolitics, but also fails to see developments in the region that are very important to traditional geopolitics. This book aimed to shift away from the restrictive understanding that the New Great Game literature offers through its reliance on realist doctrines and it aimed to shift towards more cautious, synthetic, and analytical ways of discussing the Caspian Sea region.

This book asked the question: which new insights in cooperation and conflict are provided by revised functionalism in comparison with the New Great Game narrative? Should these new insights lead to a re-evaluation of the regional dynamics? More specifically, this book asked: how did issue-specific and technical cooperation on environmental issues in the Caspian Sea region reduce the likelihood and severity of regional conflicts and reduce

DOI: 10.4324/9781003189626-7

Conclusion 177

perception of insecurity? How have the Caspian littoral states' perceptions of the regional cooperation been socially shaped and redefined by working together on transnational infrastructure projects? Have the BTC and the SGC projects changed the value and role of the regional conflicts and, if so, how? Who are the key actors besides states that are involved in shaping and constructing the Caspian Sea region's politics and how do their preferences (political and economic) and networks affect the capacity, opportunity, and will of governments (e.g., ministries, parliaments, presidents etc.) to cooperate?

I studied three interrelated cases, all of which unfolded in the last decade, namely the Caspian Environmental Program (CEP), the Baku-Tbilisi-Ceyhan (BTC) pipeline project, and the Southern Gas Corridor (SGC) project. I aimed to show and explain the as-yet-undiscussed and neglected aspects of the recent developments in the Caspian Sea region. By using these inter-linked cases, this book mainly aimed to analyse the Caspian Sea region per se, rather than discussing conflict and cooperation either in the South Caucasus or in Central Asia as that has already been described quite thoroughly. This enabled me to dig deeper and offer a more systematic, comprehensive, and critical analysis of the Caspian Sea.

An alternative image of the Caspian Sea region

By discussing the current state of the region, chapter 1 showed that the New Great Game literature does not help us understand cooperative competition and destructive conflict in the Caspian Sea region. The relevant literature repeats a political and academic debate that goes back to the 19th century, which argues that the essence of relations is still struggle for power and dominance. More specifically, chapter 1 illustrated that in addressing Caspian Sea region's natural resources developments (infrastructure projects and ecological issues), the relevant literature lacks knowledge of the Caspian Sea region and its specific circumstances; instead it knows the rules to a certain game and applies those rules to the situation in the region. Within this discussion, interests, identities, social contexts, and principles are understood to be fixed, i.e. not prone to change or to any sort of adjustment. Ecological issues are depicted as either a tool used by states to block infrastructure projects or as a reason for conflict. In the same vein, both states in the region and external states (Russia, Iran, Armenia, and China) have been identified as the main players behind every single issue or threat in the planning and construction phases of transnational infrastructures in this discussion. The relevant literature also predicted transnational projects would trigger rivalry and even war in the region following their construction (e.g., in Nagorno-Karabakh). The relevant scholarship assumes and pretends that it sufficiently covers three phases (planning, construction, and post-construction) of transnational infrastructure projects. In reality, the relevant literature constantly repeats fixed arguments about developments in each of these three

178   *Conclusion*

phases. It does not recognize or explain the specific changes, processes, and developments that occur in each phase and that are geopolitically important. Chapter 1 showed that this understanding of the natural resources offered up the misleading conclusion that if there are natural resources, there will always be conflict and rivalry. In doing so, this chapter showed that the state-centric assumptions of the New Great Game literature have offered explanations that are too simplistic to be helpful in trying to understand the complexity of the contemporary Caspian Sea region. Against this established backdrop, this book posited that it is not sufficient to think about and scrutinize natural resources only in terms of rivalry and inter-state war. Viewing the Caspian Sea region as a geopolitical battleground obscures important layers of a more complex reality, as well as the underlying dynamics of material and non-material interdependency.

In order to dismantle the simplistic and dominant New Great Game literature conception of the contemporary Caspian Sea region and unpack its complexities, this book found different insights. These insights include the role of actors besides and beyond states, socialization, spill over, the role of shared issues, changing preferences, and the importance of having a technocratic starting point. By using a social constructivist lens, chapter 2 has advanced and slightly broadened these insights. This cross-fertilization between functionalism and social constructivism has offered more comprehensive and inclusive reference points for explaining the complex, interlinked dynamics and salient issues between the Caspian Sea littoral states, such as the specific form their cooperation takes and the types of interdependent relations between them. Additionally, this cross-fertilization between functionalism and constructivism has formed a critical and innovative challenge to pessimistic traditional thinkers, stuck in an ontological swamp of the 19th century.

I addressed five main empirical points, which are missing from the relevant scholarship. The first key point is the increasing role of actors beyond and besides states, such as TNCs, NGOs, and IGOs in the Caspian Sea. The aim of this work was not to show whether they matter or play a role because the literature on this topic has already sufficiently established this. The main point of this work was instead to show how and in what way these actors play a role in constructing a framework for interaction and articulating new interests and norms in the Caspian Sea region as their roles have previously been too narrowly understood and described. In this sense, the main aim of this book was to unpack the tools and techniques they used in the socially constructive aspects of their functioning. In the 1990s, external and regional great powers (the US, China, the EU, Turkey, Iran, and Russia) were depicted as the main actors in the Caspian Sea region. Later the newly independent littoral states (Azerbaijan, Kazakhstan, and Turkmenistan) were also included within the existing discussion. By showing and explaining the role and significance of other actors, I moved one step further by de-emphasizing, if not undermining – but at the very least nuancing – the Great Game framework.

Conclusion 179

The three case studies showed that BP, the UNEP, the UNDP, the EBRD, the GEF, the AIIB, and the World Bank are the main players in the Caspian Sea region who offer technical, political, economic, social, and security assistance. They frame issues, help set agendas, and mobilize financial support. Although states are depicted as the leading actors in the Caspian Sea region, the three case studies showed that these non-state and intergovernmental actors are indeed the drivers behind every project. More specifically, by using their leverage in international political and economic networks, these actors contribute to the transnational infrastructure projects (the BTC and the SGC); offer solutions for shared problems (e.g., environmental pollution); and facilitate discussion, creating a habit of cooperation and dialogue among the governments of the Caspian littoral states.

Chapter 3 showed that the UNEP, the UNDP, the GEF, and the World Bank are the main technocratic actors who initiated, facilitated, and funded the environmental cooperation among the governments of the Caspian littoral states. Chapter 3 illustrated that by using their technical, economic, and political leverage these actors brought the littoral states under the common umbrella of the CEP which is an issue-specific program. Chapter 3 illustrated that the common environmental issues could be framed as an apolitical and functional opportunity for the Caspian littoral states' governments to work together. The governments' main goal is not to address environmental issues per se, but to improve the interactive atmosphere and practice the habit of dialogue under an apolitical umbrella. Therefore, the CEP has more effects than its environmental policy outcomes. The littoral states' preferences and interests have thus changed as the result of environmental cooperation and joint projects. In the same vein, chapters 4 and 5 showed that without the systematic support of energy companies and international financial institutions, transnational infrastructure projects (the BTC and the SGC) would never have been completed successfully. These actors have all made their contributions to cooperation and security, in line with their own distinctive set of goals and objectives. Therefore, the collapse of the Soviet Union not only led to the independence of Azerbaijan, Kazakhstan, and Turkmenistan, but also facilitated the involvement and emergence of TNCs, NGOs, and IGOs in the Caspian Sea. This means that the Caspian Sea region is no longer the exclusive playground of states, either those in the region or external powers, but that inter-governmental and non-governmental actors have also started playing significant roles in the different fields of cooperation. Therefore, the cooperation in the Caspian Sea region should be placed in a global, non-exclusively-governmental context.

The second main empirical point is the importance of shared technical issues, namely the pollution of the Caspian Sea damaging its ecology and the construction of the transnational infrastructure projects. The three case studies illustrated that these functional challenges encouraged multiple actors (state, non-state, and semi-state) to cooperate because their connection and interaction were needed to face the functional challenges in the Caspian Sea

180 *Conclusion*

region. Environmental cooperation on the issue of pollution was functional for states, private companies, and intergovernmental actors because it created vested interests, and it was a useful entry point into the regional dynamics and promised shared future gains. It was functional for the governments because it allowed them to work towards solutions for a common problem and learn how to deal with it. The environmental cooperation was also functional because the governments receive money from other actors to deal with these issues, which keeps them at the bargaining table. It was functional also for environmental IGOs because they got a foothold in the Caspian Sea region and could start to address the issue of protecting its ecology. This cooperation eventually fostered further cooperation and spilled over to other issue areas such as the discussion of the legal status of the sea. Chapter 3 illustrated that the CEP was not an isolated case of low politics or a niche area compared to traditional geopolitics but had an interdependent relationship with other issue areas, such as the discussion of the sea's legal status and pipeline construction. In contrast to the outcomes predicted on the basis of geopolitical assumptions, chapter 3 illustrated that the environmental requirements within the Legal Status Convention cannot be explained without reference to how the environmental interests of the governments of the littoral states were redefined and constructed under the CEP and later the Tehran Convention during the early 2000s. Chapter 3 illustrated that understanding how the interests and preferences of the Caspian Sea governments were established is the key to explaining a broad range of developments in the region, which the relevant (neo)realist literature has either misunderstood or neglected to do. While discussing the CEP program however, this book had to focus on non-environmental influence of the program only. In this regard, further research should consider the possible environmental influence of the program, such as the change in pollution level, fish stocks, the rise of the sea level, and biodiversity.

Another functional issue that brought multiple actors together is the construction of transnational infrastructure projects. This book has argued that the complexities and value of infrastructures are only narrowly understood by the relevant realist scholarship. By discussing three phases of the BTC and the SGC infrastructure projects, chapters 4 and 5 showed challenges and restrictions that arose beyond and besides those stemming from geopolitics. This book conceptualized the transnational infrastructure projects as consisting of three intertwined phases firstly because they are complex undertakings. I used the three phases as an heuristic tool to comprehensively analyse the pipelines a material artefacts. Secondly, each phase has its unique challenges, changes, actors and game results, which affect the other phases and the infrastructure development. Unlike the realist literature, chapters 4 and 5 illustrated and explained the unique role of different actors, challenges, and developments in each phase. The geopolitical literature argues and assumes that it covers these phases but, in reality, it constantly reproduces the same arguments and explanations in the three phases.

Conclusion 181

While the geopolitical challenge faced by actors cooperating in the Caspian Sea region is one of the pieces of the puzzle, it does not represent the full picture. In this regard, I showed that it is necessary to address interconnected construction challenges. These challenges include environmental issues, workers' protests, extra financial costs, low energy prices, NGO protests, and technical difficulties, which increased the cost of the projects and halted them from time to time. Despite their diversity, they have common features. These issues respect no national or international boundaries and cannot be resolved through unilateral national action. They created a strong functional need for collective action because the cooperation of multiple actors was necessary to address and manage these challenges. On the one hand, these challenges showed that simply signing energy contracts does not mean that natural gas or oil will flow. Rather energy will flow only when these neglected technical issues have been properly addressed. On the other hand, these complex difficulties brought multiple actors together (state, private, intergovernmental, non-governmental). The New Great Game literature misses that the SGC and the BTC are not just state properties. There are also non-state shareholders, who deal with technical and non-technical challenges during the construction phase. Therefore, it is necessary to consider the developments in the three phases of transnational infrastructure to attain the full picture. However, it is worth noting that the BTC and SGC projects are specific cases, ones in which pragmatic and issue-specific cooperation can be observed. When using the same analytical structure (planning, construction, and eventual use of infrastructure) scholars should now consider regional differences and characteristics as well.

The third key point, in line with the previous one, is that the BTC and the SGC have created constructive competition in the region because they influenced, changed, and shaped the relationship between the Caspian littoral states after their construction. As explained above, the littoral states started to experience and establish the practice of cooperation and interaction under the CEP as it function as icebreaker between the governments of the littoral states in the 1990s and led to two agreements signed by the Caspian littoral states: the Tehran Convention and the Legal Status Convention. Chapters 4 and 5 have shown that the stage for cooperative habits was not limited to environmental and legal agreement but it continued and became more compelling throughout the BTC and the SGC projects. More specifically, these pipelines led to non-calculative cooperation behaviour and offered the littoral states a functional way to interact. It was non-calculative because in the planning phase Kazakhstan, Russia, and Turkmenistan were not part of the project, but following the construction of the BTC, these countries have started to use the pipeline to transport their resources since it offers them an alternative transport opportunity for their natural resources. This infrastructure is functional because it offers the possibility of contractual and material cooperation as well as adherence to international standards. It is also an alternative to the unrealistic goal of political integration which helps

182 *Conclusion*

the littoral states bypass the thorny issues of nationalism and political difference while still creating material interdependence in the long run.

The fourth key point is that the Caspian Sea region is driven by different functional pursuits than in Western Europe was in the 1950s and the governments of the littoral states are responding to a different set of converging interests. As mentioned in my introduction chapter, two studies (Blum 2002; Petersen 2016) used classical functionalism to explain developments in the Caspian Sea region. In contrast to Blum and Petersen's conclusions, I found that functionalism is capable of explaining constructive cooperation among the Caspian littoral states. Unlike Blum and Petersen, I did not analyse and judge the performance of cooperation in the Caspian Sea against the benchmark set by Europe in the 1950s. Rather, my revised functionalism offers a less ambitious and more realistic framework to explain developments in the Caspian Sea region. In turn, the three case studies illustrated that the habit of cooperation was developed by dealing with the shared environmental issues and it continued and spilled over into the signing of the Legal Status Convention. This functionalist cooperation continued and grew stronger through the BTC and the SGC projects. Although the governments of the littoral states have signed a number of documents, regulations, and agreements to expand their cooperation in other areas, such as in technology, agriculture, and industry, the habit cooperation has not spilled over to anything beyond the transportation of natural resources. This is because non-oil and non-gas industry only represents a small share of their total exports. Since there is a lack of production and development in non-oil and non-gas industries, there is limited room for expanding cooperation to different sectors or issue areas. In this regard, economic and political agreements, document signings, or treaties would only start to play an actual role if the littoral states develop their non-oil and non-gas industry sectors.

The Caspian littoral states aim to strengthen their sovereignty, regime survival, and the position of their rulers and prevent the intervention of other actors by cooperating on specific issues, creating specific organizations, or interacting with other actors, unlike Western Europe did in the 1950s. Their governments aim to address the needs of the authorities rather than addressing the needs and rights of citizens. Therefore, functionalism is mainly in service of ruling elites in the Caspian Sea region. These findings also show that the Caspian Sea region has its own functional objectives, impulses, and approaches to cooperation. In contrast to Western Europe, the Caspian littoral states do not aim for integration per se, because the littoral states view integration as a loss of their sovereignty and freedom of decision making. The littoral states rather aim for functional cooperation because cooperation means working together for shared issues without losing autonomy. However, due to the scope of the book, I could not discuss how and in what way transnational infrastructure project strengthened the elites in authoritarian states and helped them establish and maintain a neo-feudalist government structure in the Caspian Sea region (Fails 2019; Guliyev 2012;

Heinrich and Pleines 2012). Further research should shed light on these aspects.

All these points together illustrate that the Caspian Sea region is not a hopeless or desperate place, full of conflict and rivalry. More concretely, the three case studies showed that interests, identities, the practice of cooperation, conflict, and competition are not fixed but they emerge and then change over time. While these findings create a less pessimistic view, they do not mean that the Caspian Sea region is an ideal place or a paradise for cooperation and interaction. Rather these findings mean that it is necessary to understand the complexity, interdependent nature and interconnected dynamism in the region. The three case study chapters illustrated that despite the existing conflicts, competition, and geopolitics, the Caspian littoral states have been cooperating on shared issues since the end of the Cold War. This cooperation is not a standalone or isolated area but it has autonomy in the face of geopolitics and conflict. When one zooms out, one can see that there are several unsolved issues and barriers, but when one zooms in one can see that cooperation and dialogue are ongoing and intended to solve and manage the shared issues in a way that is tailored to the region. Whether this way is right or wrong is another question, but it is necessary analyze it for its own sake rather than depicting the Caspian Sea region from a black and white perspective.

Bibliography

Blum, Douglas. 2002. 'Beyond Reciprocity: Governance and Cooperation around the Caspian Sea.' In *Environmental Peacemaking*, by Ken Conca and Geoffrey Dabelko, 161–190. Baltimore: The John Hopkins University Press.

Fails, Matthew. 2019. 'Oil Income and the personalization of autocratic politics.' *Political Science Research and Methods* 8 (4): 1–8.

Guliyev, Farid. 2012. 'Political Elites in Azerbaijan.' In *Challenges of the Caspian Resource Boom: Domestic Elites and Policy Making* by Andreas Heinrich and Heiko Pleines, 117–131. New York: Palgrave.

Heinrich, Andreas, and Heiko Pleines. 2012. *Challenges of the Caspian Resource Boom: Domestic Elites and Policy Making*. New York: Palgrave.

Petersen, Alexandros. 2016. *Integration in Energy and Transport*. London: Lexington Books.

Index

Page numbers in *italics* indicate Figures.

Abdullayev, Rovnag 128
Actor-Network-Theory (ANT) 70n8
Afghanistan 14, 17, 21–22, 25, 145–146, 166
Agreement on Conservation and Rational Use of the Aquatic Biological Resources of the Caspian Sea 87
Agreement on Cooperation in Emergency Prevention and Response in the Caspian Sea 87
Agreement on Cooperation in the Field of Hydrometeorology of the Caspian Sea 87
Agreement on the Security Cooperation 87
Aktau Protocol 92, 98, 101
Aliyev, Natig 156, 164
Alma-Ata Declaration 85
Almaty Declaration 81
Anglo-Persian War of 1856–57 14
Anglo-Russian Convention 14–15
Ankara Declaration 111
Araz-Sharg-Alov field 1
Armenia: as BTC pipeline rival 113; Nagorno-Karabakh conflict 113–114
Armenia-Turkey relationship 146, 147
Ashgabat Declaration 164
Asian Infrastructure Investment Bank (AIIB) 161
Azerbaijan: Aliyev, Natig 164; bilateral agreement with Turkmenistan 127–128; Commonwealth of Independent States and 85; economy 119, 121; energy agreements 2;

Kapaz/Sardar hydrocarbon field 1–2; Kepez (Serdar) field 127; Nagorno-Karabakh conflict 113–114; natural resources of 1; oil production 123; oil reserves 123; Production Sharing Contract and 111; SGC project costs to 156; Shahbazov, Parviz 164; United States relationship with 146
Azerbaijani oil consortia 18
Azerbaijan-Turkey relationship 147–148, 166
Azeri-Chirag-Gunashli Deepwater (ACG) oil reserves 111
Azeri-Chirag-Kepez oil fields 127

Baker, James 115
Baku-Novorossiysk pipeline 2
Baku-Tbilisi-Ceyhan pipeline *see* BTC pipeline project
Banca Intesa 118
Barroso, José Manuel 149
Baylarbayov, Vitaly 154, 156
bilateral agreements 84–85
Bogdanchikov, Sergei 128
British Petroleum (BP): BTC pipeline project investment 122–123; security standards developed by 160; Southern Gas Corridor (SGC) project 141; supporting CEP 82; supporting TAP companies 159
British-Russian rivalry 13–14
Broccoli, Barbara 3
Bryza, Matthew 146
BTC pipeline project: as alternative transport route 162; background of 111–112; as a case study 7;

Index 185

construction delays 117–118; construction phase 114, 116–118; constructive competition 181; cooperation habits and 110; cost overruns 118–119; delays in 131; economic challenges 118–119; engineering failures 117; financial institutions investing in 124; as functional for multiple actors 132; hydrocarbon resources 127; international investor concerns 117; Kazakhstan joining 126; land acquisition and compensation process 118; list of actors *124*; material integration opportunity 126; New Great Game literature on 113–114, 131; operation phase 126; opposition to 119; planning phase 113, 114–116; post-construction phase 127–130; postponement of 21; private and public lenders 123–126; risk mitigators 125; rivals to development of 113; Rosneft and 128; security measures 122–123; shareholders 120, *121*; social and environmental challenges 119–120; social protests against 119; socio-economic impact of 126; as strategic 131–132; technical challenges 117–118; throughput capacity 116; timeline 112, *112*; transnational infrastructure of 130; Turkmenistan transferring oil through 127; United States' role in 145–146

Bush, George W. 25

Caspian Environmental Information Centre (CEIC) 82, 94

Caspian Environmental Program (CEP): Aktau Protocol 92; Blum's study on 5; British Petroleum supporting 82; as a case study 6–7; economic leverage 91–94, 104; environmental cooperation 80–84; environmental framework 91–92; establishment of 91; as example of mutual cooperation 100; as issue-specific program 81–82, 103; list of actors *83*; networking meetings 94–96; New Great Game explanation for 88–90; phases of 83–84, 92–93; side-lining political attitudes 99; socialization under 95–96; Strategic Action Plan (SAP) 91; support for 81–82; technical

expertise 96–99; Tehran Convention 79, *82*, 84; timeline *82*

Caspian-Pipeline-Consortium (CPC) pipeline 25

Caspian Sea region: academic and media attention for 2; alternative image of 177–183; as a border lake 85; as a condominium 85; decline in US interests in 145–147; as enclosed sea 85; energy reserves figures 115–116; environmental issues (*See* environmental issues); functional challenges in 179–180; geo-strategic position of 1–5; intergovernmental actors 179; legal status of (*See* legal status of the Caspian Sea); natural resource reserves of 21; non-state actors in 179; oil and gas resources of 2–5; sea level fluctuations 78

Caspian Security Agreement 100, 103–104

caviar trade 2, 51, 79, 89–90

Central Asia-China Pipeline 163

China: Central Asian states' dependence on 17; diversifying imported natural gas sources 142; One Belt, One Road project 20; as part of SGC 163; role in transnational infrastructure projects 20; as winner of New Great Game 24

classical functionalism: assumptions 53–54; automatic spill-over and 47–48; core observations of 39–40; critiques of 47–52; state fixation and 41; *see also* functionalism

Clinton administration 111–112, 146

Cohen, Ariel 113

Commonwealth of Independent States (CIS), founding treaty of 85

Conference of Parties (COP) 84, 94, 101

Consolidated Contractors International Co. 119

constructivist spill-over 48

Contract of the Century 2

cross-border infrastructure 57–59 *see also* transnational infrastructure

cultivated spill-over 47

Denison, Michael 17

development banks 64

dialectic spill-over 67

186 *Index*

Di Maio, Luigi 155
domestic infrastructure 57–58

economic interdependence 59–60
economic leverage: of international
actors 62–63, 91–94; of multinational
energy companies 120–122
economic sanctions 87, 93, 111, 146,
155, 159
Emiliano, Michele 153–154
Enagas 157–158, 159
energy companies 120–123
environmental cooperation 62, 80–81,
88, 90, 99–104, 179–180 *see also*
Caspian Environmental Program
(CEP)
Environmental Impact Assessment
(EIA) protocol 98, 123, 144
environmental issues: bilateral/trilateral
agreements on 87–88; marine
biodiversity loss 78–79; overfishing 79;
pollution 180; sea level fluctuations
78; with Trans Caspian Pipeline
89–90; water pollution 79; *see also*
Caspian Environmental Program
(CEP)
environmental resources 20–21
Eom, Gu-Ito 113–114
Espoo Convention 98
Eurocentrism 5, 70, 167
European Bank for Reconstruction and
Development (EBRD) 119, 121,
123–125, 159–163
European benchmark 70
European Coal and Steel Community
(ECSC) 38, 44, 45
European Commission 140, 149, 150,
161
European Economic Community (EEC)
38, 50
European style integration 5, 49, 52, 102,
104
European Union: Connecting Europe
Facility funding instrument 161;
funding for Nabucco project 140;
resistance for TAP project 148–149;
seeking expansion of SGC project
143–144; Technical Assistance for the
Commonwealth of Independent States
program 82
EXIM Bank 124
Export Credit Guarantee Department
(ECGD-UK government) 117, 124

Extractive Industry Transparency
Initiative (EITI) 125

First Anglo-Persian War of 1838–42 14
First Caspian Economic Forum 165–166
First Caspian Summit 87, 88–89
Five Star Movement party 155
Fourth Caspian Summit 87
*Framework Convention for the Protection
of the Marine Environment of the
Caspian Seasee* Tehran Convention
functionalism: actors' loyalties and 44;
characteristics of 37; cooperation for
the common good and 42; European
integration and 52; from global to
regional level 42–43; integration and
46–47; linguistic functions of 51;
neofunctionalism overlap with 40;
political vs. technical 50–51;
popularity of 38; principles of 50;
ramification approach 45–47; regional
cooperation and 51–52; in service of
ruling elites 182; as social constructivist in character 37–39, 52–54,
178; spill-over process 46–48;
stagnation phase 48; state fixation
toward international politics 40–41;
technical cooperation 68–69;
Tennessee Valley Authority as
example of 42; unique features of 39;
see also classical functionalism
functional spill-over 47

Gazprom 147, 155
Georgia 119
Gerebizza, Elena 154
Global Environmental Facility (GEF) 7,
81, 91, 93, 97, 99, 104, 179
global interdependency 66
Great Britain: attacking Afghanistan 14;
Russian rivalry with 13–15
Great Game 14 *see also* New Great
Game literature, Old Great Game
Greece, supporting TAP project 149–150
Grillo, Beppo 153

Haas, Ernst B. 38
hydrocarbon fields 1–2

induced spill-over 44–48
infrastructure *see* cross-border
infrastructure, transnational
infrastructure

Index 187

Interconnector Turkey-Greece-Italy (ITGI) projects 148–149
interest politics 44
intergovernmental actors 179
International Finance Cooperation (IFC) 118
international governmental organizations (IGOs): economic leverage and 63–64; as functionalist agencies 52–53
International Labour Organization (ILO) 43
International Monetary Fund (IMF) 64
International Telecommunications Union (ITU) 43, 56–57
International Telegraph Union 43
Iran: bilateral agreements with Russia 84–85; as BTC pipeline rival 113; economic sanctions imposed on 111; interest in joining SGC project 163; lacking geo-economic clout 27; preventing TCP project 144; proposing environmental protection regional organization 81; Treaty of Friendship 85; US sanctions against 159
Isayev, Afgan 156
Ismailzade, Fariz 18
Italy, supporting TAP project 149–150
Izvolsky, Alexander 14

Journal of Central Asian Survey 15

Kapaz/Sardar hydrocarbon field 1–2
Kazakh oil 129
Kazakhstan: Commonwealth of Independent States and 85; desertification risk in 78; hydrocarbon resources 127; interest in joining SGC project 163; joining BTC pipeline project 126; natural resources of 1
Kepez (Serdar) field 127
Khagani, Mahmoud 128
Kim (Kipling) 13, 27
Kim, Younkyoo 113–114
Kipling, Rudyard 13, 27
Kleveman, Lutz 3

Lazio Regional Administrative Court (TAR) 154
Legal Status Convention: *ad hoc* working group 86; as comprehensive agreement 100, 102; formation of 84–88; New Great Game explanation

for 88–90; on shipping across Caspian Sea 129; signing of 79–80, 87–88; timeline *86*; undersea pipelines and 162, 164; use in preventing TCP project 144
legal status of the Caspian Sea: of Caspian seabed 103; contested 89; delimitation options 85; ending uncertainty of 85–86; environmental cooperation and 100–101; history of 84–86; military security and 21–22; New Great Game literature 88–90; oil field ownership and 115; SGC project and 144; as uncertain 1–2; *see also* Legal Status Convention
Libanidze, Tamar 119
Lukoil 114, 128–129, 155, 158, 161

March, James G. 45
marine biodiversity loss 78–79
Medvedev, Dmitry 100–101
military security 21–22
Mitrany, David: on economic leverage 63; on functional agency's purpose 40, 43; functionalism principles 50; importance of cooperation 46; on New Deal 42; as policy advisor 64–65; on regional cooperation 51; state fixation and 40–41; on technical cooperation 56; on transnational networks 60; on unity within diversity 41–42; *Working Peace System, A* (pamphlet) 37–38
Morningstar, Richard 146–147
multilateral development banks 64

Nabucco project 140–141, 148–149, 150 *see also* Southern Gas Corridor (SGC) project
Nagorno-Karabakh conflict 114–115, 143
National Environmental Action Plan (NEAP) 91
National Iranian Oil Company (NIOC) 146, 158, 159, 163, 166
NATO Partnership for Peace (PfP) program 21, 22, 31n4
natural resource reserves 21, 26, 27, 130
Navigation Agreement 85
neofunctionalism 38, 40, 44, 48
New Deal 42, 57, 70n5
New Great Game literature 4; on BTC pipeline 113–114, 131; Caspian Environmental Program and 88–90;

188 *Index*

cultural/religious dominance and 30n3; environmental cooperation and 103; environmental resources 20–21; as an explanatory paradigm 12; external actors and 18; external players 25; external powers as actors 18; Legal Status Convention 88–90; naval advancement and 21–22; neorealist approach 24; non-governmental actors' influence 18–19; Old Great Game vs. 16; recognizing regional states 16, 23; relationships between great powers and regional states 25; role of regional actors 17–18; on SGC project 141–145; shortcomings in study of 27–30; transnational infrastructure as new round of 19; winners of 23–24; *see also* Great Game

Nicolson, Arthur 14

non-governmental organizations (NGOs) 52–53, 63, 152

non-renewable sources 20

Obama administration 146

oil reserves *see* natural resource reserves

Old Great Game: British-Russian rivalry and 13–14; concept of 13–16; goals of 13, 15; New Great Game vs. 16

Olsen, Johen P. 45

overfishing 79

Partnership for Peace (PfP) 21, 22, 31n4

Petronas 158

political spill-over 47

"polluter pays" principle 98

Production Sharing Agreements (PSAs) 121–122

Puglia Regional Committee on the Environmental Impact Assessment of TAP project 153

Putin, Vladimir 25

ramification 40, 45–47

Rasmussen, Anders Fogh 154

regional development banks 64

regional integration 4, 30, 38, 49, 59 *see also* Trans-Adriatic Pipeline (TAP)

revised functionalism 9, 39, 52–55, 69–70, 91, 102, 120, 165–167, 182

revised functionalism, logic of 9

Richardson, Bill 111

Roosevelt, Franklin D. 70n5

Rosneft 128

Russia: blamed for TAP protests 154; as BTC pipeline rival 113; Caspian Sea region policies 25–26; changing pipeline direction to Turkey 142; expansion of 14–15; Gazprom 147, 155; lacking geo-economic clout 27; Lukoil 114, 128–129, 155, 158, 161; oil production 115–116; preventing TCP project 144; as SGC project rival 142; US sanctions against 159; as winner of New Great Game 23–24; *see also* Soviet Union

Russian energy companies 122

sea level fluctuations 78

Second Caspian Summit 87

Sefcovic, Maros 141

SGC Closed Joint Stock Company (SGC-CJSC) 156

Shahbazov, Parviz 164

Shah Deniz (SD) consortium 26, 158

Shah Deniz II project 158, 159

Shah Deniz natural gas 141, 142–143

Siddi, Marco 143

social constructivism 37, 52–55, 178

social interaction 54–55

socialization processes 9, 38, 45, 55, 59, 62, 94–102

South Caucasus Pipeline (SCP) consortium 25, 31n5, 141

Southern Gas Corridor (SGC) 7, 114, 127, 132n4

Southern Gas Corridor (SGC) project: Azerbaijan's investment share 156, 158; background of 140–141; barriers for 148–151; construction phase 143, 151–157; constructive competition 181; economic challenges 155–157, 166–167; energy companies involved with 157–160; environmental protests 143; estimated costs of 155–156; European Union seeking expansion of 143–144; historical settlements discovery 152; international loans for *161*; Italian opposition to 153–154; list of actors *158*; as mediating interface 162; Nabucco project as precursor to 140–141; New Great Game literature on 141–145; olive tree transport 152; pipelines joining in with 141; planning phase 142, 145–151; post-construction phase

162–166; practice of cooperation 167; private and public lenders 160–162; as Russian gas rival 142; security for 159–160; security threats 143; shareholders 146; social/environmental obstacles 152–155; technical challenges 151–152

South Stream 142, 145, 148

Soviet-Iranian Trade and Navigation Agreement 9n1

Soviet Union: bilateral agreements with Iran 84–85; Britain's rivalry with 13–15; collapse of 179; dissolution of 1; Treaty of Friendship 85; *see also* Russia

spillback 48

spill-over process 46–47, 66–68

state fixation 40–41

State Oil Company of the Azerbaijan Republic (SOCAR) 118, 128, 147, 154, 156–160

State Oil Fund of Azerbaijan (SOFAZ) 125

Strategic Convention Action Plan (SCAP) 92

Swanstrom, Niklas 16–17

Talbott, Strobe 115

Technical Assistance for the Commonwealth of Independent States (TACIS) program 82

technical cooperation 56–57, 58, 68–69

Tehran Convention 79, *82*, 84, 91–92, 144, 164 *see also* Caspian Environmental Program (CEP)

Tennessee Valley Authority (TVA) 42, 70n5

Third Caspian Summit 87, 100–101

Titan D 122

Trans-Adriatic Pipeline (TAP): construction phase 151–157; contested in Puglia region 153–154; European Union's lack of support for 148; Greece's support for 149–150; Italian opposition to 153–154; Italy's support for 149–150; Nabucco project competing against 148–151; projected completion date 156

Trans-Anatolian-Gas Pipeline (TANAP) 141, 142–143, 150, 161

Trans-Caspian oil transport system 126–127

Trans-Caspian Pipeline (TCP) 89–90, 141, 144, 163–165

transnational corporations (TNCs): as functionalist agencies 52–53, 64–65; global developments and 65; impact on home governments 65

transnational energy pipelines 4

transnational infrastructure: actors' interdependencies 59–60; of BTC pipeline 130; as conflictual 59; economic development and 58; facilitating socialization 59; international actors and 56–57; managing access 19; as mediating interface 59; as new round in Great Game 19; pipeline development opponents 19–20; power politics influencing 20; technical cooperation 56–58; *see also* cross-border infrastructure

transnational infrastructure projects: actors roles in 29, 179; China's role in 20; construction of 19, 179–180; as mediating interfaces 9; network of actors 120–126; regional cooperation 176–177; *see also* BTC pipeline project

transnational networks: diverse actors' interactions 69; economic leverage and 62–64; enhancing flexibility 62; Mitrany on 60; roles 61; socializing function 61–62; as value add 61–62

Treaty of Friendship 9n1, 85

Treaty of Versailles 43

Turkey-Armenia relationship 146, 147

Turkey-Azerbaijan relationship 147–148, 166

Turkish-Armenian rapprochement 147–148

Turkish Petroleum (TP) 158

Turkmen gas 127

Turkmenistan: bilateral agreement with Azerbaijan 127–128; Commonwealth of Independent States and 85; desertification risk in 78; interest in joining SGC project 163; Kapaz/Sardar hydrocarbon field 1–2; Kepez (Serdar) field 127; natural resources of 1

Turkmenistan-Afghanistan-Pakistan-Indian (TAPI) pipeline 146

190 *Index*

UK Parliament 117, 131
UNECE Environmental Performance
  Review 82–83
United Nations Development Program
  (UNDP) 91, 94, 97
United Nations Environmental Program
  (UNEP) 91, 93, 94, 97
United States: Azerbaijan's relationship
  with 146; declining interest in Caspian
  Sea 145–147; economic sanctions
  imposed on Iran 111; promoting
  TAPI pipeline 146
Universal Postal Union (UPU) 43, 56–57
Unsponsored Alliance of Civilisations
  Initiative 147

Vaezi, Mahmoud 163
Van Aarsten, Jozias 140
Victoria, Queen of England 14
Volga River 78

water pollution 79
Western energy companies 122
Working Peace System, A (Mitrany)
  37–38
World Bank 64, 91, 94, 97
World is Not Enough, The (film) 3,
  176
WorleyParsons 117

zero-sum competition 12, 26, 44, 176

Printed in the United States
by Baker & Taylor Publisher Services